Victims of Commemoration

Contemporary Issues in the Middle East
Mehran Kamrava, *Series Editor*

Select Titles in Contemporary Issues in the Middle East

Generations of Dissent: Intellectuals, Cultural Production, and the State in the Middle East and North Africa
Alexa Firat and R. Shareah Taleghani, eds.

The Lost Orchard: The Palestinian-Arab Citrus Industry, 1850–1950
Mustafa Kabha and Nahum Karlinsky

Making the New Middle East: Politics, Culture, and Human Rights
Valerie J. Hoffman, ed.

Ottoman Children and Youth during World War I
Nazan Maksudyan

Political Muslims: Understanding Youth Resistance in a Global Context
Tahir Abbas and Sadek Hamid, eds.

Readings in Syrian Prison Literature: The Poetics of Human Rights
R. Shareah Taleghani

Turkey's State Crisis: Institutions, Reform, and Conflict
Bülent Aras

Understanding Hezbollah: The Hegemony of Resistance
Abed T. Kanaaneh

———————————

For a full list of titles in this series,
visit https://press.syr.edu/supressbook-series
/contemporary-issues-in-the-middle-east/.

Victims of Commemoration

The Architecture and Violence of Confronting the Past in Turkey

Eray Çaylı

Syracuse University Press

Copyright © 2022 by Syracuse University Press
Syracuse, New York 13244-5290

All Rights Reserved

First Edition 2022

22   23   24   25   26   27   6   5   4   3   2   1

∞ The paper used in this publication meets the minimum requirements
of the American National Standard for Information Sciences—Permanence
of Paper for Printed Library Materials, ANSI Z39.48-1992.

For a listing of books published and distributed by Syracuse University Press,
visit https://press.syr.edu/.

ISBN: 978-0-8156-3754-7 (hardcover)
        978-0-8156-3751-6 (paperback)
        978-0-8156-5546-6 (e-book)

Library of Congress Cataloging-in-Publication Data

Names: Çaylı, Eray, author.
Title: Victims of commemoration : the architecture and violence
        of confronting the past in Turkey / Eray Çaylı.
Other titles: Contemporary issues in the Middle East.
Description: First edition. | Syracuse : Syracuse University Press, 2022. |
        Series: Contemporary issues in the Middle East | Includes bibliographical
        references and index.
Identifiers: LCCN 2022002540 (print) | LCCN 2022002541 (ebook) |
        ISBN 9780815637547 (hardcover) | ISBN 9780815637516 (paperback) |
        ISBN 9780815655466 (ebook)
Subjects: LCSH: Memorials—Political aspects—Turkey—History—21st century. |
        Memorialization—Turkey—History—21st century. | Victims of state-sponsored
        terrorism—Monuments—Turkey—History.
Classification: LCC NA9348.T9 C39 2022 (print) | LCC NA9348.T9 (ebook) |
        DDC 725/.9409561—dc23/eng/20220304
LC record available at https://lccn.loc.gov/2022002540
LC ebook record available at https://lccn.loc.gov/2022002541

Manufactured in the United States of America

Dedicated to Carina "Cuanna" Thuijs

Contents

Illustrations

Acknowledgments

This book is the outcome of a decade of work. It was first conceived in Lithuania and then developed, researched, written, and debated in Turkey, the United Kingdom, Germany, Sweden, Denmark, and the Netherlands. I am sincerely indebted to the following individuals who, each in their own way, contributed invaluably to the project in those countries and beyond: Ronald Jones, Meltem Ahıska, Ayfer Bartu Candan, Tuna Kuyucu, Özlem Ünsal, Can Evren, İrem Taşçıoğlu, Leyla Neyzi, Jan Birksted, Ruth Mandel, Yael Navaro, Iain Borden, Esra Özyürek, Yasemin Yıldız, Michael Rothberg, Onur Suzan Nobrega, Bilgin Ayata, Aslı Yıldırım, Benjamin Fortna, Davide Deriu, Gökçe Yurdakul, Hüseyin Diril, Evren Uzer, Feras Hammami, Hanna Baumann, Başak Ertür, Zerrin Özlem Biner, Sinan Laçiner, Önder Aydın, Önder San, Fuat Ateş, İsrafil Erbil, Gülizar Yaldız, Nevzat Dinçal, Rıza Aydın, Kelime Ata, Besim Can Zırh, Murat Güven, Serhad Solin, Brian Beeley, Banu Karaca, Charlotte Weber, Murat Çetin, Görkem Aygün, Enise Burcu Derinboğaz, Diana Dethloff, Martin Holbraad, Didem Kılıçkıran, Güray Balıktay, Mustafa İşlek, Okay Kangal, Merthan Anık, Nevin Soyukaya, Sinem Yıldırım, Tuncel Çaylı, Nesrin Çaylı, Elvan Çaylı, Mert Umur, Aysel İrtem, Cahit Koççoban, Haşim Aydemir, Mirza Metin, Berfin Zenderlioğlu, Berfu Arslan Ağırsoy, Murad Aygün, Zülfikar Tak, Irfan Babaoglu, Necmettin Ünal, Umut Kart, Gökhan Karakuş, Gözde Kavalcı, Manuela Antunes, Cale Lobba, Cecilia Bizzotto, Laura Barbi, Artur Assis, Katy Beinart, Ömer Aktaş, Günseli Ulusoy, Ali Aslan Yıldız, İsmail Pehlivan, Miraz Bezar, Bahar Başer Öztürk, Hakan Vreskala, Özge Ersoy, James Halliday, Adnan Fırat, Ramazan Ergin, Rasa Antanavičiūtė, Kostas Bogdanas, Horst Hoheisel, Güvenç Topçuoğlu, Andreas Mihalopoulos-Philippopoulos, Manca Bajec, Helene Kazan, Emre Özdamarlar,

Peg Rawes, Irit Dekel, Stamatis Zografos, Volkan Taşkın, Yelta Köm, Aslı Çavuşoğlu, Lorans Tanatar Baruh, Samuel Merrill, Timur Hammond, Gül Köksal, Tom Snow, Sefa Yerlikaya, Cevat Üstün, Vazken Khatchig Davidian, Krikor Moskofian, Joost Jongerden, Charles Stewart, Janine Su, Aykut Öztürk, Sinan Logie, Didem Özbek, Marina Lathouri, Eva Branscome, Danilo Mandic, Barbara Penner, Mario Carpo, Francisco Sanin, Ivar Björkman, Maria Paz, Lea Bonde Christensen, Omri Grinberg, Theresa Truax-Gischler, Kabir Tambar, Kyle Evered, Peggy Solic, Lisa Renee Kuerbis, Fred Wellner, Annette Wenda, Miranda Baur, Meghan Cafarelli, Allison McKechnie, and Nino Biniashvili. I apologize to anyone I may have forgotten.

The fieldwork underpinning this book used funding from University College London; Konstfack University College of Arts, Crafts, and Design in Stockholm; the German Academic Exchange Service DAAD; and the Istanbul-based art institution SALT.

Previous versions of chapter 1, 3, and 6 were published as peer-reviewed articles in *Environment and Planning D: Society and Space*, *International Journal of Urban and Regional Research*, and *Space and Culture*, respectively.

My deepest gratitude is to Sera Bal for her boundless patience and endless support.

Note on Language and Illustrations

All photographs and maps are mine unless otherwise stated. All translations to English are mine, and all italicized non-English words are in Turkish unless otherwise stated. The interlocutors to whom I refer only by first name have been given pseudonyms.

The following Turkish terms appear more than once in their original form: *cemevi* (pronounced "djemevi," place of Alevi ritual and worship), *kamu* (public, the people), *kamulaştırma/kamulaştırılma* (expropriation; literally, making public), *kamusal* (that which is public and/or concerns the people), *memleket* (native village, town, or country, whether by birth or by ancestral link), *meydan* (public/town square, and the space of Alevi ritual, worship, and judgment by peers), *şehadet* (martyrdom), and *şehit* (martyr).

As regards local government, an important distinction exists in Turkey between the mayor (*belediye başkanı*; literally, municipal president), who is in charge of the municipality (*belediye*) of a town or city, and the governor (*vali*), who governs the province (*il*) in which the town or city is located. Whereas mayors are elected by popular vote in local elections held every five years, governors are assigned to duty by the central government.

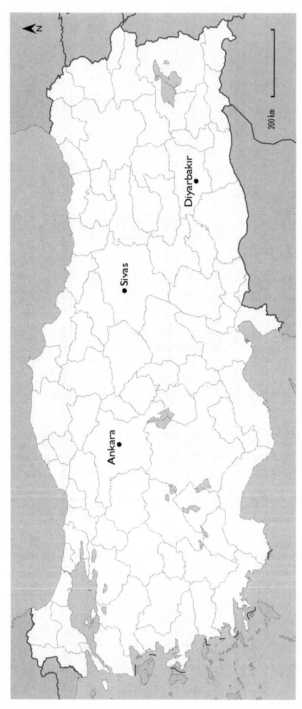

Map 1. Map of Turkey, marking the three cities of Ankara, Sivas, and Diyarbakır discussed in this book.

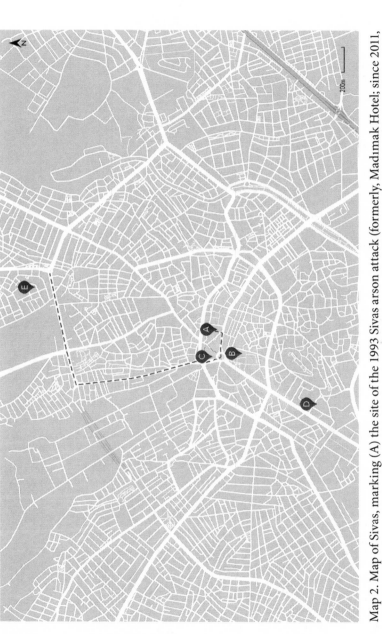

Map 2. Map of Sivas, marking (A) the site of the 1993 Sivas arson attack (formerly, Madımak Hotel; since 2011, Science and Culture Center), (B) Buruciye Madrassa (where eventual victims and survivors were first assaulted on the day of the arson attack), (C) Sivas Governor's Office (a major target of the assailants in the buildup to the arson attack), (D) main venue for 1993 Pir Sultan Abdal Culture Festival whose guests were targeted in the arson attack, and (E) Alibaba neighborhood (Sivas's "Alevi neighborhood" and departure point for annual activist-run commemorations; dotted lines indicate the route of procession).

Map 3. Map of Ankara, marking (A) Ulucanlar Prison Museum (before 2010, Ulucanlar Prison), and (B) the venue for the exhibition "September 12 Museum of Shame" held annually by memory activists.

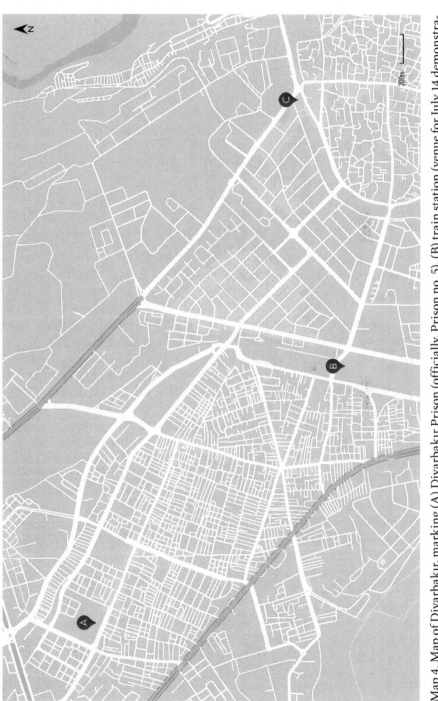

Map 4. Map of Diyarbakır, marking (A) Diyarbakır Prison (officially, Prison no. 5), (B) train station (venue for July 14 demonstrations), (C) Dağkapı Square (venue for "Civilian Friday" prayers).

Victims of Commemoration

Introduction

Architecture, Violence, and "Confronting the Past"

It is September 2011. General elections were held in Turkey just three months ago, resulting in the governing AKP's (Justice and Development Party) landslide victory and extending their rule seamlessly into its second decade. The government has hailed the result as evidence that "the coup era is over" and that "Turkey is ready to join the club of advanced democracies" (Arınç 2011). A year ago, a referendum called by the AKP government put a series of constitutional amendments to the vote. It was scheduled deliberately for September 12, the thirtieth anniversary of Turkey's last conventional and successful military coup. Recep Tayyip Erdoğan, leader of the AKP and prime minister, spoke of voting yes as key to "confronting September 12" and to "a freedom, democracy, stability, justice on a par with European standards"—"those who do not confront their past," he said, "cannot construct a bright future."[1] In the lead-up to the referendum, the government held a series of "workshops" with representatives of nongovernmental organizations and historically marginalized ethnic and/or religious minorities.[2] According to Erdoğan, the workshops

1. For Erdoğan's full speech, see "Darbelerden nemalanmadık" [The Coups Did Not Benefit Us], *Sabah*, July 23, 2010, http://www.sabah.com.tr/gundem/2010/07/23/basbakandan_carpici_aciklamalar.

2. The only constitutional minorities in Turkey are non-Muslim ones such as Jews, Armenians, and Greeks, whereas the "minorities" involved in this series of workshops were not limited to non-Muslims. Therefore, here I use the term *minority* as a shorthand for demographics organized around minoritized ethnic and/or religious identities. Exact numbers in this respect are uncertain as the country has no census that records these identities. For an excellent ethnographic study of how the very construction of "minority" as a political and conceptual category and its subsequent officializations in Turkey

1

aimed to "democratize the state" by "revising and indeed reconstructing its historical memory" (T.C. Devlet Bakanlığı 2010, 5–6). Central to that memory is a string of violent episodes dating from the twentieth century that have implicated the country's past administrations in the persecution of the minorities represented in the workshops. Representatives of such minorities have campaigned over the past decade to raise awareness about these episodes of state-endorsed violence. The campaigns have spotlighted demands for the state to recognize its role in the plight of the victims by transforming sites of violence toward a commemorative end.

I am in downtown Sivas in central-eastern Turkey. This city is at the heart of a commemorative campaign that has pioneered various calls for the country to "confront" its "past" echoed in Erdoğan's words about the referendum and the workshops. An arson attack took place here in 1993 at the Madımak Hotel—in broad daylight and before an inactive law enforcement, thousands of onlookers, and live TV cameras. It killed two of the hotel's employees and thirty-three of its guests. The latter were in Sivas to participate in a cultural festival organized by an association representing followers of the Alevi faith whose practices and rituals are distinct from those of Sunnism, Turkey's predominant denomination. Only a week after the arson, representatives of various left-leaning political parties and professional organizations launched a campaign demanding that the state designate the hotel as a "museum of shame," thereby introducing to Turkey this concept that various commemorative campaigns throughout the following decade would adopt. But the building was fast repaired to continue serving commercial purposes, including that of a grilled-meat restaurant. Come 2009, the so-called Alevi workshops presented five key demands to the government, among which was an on-site museum commemorating the arson attack. This was followed by the authorities' expropriation of the hotel. They then converted the building into a commemorative-cum-educational institution called the Science and Culture Center and opened it to the public just a couple of weeks before last June's general elections. I have come to Sivas to observe and document the outcomes of this recent development.

---

are bound up with the genocides of non-Muslims and the material dispossession involved therein, see Biner 2020.

I am standing outside the Science and Culture Center, waiting for it to reopen as this busy weekday lunchtime draws to a close. A man in his early forties approaches, together with two little girls. Confronted with closed doors, he peers about. I tell him that the building's recent conversion has made it a state-run institution, which therefore means lunchtime closure. "Thank you," he replies, and joins me in the wait. To pass the time, the man starts showing the little girls around—his daughters, as I now find out. Something startles him. Grabbing his daughters by the hand, he hurries across the street. There, the man stops outside a restaurant that happens to serve grilled meat, as had been done on the ground floor of the Madımak Hotel until a couple of years ago. Furious, the man shouts into the face of unruffled customers enjoying their lunch by open windows: "I'm originally from Sivas but live elsewhere. When I read that Madımak was becoming a museum, I started thinking of moving back here with my family. But now that I've seen you, I've changed my mind. What a disgrace—still eating kebabs here! Shame on you!" The diners seem unmoved by the man's outburst; he and his daughters leave the scene without setting foot inside the building they have come here to visit.

Scholarly appraisals of commemoration tend to approach the politics of its relationship with violence as a question of representation and/or reception—of how commemoration narrates or aestheticizes the violence and/or how the public responds to it. In so doing, they assume that commemoration is always already posterior to violence and that publicness is always necessarily nonviolent. Where the pastness of the past is considered questionable, the tendency is to praise this questionability sweepingly as a desirable effect that results from commemoration rather than problematize it as a strictly social and political matter with contrasting implications for different groups or individuals. The man's encounter with the grill restaurant indicates the need to reconsider these tendencies. The man may have come to Sivas to visit and respond to a publicly accessible space where the 1993 arson attack is commemorated. But this expectation is thrown into disarray by ongoing daily affairs around the site and the associations they trigger in the man's psyche with the very event that he hoped had long been left behind. If the encounter reveals the *past's* being anything but that, then this is a feature of neither the representation he has come to Sivas to visit nor his reception of it. The past's pastness is rendered questionable owing to continuing political conflicts and contestations that structure the seemingly nonviolent everyday but are revealed as associable with the violent past when necessary material and social factors crystallize and when there is someone to speak this crystallization out. As such, this becoming-present of the past is anything but desirable, especially for the very individual who experiences and verbalizes it.

This book departs from the scholarly tendency in appraisals of commemoration of state-endorsed violence to mistake the ideal of nonviolence and publicness for the reality that is violence's continuing presence, including in the very spaces and spheres where commemoration takes place and encounters publics. The urgency of rethinking this focus has been nowhere more salient than in the case of contemporary Turkey, whose image both in academia and elsewhere has rapidly descended from a regional beacon of democratization and prosperity to a hotbed of conflict and oppression within the space of a few recent years. I address this urgency by turning to three sites in Turkey where discourses and practices of confronting the past have crystallized. These sites are Ulucanlar Prison in Ankara, where leaders of Turkey's '68 student movement were hanged under the influence of the military; Diyarbakır Prison, where pro-Kurdish activists were tortured by the 1980 junta; and Madımak Hotel in Sivas, where an arson attack targeted the participants of an Alevi-run culture festival in 1993 before an inactive law enforcement and thousands of onlookers. *Victims of Commemoration* studies activist and official commemorations held at the three sites, architectural projects for turning them into memorial museums, and the reverberations of these commemorative acts and artifacts across the everyday life of the city where each site is located. The first comprehensive account of space's centrality to confronting state-endorsed violence in contemporary Turkey, the book is based on an ethnography conducted between 2011 and 2013, the very year when Turkey's global image began to deteriorate as mentioned above. I challenge the tendency in memory studies and postconflict studies, including those on contemporary Turkey, to understand the cultural practice of commemoration and its public import as always already posterior to or ontologically distinct from violence. The book argues that the benchmark against which to appraise commemoration is not the instances of violence and injustice it proclaims to overcome but rather those that exist alongside or within it and are at times even exacerbated by it.

The fieldwork that underpins this book began simultaneously with the first government-sponsored transformation of sites of violence at a time when "confronting the past," "democratization," and "Europeanization" were on the lips of mainstream commentators on Turkey both within the country and abroad. It ended in 2013 when Turkey witnessed widespread mass protests, causing the mainstream narrative about its administration to gradually shift from one of democracy to one of authoritarianism. Throughout these two years, I talked to the government officials involved in transforming sites of violence, observed life in and around each site, attended activist commemorations, and visited places elsewhere in Turkey and beyond where relevant commemorative initiatives were pursued. *Victims of Commemoration* is therefore the first scholarly work to take seriously the medium of spatiality that has been central to discourses and practices of "confronting the past" in Turkey. The book is also original in the ethnographically grounded nuance it adds to the prevailing image of this period as a time when the country's democracy eroded suddenly and rapidly. Its architectural focus helps reveal that such dyads as authoritarianism versus democracy, past versus present, and violence versus peace are the stuff of embodied, situated, and aesthetic experiences shaped not only by policy and discourse but also by contestations and antagonisms unfolding in concrete sociopolitical contexts.

The Architecture and Violence of "Confronting the Past"

Over the past three decades, commemoration has become one of the most widely researched topics in the humanities and social sciences. So prolific is this research that it has engendered a near-autonomous scholarly field called memory studies, shedding unprecedented light on the political work done by and through monuments, memorials, and site-specific commemorative practices. Increasingly throughout this period, scholars of memory and memorialization have come to conceptualize commemoration as not "a thing" but rather "a process" characterized by "varieties, contradictions, and dynamism" (Olick 2008, 159) and as productive of not just "meanings" about the past but also "affects and effects" in the present (Rigney 2015). They have helped understand the commemorative act or artifact as intimately linked to others separated from it, whether in space or in time. Commemoration, the scholarship has shown, operates "multi-directionally" across time; it evolves dialogically by borrowing from and cross-referencing commemorative artifacts or practices seemingly distinct from it and thus loosening the bind between memory and identity (Rothberg 2009). Influenced by "globalization," scholars have also demonstrated that commemorative artifacts and practices "travel" or "move" in space, transcending national or ethnic and cultural boundaries (Levy and Sznaider 2006; Assmann and Conrad 2010; Erll 2011; Rigney 2012; Bond and Rapson 2014). The empirical transversality characterizing this scholarship has inspired a revision of "methodological nationalisms," triggering an appreciation for the multiple "scales" across which commemoration operates, including the local, the everyday, the national, and the global (Cesari and Rigney 2014; Kennedy and Nugent 2016). This methodological revision has helped acknowledge commemoration's increasing "cosmopolitanism"—its becoming progressively more divergent, unsettling, and pluralistic rather than convergent, reassuring, and universalistic (Levy and Sznaider 2006; Rothberg 2009).

In this book, I take my cue from these various explorations of commemoration as processual, affective, multidirectional, transversal, mobile, multiscalar, and divergent. The opening vignette indicates their relevance to my material. The man's visit with his daughters to the site of the arson attack is motivated by news of its commemorative transformation. But the affective qualities of fire and its inextricable association with the site, which derive from not just the blaze but also its aftermath when part of the building served as a grill restaurant, prove difficult to obliterate. The otherwise mundane business of serving and having lunch across the street from the building attacked by arsonists therefore becomes embroiled in the overlapping of diverse spatial scales and the temporalities associated with them. So processual does this embroilment render commemoration that it precludes the seemingly straightforward act of a family visit to a site transformed partly to encourage such visits; it renders the outcome of the architectural transformation virtually irrelevant to commemoration.

That said, much of the empirical material discussed in this book is also a call to critically reconsider methodological tendencies that have persisted among memory studies scholars throughout the past three decades of its evolution into an autonomous scholarly field. The first tendency is the assumption that violence and its commemoration each constitute a discrete and singular event. The opening vignette foreshadows some of the reasons why my empirical material might call this assumption into question. The man's encounter with the grill restaurant across the street from the former Madımak Hotel upends his presupposition that the arson attack is over and done with. The site's transformation may have motivated both his visit and his plans to move to Sivas. But this motivation is reversed and replaced by the lack of a sense of closure that his encounter with the diners makes him feel regarding the arson attack. Such qualities as processuality, affectivity, multidirectionality, transversality, mobility, multiscalarity, and divergence, which imply a lack of closure, of calculability, and of completion, therefore characterize not only the man's memory of the arson attack being commemorated but also the very ontological distinction between violence and its commemoration. In bringing this distinction into question, the vignette also points to the second methodological tendency worthy of reconsideration. It indicates that incompletion, incalculability, and the absence of closure may not be so categorically emancipatory as many a proponent of memory studies would like to assume or that the very ability to prefer these over completion, calculability, and closure might itself be implicated in the unequal relations of power resulting from violence in the first place.

In reconsidering these tendencies, I take my cue from Robin Wagner-Pacifici's problematization of the idea that commemoration pertains only to "the aftermath, after-effects, or afterlife of" the event being commemorated (2015, 22). She proposes to understand commemoration instead as "part and parcel" of the continuing development of the event (2010, 1362; 2015, 26). The misunderstanding that commemorative representations are merely "memory" and thus ontologically distinct from the events being represented becomes especially problematic in the case of violent events (Wagner-Pacifici 2015, 23). The violence that marks the "past" being commemorated is often readily acknowledged. But the ways in which the "cultural" work of that past's being named, appropriated, and displaced in its apparent "aftermath" might be entangled in the very violence being commemorated is often overlooked (Wagner-Pacifici 2010, 1358; Wagner-Pacifici 2015, 22). The segment of memory studies literature that focuses on spatial memorialization has been especially affected by this problem. Monuments and memorials are explored in terms of their various processual and relational aspects, including the contestations and controversies surrounding their design and construction (Wagner-Pacifici and Schwartz 1991; Linenthal 2001, 117; Foote 2003, 6; Carrier 2005, 228; Stevens and Franck 2016, 236; Young 2016, 16), their relationships to the urban settings in which they are located (Aguilera 2014, 110), and the myriad ways publics interact with them (Wagner-Pacifici and Schwartz 1991, 416; Foote 2003, 27–32; Young 2016, 155–83). This multifarious exploration has influentially demonstrated the significance of memorialization as pertaining not only to representation of the past event but also to various present-day events involved in its cultural production and reception. But it has left intact the methodological problem that the event being memorialized, that is, "violence," is singular, complete, and readily locatable in time, and therefore ontologically distinct from the events surrounding memorialization, that is, "culture."

The built environment offers an apt medium through which to approach this problem. Take Andrew Herscher's work on the 1990s destruction of architectural heritage in former Yugoslavia (2008, 2010). He echoes anthropologist Allen Feldman's observation that violence has conventionally been understood as "a surface expression of 'deeper' socio-economic and/or ideological contexts" and therefore as devoid "of any intrinsic semantic or causal character" (1991, 19). This understanding, for Herscher, overlooks violence's function as "a key process of delegation, . . . a way for its perpetrators to arrogate a collective identity, as opposed to simply mediate an identity that preexists its violent performance" (2008, 41). In acknowledging the "exploratory" potential of violence, he seeks to grant it the same sort of semantic autonomy that "humanist discourse" assigns to "culture," including architecture (2010, 3–4).[3] This acknowledgment

3. What Herscher is doing here, therefore, is not only to advance the more obvious argument against those who see violence as "senseless barbarism," but also to argue against those such as Bevan (2006) who have studied destruction as a rational and

avoids reducing violence's architectural implications to "senseless barbarism" or to "targeted destruction" (Herscher 2008, 41) and legitimizes the application of methodologies employed in analyzing culture to the study of violence. Similarly, critical geographers Derek Alderman, Joshua Inwood, and James Tyner advocate a shift of focus in analyses of the relationship between landscape and violence. The shift involves extending the semantic attention paid to landscape's role in commemorating violent histories to the ways in which it produces and is produced by violence (2014, 906–7).

In this book I work from such critical reconsiderations that have explored violence and culture as mutually entangled rather than antithetical. If they have attended to this entanglement by analyzing the culture that inheres in violence, I venture to its flip side. I attend to the violence that inheres in culture or, better put, in cultures of commemoration as they become manifest through the built environment. This attention builds on various retheorizations of violence that have been formulated since the late twentieth century, which have shown it to be much more

---

ideologically motivated phenomenon and thus one whose function is simply to represent or manifest preordained meanings and agendas. Bechir Kenzari (2011a, 13–14) has echoed Herscher's point, going on to argue that a "reflection upon the reality of violence in relation to architecture must first take into account and come to terms with the history of the rites of construction" that is itself replete with violent conduct (2011b, 151). Herscher's book includes a useful historiette of architectural and artistic destruction as cultural production (2010, 7–10) and that of destruction's centrality to urban-architectural modernization (25–27). For a compilation of brief yet wide-ranging essays that pioneered the scholarly discussion on the relationship between architectural space and violence, see the April 1993 issue of the journal *Assemblage*. Beatriz Colomina's (1993) essay in that compilation is especially pertinent as it shows, through Le Corbusier's defacement of Eileen Gray's house E-1027, how latent yet inherent an aspect of architecture that violence is, even in the case of works and architects associated with the canons of architectural history. This pathbreaking *Assemblage* issue was followed by renowned architect Bernard Tschumi's (1996, 122–38) consideration of violence's role in architecture as a systemic and structural force rather than one that materializes exclusively through destruction. For a recent survey of terms that scholars have developed to conceptualize architectural destruction, see Boano 2011, 41–42.

than just readily discernible outbursts of physical aggression. Slavoj Žižek, for instance, has termed the latter "subjective violence"—violence inflicted by a specific subject on another—and has distinguished it from "objective violence" (2008). This second type of violence recalls Paul Farmer's notion of "structural violence" (2004), which he developed after Johan Galtung (1969). While Farmer's and Žižek's concepts undoubtedly differ from each other in important ways (Van der Linden 2012), they are comparable in terms of their shared concern for an analysis of violence that takes into account the semantic and economic structures framing social relations found in particular contexts. More specifically, for Žižek, "objective violence" has two subsets: "symbolic violence," which involves "language" and "its imposition of a certain universe of meaning," and "systemic violence," which concerns "the smooth functioning of our economic and political systems" (2008, 1). The built environment is among the foremost realms where the two subsets overlap, as architecture has long served both symbolic and economic agendas. The overlap is arguably nowhere more salient than in cases of spatial commemoration; the very semantic instrumentality of monuments, memorials, and memorial museums is often seen as a justification for the disproportion between costliness and practical usefulness that characterizes them and that is otherwise widely frowned upon in architecture.

Exploring cultures of spatial commemoration for their entanglement in violence is not to suggest that they are a form of "objective" or "structural" violence. Doing so would be to assume that "violence" as well as "space" is easily contourable and that the former operates uniformly across the latter. Commenting on Farmer's Galtung-inspired conceptualization of "structural violence," Loïc Wacquant has outlined three reasons such an assumption might debilitate the concept's analytical potential (Farmer 2004, 322). First, it overlooks the unequal distribution of violence's effects across the bodies populating a given space; in fact, for many of its direct victims, "structural violence" is not invisible or difficult to contour, as they feel its effects in physical and readily discernible ways. Second, conflating instances of violence traceable to specific culprits with those involving consensual subordination through power relations flattens the varying degrees of responsibility involved in each instance.

Finally, the anachronistic collapsing of various phenomena from across history under the same heading of "structural violence" overlooks the importance of historical context and the meaning each such phenomenon carried at the time of its occurrence. Jenna Loyd's take on the concept has sought to amend these shortcomings. Instead of understanding "structural violence" as operating uniformly across space in the abstract, she has proposed to conceptualize the structurality in question as involving context-specific spatial imaginaries that derive from unaccounted-for histories of violence and that facilitate the continued infliction of observable harm on members of particular sociopolitical groups (2012).

Victims of Commemoration directs the methodologies used in analyzing violence to the study of commemorative artifacts and practices. It explores the ways in which these artifacts and practices might be entangled in structural or objective violence. But, in so doing, the book also follows the above-mentioned critical perspectives that have helped nuance precisely what the adjective *objective* or *structural* might entail in this context. This means to avoid compartmentalizing violence into distinct forms and/or scales that operate in mutual isolation or with identical effects across time and space—hence the book's exploration of spatial commemoration's symbolic and systemic violence as operating in tandem and with sociopolitical selectivity. Reasons that justify this exploration are twofold. The first involves commemoration's role in semantically obfuscating the decisively sociopolitical nature of why violence targets the victims it does. The second reason concerns spatial commemoration's systemic role in gradually institutionalizing this semantic obfuscation as the basis of the only legitimate meaning attributable to the violence, and in so doing authorizing new violent episodes inflicting observable harm on subjects sociopolitically comparable to those targeted previously. If students of commemoration must avoid taking it for granted as indexing the aftermath of violence and focus instead on how it might operate as violence's medium, they must also refrain from essentializing this operation as spatially and temporally uniform or, better put, as sociopolitically indiscriminate. *Victims of Commemoration* therefore argues that only by attending to commemoration's entanglement in asymmetrical power relations formed by violent histories and formative of new forms of symbolic and systemic violence with observably harmful effects might its promise of "confronting the past" be reclaimed. It is with such attention that the book also presents critical analyses of relevant practices marked by just this sort of a reversal that renders spatial commemoration a medium of empowering those marginalized by violence rather than one of further disempowering them.[4]

"Confronting the Past" in Twenty-First-Century Turkey

Prior to their proliferation in the 2010s, discourses and practices of "confronting the past" (*geçmişle yüzleşme*) had already been in circulation in Turkey for more than a decade and a half. Their origins indeed lie in the immediate aftermath of one of the episodes of violence discussed in this book: the Sivas arson attack of 1993. Just a week after the attack, when anger among victims' relatives and their sociopolitical allies had barely, if at all, given way to grief and mourning, a group of representatives from various left-leaning political parties and professional organizations launched a commemorative campaign. They demanded that the state turn the charred remains of the Madımak Hotel into a memorial museum, citing "Europe's World War II sites" bearing "fascism's inhumanity" as a model (Ekinci 1993). As the millennial turn saw Turkey become a candidate for European Union membership, the campaign not only mustered growing support among representatives of Turkey's Alevis but also inspired various other sociopolitical groups to pursue such campaigns. Among the latter was a campaign on the Ulucanlar Prison in the capital, Ankara, notorious for having witnessed the military-endorsed hanging of Turkey's revolutionary youth leaders in 1972 and the government's violent crackdown on socialist prisoners on a hunger strike in 2000. Following the prison's evacuation in 2006, the local Chamber of Architects and former left-wing political convicts launched a campaign demanding its conversion into a

---

4. My emphasis here on the question of power in explorations of victimhood and particularly on the imperative to avoid reproducing violence's effects on victims by producing knowledge about them in ways that deprive them of agency is not unprecedented. It follows recent scholarship that has attended to such an imperative (Stølen 2007; Fassin and Rechtman 2009; Jensen and Ronsbo 2014).

memorial museum. Another such campaign concerned the Diyarbakır Prison located in the eponymous city in Turkey's Southeast that is its largest predominantly Kurdish-inhabited one and the unofficial capital of northern Kurdistan. The prison is infamous for the torture of Kurdish political prisoners under the junta instituted by the violent coup of September 12, 1980, and, as such, became the subject of a memorial museum campaign launched in 2009 by a group of activist initiatives associated with the pro-Kurdish political movement.

As the 2000s gave way to the 2010s, campaigns for memorial museums reached unprecedented visibility and began yielding practical results. In 2011 the government redesigned the Ulucanlar Prison as a museum as well as turning the site of the Sivas arson attack into a commemorative-cum-educational institution. Around the same time, senior cabinet members including Prime Minister Erdoğan declared their willingness to close down the Diyarbakır Prison and/or turn it into a museum. Importantly, these developments unfolded in a political climate framed by a government initiative known popularly as Democratic Opening (*Demokratik Açılım*) that saw cabinet members meet with nongovernmental actors and representatives from historically underrepresented groups such as Kurds, Alevis, and non-Muslims. Senior cabinet members heralded the initiative as an opportunity for "the state to revise its memory" (T.C. Devlet Bakanlığı 2010, 6, 17). The initiative marked the lead-up to the constitutional referendum that, as mentioned earlier, was scheduled to fall on the thirtieth anniversary of the 1980 coup and in which the government vigorously campaigned for a yes vote as itself a means of confronting the past.[5]

5. The 2010s also witnessed unprecedented broadening of the sociopolitical spectrum across which campaigns for memorial museums were launched. The PKK (Kurdistan Workers' Party) embarked on a project to turn a house where thirty-three of their members were killed in a 1992 skirmish with the army into a museum. The Turkish army's December 2011 air strike that killed thirty-four civilians in the village of Roboskî near Turkey's border with Iraq—an attack whose exact perpetrators have yet to be found and brought before justice—has since its first anniversary become the subject of an architectural competition for an on site memorial museum, led under the slogan "Justice Emerges from the Site of Injustice" by activist organizations claiming the victims' legacy. The AKP

The fieldwork underpinning this book took place at this historical juncture and involved the sites of state-endorsed violence in Sivas, Ankara, and Diyarbakır mentioned above. Between 2011 and 2013, I talked to activists campaigning for memorial museums at these sites and state officials to whom the campaigns were addressed. Overall, the ethnography involved not only the designers, sponsors, managers, users, and visitors of commemorative spaces but also those who contest, pass by, inhabit the vicinity of, or refuse to engage with relevant sites. The material that features in my ethnography among these individuals draws on local and national newspapers, architectural plans, archival documents, TV coverage, documentaries, and photography alongside buildings, cityscapes, and landscapes. I conducted an ethnography of commemorative initiatives in the three cities and beyond, including villages hosting self-funded memorials to victims. Throughout this fieldwork, I explored not only the political possibilities and limitations of relying on site-specific memorialization in the pursuit of recognition of and justice for victims of state-endorsed violence but also the following context-specific question: How would these political possibilities and limitations as well as the victimhood they represented be affected by the becoming-mainstream of campaigns for the commemorative transformation of sites of state-endorsed violence?

The Aesthetics of Confronting the Past and the Question of Power

The politics of cultural production in Turkey that aims to "confront the past" has been the subject of a growing body of critical scholarship over the past decade. One strand of this scholarship relevant to this book focuses on the forms and media—the aesthetics—involved in discourses and practices of confronting the past. It distinguishes between those forms and media that subscribe to dominant aesthetic regimes—regimes of visibility, audibility, and tangibility—and those that do not. The former are

---

government itself launched and completed a memorial museum project on Yassıada, the island off Istanbul that witnessed the 1960 junta's trials of the then ruling DP (Democrat Party) members whose political legacy Erdoğan's ilk have long upheld.

criticized for tending toward closure and thus separating the past from the present. The criticism is that this tendency locates violence solely in the past and thus legitimizes emergent power asymmetries laden with their own violent potential. Self-proclaimed challenges to dominant discourses and practices of confronting the past are also evaluated in light of this focus on forms and media. Whether for better or for worse, the sociopolitical function of attempts at mediating past violence is therefore seen as deriving primarily from their aesthetics understood mainly as a question of form or medium. In this book I take my cue from this critical literature in attending to the aesthetics of mediation and its potential to affect power relations virtually independently of mediators' intentions. But I also seek to contribute to the literature by reconsidering the idea that any given instance of mediation engenders only one sort of effect on power. I propose to approach such effects instead as hinging, if partly, on *political work proper*—the work of organizing and mobilizing that is undertaken by, addressed to and generative of *collectives*. I suggest that the sort of spatial focus adopted in this book enables such an approach.

Any survey of the emergence of "the past" as a significant interest in ethnographically informed literature on Turkey must begin with analyses of the transformations that affected the republic's founding ideology, Kemalism, around the millennial turn. Simultaneously with momentous developments at the end of the twentieth century, such as Turkey's integration into global markets and the disintegration of Cold War–era ideological camps, Kemalism grew out of the conventional bureaucratism and institutionalism that had been its modus operandi since the republic's inauguration in the 1920s. Personified in its founder Mustafa Kemal's cult, the republic's secularist ideology became, according to Yael Navaro-Yashin (2002), the stuff of a "public" cult—a sort of "state fetishism" with more than secular qualities such as magic, myth, emotionality, and spirituality.[6] Esra Özyürek (2006) observed the cult's "privatization" through commodification as well as personalization. Both these ethnographies therefore featured "the state" as having expanded its influence by

6. In making this point, Navaro-Yashin echoes Taussig 1997.

becoming an object, whether one of desire, fear, and reverence (Navaro-Yashin 2002) or one of loss, mourning, and nostalgia (Özyürek 2006). The "Turkish modernity project" was no longer just the stuff of History; it had become the subject of histories and memories (Neyzi 2002). Accordingly, a culture of "public memory" emerged in Turkey, whose publicness derived from its being not only collective but also contested (Özyürek 2007).

As plural and contested interpretations of Turkey's twentieth century moved from the political fringe to the mainstream in the mid-2000s, critical scholarship on the subject turned toward nascent power relations this move upheld. Scholars have since criticized mainstream approaches to histories of violence for tending toward closure and in so doing masking troublesome continuities that link the past to the present (Ahıska and Kırlı 2006; B. Karaca 2011; Maessen 2014; Kaya 2015). They have considered this tendency as characterized by a certain aesthetic—an unquestioning preference for presence. Writing on the celebratory reception of the authorities' expressions of regret and condolences for past violence that implicates their predecessors, Bilgin Ayata and Serra Hakyemez (2013), for instance, have criticized the assumption that acknowledging violent histories verbally suffices to ensure accountability and justice without attending to the questions of by whom, where, when, and precisely how the acknowledgment is expressed. Challenges to such mainstream acknowledgments of past violence have not been free from criticism, either. Scholars have criticized, for at least two reasons, particularly those challenges to mainstream commemoration that have been oriented toward making victimhood visible. The first reason is that this orientation risks reproducing the objectifying gaze that underpinned the violence inflicted on victims in the first place (Iğsız 2008; Neyzi and Darıcı 2015; Spence and Kotaman Avcı 2013; Tambar 2014, 77–106). Second, it risks erasing the historical persecution of various other individuals and groups who may not have had the sort of representation available to those fixated on making their own victimhood visible (Mills 2010; Törne 2015). Following this critique through, scholars have turned to the progressive political potential of cultural practices that prioritize silence or inaudibility over voice (Schäfers 2018; Tambar 2017) and absence over presence (Suner 2009, 2011), or those that escape dominant genres of audibility and visibility by, for instance, using voice for its material qualities rather than simply metaphorical ones (Schäfers 2019).

Few commemorative forms, genres, and/or media are more markedly obsessed with presence (not least one grounded in dominant regimes of visibility) and with a tendency toward closure than those featured in this book: a memorial museum, a culture center, monuments, name lists, and memorial processions. Yet, as this book evinces throughout, the effects they are made to produce are far from being reducible to the objectification of victimhood, the legitimization of emergent power relations, and the effacing of other violent histories than those they directly commemorate. This is not to say that aesthetics is not relevant to commemoration's sociopolitical effects. If anything, attention to aesthetics helps to show that commemoration's effects are irreducible to commemorators' identities and to appreciate the political generativity of commemorative practice. It therefore resonates with recent anthropological literature on state-citizen relations in Turkey. As indicated above, this literature has cautioned against reifying "the state" and "civil society" as anthropomorphic concepts—whether benign or malign—that preexist the messy, day-to-day, and conflict-ridden situations through which each concept assumes its political function (Navaro-Yashin 2002; Biner 2011). These situations include commemorative ones, and aesthetics serves as a useful theoretical lens for grasping how their political function arises significantly from the genres, media, and forms through which they render commemoration available to the senses and/or to an embodied rationality (Rancière 2004). Nevertheless, recent critical analyses mentioned above, which have tended to center commemoration's aesthetics-as-politics on absence (or silence) and presence (or voice), warrant reconsideration. Even as scholars have aimed to problematize dichotomizing understandings of presence and absence that assume a certain politics (whether progressive or regressive) to inhere in the one or the other, their approach to aesthetics has remained fixated on aesthetic properties, including genre, form, or medium. Doing so has risked reproducing the reification of "state" versus "nonstate" this time as an aesthetic (rather than an anthropomorphic) dyad—whether by focusing politics squarely on presence versus absence or by replacing this focus with one on metaphor versus materiality.

My worry is that such an approach to aesthetics might fall short of the very critical-analytical project of attending to power relations that preoccupies the growing literature on discourses and practices of "confronting the past" in Turkey. In saying this I follow Andrew Herscher's counterposing Foucauldian "countermemory" to "countermonumentality," the latter being the best-known aesthetically focused conceptualization to have come out of the recent strand of critique leveled against closure-driven and presence-oriented commemorative cultures the world over. "If discourse on the countermonument suggests a countermemory that is permanently open to discussion, renegotiation, and contestation, discourse on countermemory suggests contestation with oppressive regimes of power" (Herscher 2014a, 467). Commemoration therefore assumes its contrarian character through the *organized political* work of *collectives* who continue to face the disempowering effects of violent histories and who challenge these effects by confronting those empowered by the same histories. Neither the events constituting "the past" being commemorated nor the political effects achievable through aesthetic properties of commemoration preexist such confrontations and the collective work that underpins them. Categorical interpretations of the drive toward closure as oppressive or certain aesthetic properties (for example, absence rather than presence, materiality rather than metaphor) as politically potent, then, risk overlooking the asymmetries of power that structure the very obligation to continually renegotiate a violent history or to refrain from making visible or audible (or from metaphorizing) one's disempowerment by that history. Such categorical interpretations also risk denying the historically disempowered the opportunity for political progress, overlooking the possibility that they might draw on the political confidence amassed by closing the lid on one set of historical disempowerments to solidarize with endeavors that seek to overcome other histories of disempowerment. The question, then, is not whether commemoration's aesthetics is closure driven, presence oriented, or materialist (in the sense indicated above). It is, rather, who might be empowered or disempowered by presence (and/or absence), closure (and/or lack thereof), or materiality (and/or metaphor) and how, if at all, these forms of empowerment and disempowerment might challenge or perpetuate their violence-induced historical precedents.

Why might spatially focused ethnography be an appropriate method for exploring commemoration as such a question? The spatial focus is appropriate not only because of architecture's significance to recent discourses and practices of "confronting the past" in Turkey, as evinced by the preoccupation across the social spectrum with museum and monument building. The focus on space is appropriate also because it avoids assuming that commemoration's effects on power and entanglements in histories of violence are predetermined by the presumed ethnic or ideological affiliation of its authors and its audiences, while also refusing to replace this assumption with a sharp turn toward the subject and subjectivity as the only sociopolitical category relevant to commemorative politics. A focus on the spatialities that commemoration produces and through which it takes effect helps trace its effects that transcend ethnic or ideological affiliations (Feldman 1991) while also retaining the focus on collectives that undertake, that are exposed to, and that transform through organized political work (Saldanha 2012). This is not to argue that the mutually entangled effects of commemoration and violence are possible to locate only in particular physical spaces (Navaro-Yashin 2002) but rather to suggest that they are made sensible through their spatial qualities (Navaro-Yashin 2003) and are made so *collectively*: by collectives and for collectives. The spatial ethnography offered in this book therefore approaches commemoration as the not necessarily physical site through which both power and counterpower operate as extensions of the disempowerment and empowerment produced by histories of violence. In practical terms, throughout the fieldwork behind this ethnography, I returned repeatedly to each commemorative setting in order to account for commemoration's unevenly distributed sociopolitical effects while also tracing its aesthetically charged mediations and reverberations at other times and places. Doubtless, no single ethnography can claim to be socially all-encompassing, and mine has centered on those upholding the legacy of victims. This is because they are the ones to have both felt most directly how commemoration's power-laden effects entangle it in the very violence it commemorates and endeavored to pose the strongest organized challenges to this entanglement. That said, this book presents an ample amount of empirical material involving various other individuals and groups, too, but does so with a view to furthering the political objectives pursued by those upholding the victims' legacy.

Outline of the Book and Its Main Argument

Victims of Commemoration argues that, in early 2010s Turkey, the (spatial) politics of the relationship between commemoration and violence was irreducible to a question of representation or reception. Commemorative endeavors at sites of violence led to unexpected encounters with histories of state-endorsed violence seemingly different from yet entangled with those being commemorated, such as the Armenian genocide of 1915–16. Securitization of space during activist-led commemorations antagonized activists highlighting the victims' sociopolitical particularity as conspirators against the nation, meanwhile causing them to feel victimized. Relics of violence whose authenticity the authorities boasted as an enhancement to commemoration came to be repurposed in violent threats against present-day oppositional figures. The book therefore shows that the question of victimhood was central to commemoration not only as a matter of historiography but also as the stuff of embodied experiences produced spatially at sites of state-endorsed violence.[7] It moreover charts a process in which victimhood's being experienced as such caused a shift among those seeking recognition of and justice for victims. I argue that this shift was away from an understanding of victimhood as subjection to one that considered it as the basis of subjectivation, particularly by reclaiming the agency to historicize in nonidentarian ways the violence that caused the victimhood in the first place. The book's outline reflects this process and the shift it witnessed.

7. The book therefore charts a process that bridges Jensen and Ronsbo's (2014) distinction between victims and victimhood. Being a victim, for them, requires the experience of suffering, whereas victimhood is a sociopolitical construction, albeit one with significant material import, which it gains through political contestation as well as biopolitical governmentality. The process charted in this book is one wherein the political and biopolitical mechanisms invoked by Jensen and Ronsbo not only produce new experiences of suffering but also suppress and, in so doing, sometimes even worsen existing ones.

Following the introduction, *Victims of Commemoration* comprises seven chapters distributed across three parts. Part 1 is themed "Nationalizing Victimhood" and discusses the two sites of state-endorsed violence that the government has transformed toward a commemorative end. It argues that these transformations sought to nationalize victimhood, as they were based on conspiracy theories regarding Turkey's histories of state-endorsed violence being plots against the entire country. Moreover, it shows how this conspiracy theoretical understanding of history has characterized not only the transformation of the two sites but also the seemingly liberal conditions under which memory activists have been allowed to stage alternative commemorations on site. Titled "Commemoration as Conspiracy in Sivas," chapter 1 discusses the commemorative-cum-educational transformation of the Madımak Hotel and the commemorations held at the site by memory activists. It shows how the fact that many of the memory activists invested in commemorating the arson attack on site live outside Sivas has been rendered the stuff of conspiracy theories that portray them as outsiders, whereas the reason many of them fled Sivas or Turkey in the first place was state-endorsed violence. The chapter demonstrates that this portrayal is reinforced by way of the authorities' securitization of space during activist commemorations. It argues that the visual and spatial connotations of such conspiracy theoretical concepts as "exogenously focused" and "dark plot" have affected site-specific commemorations not only figuratively but also physically. Chapter 2 is titled "Depoliticization of Violence at Ulucanlar Prison Museum." It shows that the way Ulucanlar Prison Museum has represented episodes of state-endorsed violence has depoliticized and decontextualized them; even when the museum has given a platform to victims of state-endorsed violence, it has done so only by detaching them from their ideologies and the political projects they pursued. The chapter concludes part 1 by arguing that the Turkish authorities' conspiracy theory–inspired transformations of sites of state-endorsed violence not only depoliticized the country's violent histories by nationalizing victimhood but also forged a continuity between alleged past conspirators and present-day activists endeavoring to highlight the victims' sociopolitical specificity, thereby exposing the latter to nationalist aggression.

Titled "Protesting Victimhood," part 2 examines spatially charged discourses and practices of publicness that have figured in both activist-led commemorations and in the authorities' attempts to manage and promote sites of violence following their commemorative transformation. It draws on critical theoretical perspectives developed since the 1990s to consider conventional models of public space as entangled in violence. Chapter 3 is titled "Spatial Entanglements between Violence and Publicness in Sivas." It offers an ethnography of conventional and contrarian imaginaries of public space that have featured in commemorations of the Sivas arson attack. It unpacks several context-specific and historically grounded notions that have been central to these imaginaries and discusses their associations with the state, citizenship, and faith. Chapter 4, "Commemorating Diyarbakır Prison Victims in Public," discusses how publicness has served as both a restrictive measure and a dissentient imaginary in commemorations of coup-era torture at the Diyarbakır Prison. Chapter 5 explores both the ways the government has invoked publicness to legitimize its architectural transformation of the Ulucanlar Prison into a memorial museum and the counterpublic imaginaries with which this invocation has been met by former political convicts as they have staged their own commemorative exhibition. Against the tendency in relevant scholarship to identify such imaginaries as unscripted and performative versus rational and legislation facing, this chapter concludes part 2 by showing how Turkey's memory activists have not refrained from engaging conventional models of public space while also developing and mobilizing contrarian ones.

Part 3 is titled "Self-Reflexive Victimhood." It explores the concepts of shame and martyrdom that memory activism in 2010s Turkey has featured prominently, particularly through spatially charged discourses and practices of witnessing that arose from and grappled with violence's destructive impact on subjectivity. Titled "Spatial Testimony in Sivas," chapter 6 explores the spatial underpinnings and consequences of shame and martyrdom—two concepts that have figured heavily in the commemorative repertoire around the Sivas arson attack. Whereas discourses and practices of "confronting the past" in Turkey have tended to take witnessing for granted as an all-encompassing experience, this chapter demonstrates its sociopolitical specificity. It shows how these specific experiences of witnessing have not only rigidified memory activists' subject positionality vis-à-vis histories of violence (for example, leading to greater identification with victims) but also ambiguated it in a way that prompts self-reflection. The chapter considers this self-reflection central to how witnessing has informed the affective trope characterizing activist campaigns for the state to turn the site of the Sivas arson attack into a "museum of shame." The centrality, argues the chapter, has rendered the site conducive to not only remembering the arson attack but also encountering, if unanticipatedly, other episodes than those commemorated by the activists—episodes such as the Armenian genocide of 1915–16. Chapter 7 returns to the case of Diyarbakır to further explore what unanticipated encounters of the sort discussed in chapter 6 might entail for testimony in the spatial mode. Titled "Testifying to Diyarbakır Prison, Architecturally," the chapter shows how acts as ordinary as painting a wall become poorly anticipated but technologically informed and historically situated gateways into witnessing and bearing witness to violence. It argues that such unanticipated encounters enable those identifying with the victims to historicize episodes of state-endorsed violence anew upon every encounter. The chapter concludes part 3 by considering these encounters a scholarly call for appraising the reclamation of victimhood beyond confinement to a passive victim identity and for attending to the ways it hinges on the right to historicization as a form of social and political agency.

Victims of Commemoration closes with a coda that outlines the insights the book offers into more recent developments in Turkey and its environs where political violence has flared up in a markedly urban-spatial way, including the 2013 Gezi Park protests and the war that unfolded in predominantly Kurdish-inhabited cities in 2015–16. The coda rewinds these recent and widely known developments to a yet-to-be-publicized episode from the fieldwork that underpinned this book. This episode, which took place at a time when Turkey was internationally celebrated as a regional beacon of democratization and prosperity, involved my expulsion from the field and led to a high-level bureaucrat's threats of prosecution despite his previous authorization of my work. Tracing an arc from this fieldwork episode to the recent flare-up of violence in Turkey, the coda concludes by interrogating the ways the spatial ethnography of commemoration and the ethnographer are entangled in the linkage between bodily, symbolic, and systemic violence sustained or challenged through commemorative practices and artifacts.

Fieldwork Positionality and Space's Role in It

Having been born in Turkey and spent the first twenty-three years of my life there, I moved abroad for my graduate studies a couple of years before the start of the fieldwork that led to this book. What might this profile have meant for my positionality in the field? Since the advent of the poststructuralist critique of objectivity, reflecting critically on the fieldworker's subject position in the field has become a near imperative in ethnographically informed scholarship. While at the outset of this critique, the problematization of anthropology's colonial origins led ethnography "at home" and by "insiders" or "natives" to emerge as contrarian modalities of representation, over time the very indigeneity at work here came to be problematized. The multiple factors bearing upon the construction of identity, such as ethnicity, racialization, faith, class, and gender, threw being "native" into sharp relief as not only ever changing but also profoundly pluralized and differentialized across the "homes" and "insides" it inhabited (Wolf 1996; Ryang 1997; Navaro-Yashin 2002, 14; Kusow 2003; Butz 2010, 149). Recently, this problematization itself became subject to criticism for leaving intact the native versus nonnative dualism (or its spatial counterparts of insider versus outsider and home versus away). Whether conceived as dichotomous or continual, the dualism was left intact as the only possible axis along which to understand the implications of fieldworker positionality (Ergun and Erdemir 2010; Razon and Ross 2012; Takeyuki 2015). Notwithstanding its critical potentialities, this latest strand of critique has continued to approach fieldworker-interlocutor relations as a question of *being* or belonging and one in which space features primarily as a delineator of positionality whether socially or physically (that is, delineating it through such concepts as inside, outside, home, and away). Thus sidelined is the question of *thinking* and *doing*, and the ways in which space shapes thoughts and deeds in the field rather than simply serving as their container, while undoubtedly also being shaped by them. My fieldwork did sometimes affirm the continuing importance of spatially delineated notions and experiences of being or belonging, but many of the interactions I had in the field also threw it into question.

My fieldwork involved two types of interlocutors. The first constituted the smaller group; these were the people with whom I had close contact and in-depth conversations. The second, larger, group consisted of numerous others with whom I crossed paths for interviews or brief exchanges. The first introduced me to the second and often accompanied my initial encounters with them. Nearly invariably, the question *"Memleket nere?"* prefaced my encounters with the second type of interlocutors, as it does most daily exchanges between strangers in Turkey. *Nere* is vernacular for "where," and *memleket* translates as "homeland." The question often concerns not only the addressee's homeland but also that of their parents and, most commonly, the paternal side. My answer, however, tends to begin with my maternal side, owing mainly to the proximity between its geographical origin and the region of northwestern Turkey where I was born and brought up. My maternal side is *macır*, informal for *muhacir*. This is the Ottoman Turkish word for "migrant" that, in modern-day Turkey, denotes citizens hailing from the Balkans whose Muslim ancestors were forced to relocate to Anatolia in the early twentieth century when they were racialized as Turks amid various projects of ethnic homogenization pursued by nation-states that replaced the crumbling Ottoman Empire in the region. Most Alevi interlocutors responded favorably to my maternal origins, not least because, under the Ottomans, the Balkans hosted a significant Bektashi population whose belief systems many Alevis consider akin to their own (Mélikoff 2004). Indeed, many insisted that, if I search hard enough, I might well discover being of Alevi-Bektashi origin, despite my clarifications to the contrary. However, many were somewhat disappointed when I went on to state my paternal homeland as a town near Afyon's border with Konya, a central Anatolian province long stereotyped as the "bastion of (Sunni) Islamic conservatism" (Sfeir 2007, 111). In northern Kurdistan or Turkey's predominantly Kurdish-inhabited Southeast, the response often marked me as "a Westerner through and through."

That the question "Where are you from?" prefaces fieldwork encounters is not unprecedented (Stoneall 1983; Raj 2003; Myers 2006; Razon and

Ross 2012). What did render my case somewhat different from these precedents, however, was the question's relative insignificance to my fieldwork.
The first type of interlocutors not only did not prioritize it much but also
often intervened to promptly get it over with whenever the second type of
interlocutors asked the question. Note how my company across Alevi villages in Sivas province's Emlek region began to intervene when he realized
the difficulties the second type of interlocutors were having in grappling
with my extended answer to the question. In Ortaköy, he introduced me to
inquisitive villagers as "Örenyurtlu"—as someone from the nearest Sunni
village of Örenyurt. According to him, this would "make things easier for
everybody, because when people ask you where you are from, all they want
to know is whether you are Alevi or Sunni." In the village of Kaymak, I
came to be introduced as someone "from Karavuz," the nearest Sunni village. In bigger cities such as Ankara, I was even called "English," in reference to the country in which I lived and worked. Undoubtedly, everyone
involved knew that such references were not grounded in factuality, as
signposted by grins and giggles. The effect they made, then, was neither
the eradication nor the amplification of difference but rather its familiar-
ization by mapping it onto political geographies known to interlocutors.
Being called a "Westerner through and through" in northern Kurdistan
had a similar effect; it used a geopolitical category that, however broad
and ambiguous in its physical content, was a most familiar marker of
non-Kurdishness.

If the question of *memleket* was not singularly significant to fieldwork, then what was? More significant than this question was the content
of the work. Content featured prominently in my exchanges with interlocutors first because many of them were personally invested in intellectual and cultural production. Indeed, some were ethnographers and/or
historians themselves; Turkey's ethnic, religious, and political minorities
have not only been the subject of many scholarly ethnographies but also
enjoy a long-established tradition of writing about their own histories and
affairs in forms ranging from community biographies to political analyses of violent episodes that have targeted them. This confronted me with
the question of what new insight I could possibly produce when the sort

of issues I had set out to explore had already been covered at great length, not least by those affected by them. In response, I acknowledged existing and extensive explorations of the subject matter. But I also noted that a spatial focus was largely missing from such explorations, even as recent developments surrounding the debate around them had thrown into sharp relief space's importance to the subject. I clarified that my research centered not on the ethnic, religious, or political minorities targeted in episodes of state-endorsed violence (that is, Kurds, Alevis, or revolutionaries) but rather on architecture's role in remembering and forgetting these episodes. Many interlocutors welcomed this response and then went on to use me as a sounding board for brainstorming ideas on architectural commemoration. This is where many self-reflexive accounts of fieldworker positionality and its potential impact on fieldwork might fall short, as they consider space simply as a marker of who the researcher or the interlocutor *is* rather than as the ever-changing medium of what not only researchers but also interlocutors *do* and *think* through the research and what new perspectives these thoughts and deeds might offer relative to existing ones pertinent to the subject matter. In my case, positionality featured more as such a question of doing and thinking through space than as one of being in space.

That those in the field expressed greater interest in what I do than who I am does not mean that their perceptions regarding the political significance of my work's spatial focus were identical from the get-go. Consider some of the encounters I had with state officials and other individuals who do not actively uphold the legacy of victims. While they, too, welcomed the spatial focus of my research, I came to notice that many did so by depoliticizing architecture and space. A case in point was my first meeting with the deputy governor of Sivas province in charge of the Madımak Hotel's transformation into the Science and Culture Center. When I told him about my interest in the Madımak Hotel as one among Turkey's various sites subject to commemorative campaigns, he exclaimed that "they are all very political places!" I confirmed that such sites had been at the center of much political contestation but underexplored as architectural spaces. While this helped resume the conversation, the deputy governor periodically felt obliged to confirm that my "field of study is architecture and space, right?" Similarly, when I went to Sivas municipality's planning department to ask for permission to access their archives, the officers were alarmed by the name Madımak, but, upon hearing about my architectural focus, they smiled and said, "How nice." One of them asked where I went to college. We turned out to be fellow alumni, and she facilitated access. Right-leaning non-Alevi young adults with whom I became acquainted in central Sivas found my research refreshing as one that approached the arson attack through a prism other than the binary of Alevism versus Sunnism or that of secularist leftism versus religious rightism, expressing a sense of stigmatization by such binarisms. The assumption characterizing such responses was that architecture and space were somewhat free from politics and social conflict.

But those who may have adhered to this assumption gradually confronted its invalidity as they further familiarized with my research and encountered some of what it revealed early on about the political energies harbored by urban and architectural space, including spaces they inhabited daily. While, as will be detailed in the book's coda, these encounters did not always benefit my research in a pragmatic-logistic sense, they have underscored that taking space seriously as a critical and analytical focus for ethnography requires approaching fieldwork positionality as a question of thinking and doing rather than simply one of being. Recent attempts to methodize such a focus through the concept of "spatial ethnography" have reiterated the twofold role that space plays in social relations; space may serve as the scene of social relations just as it may shape them actively, if often slowly and inconspicuously, by prompting its inhabitants into new thoughts and deeds (Low 2017; Cuff et al. 2020, 87–96). The first role is what makes space seem a nonthreatening starting point for fieldwork interactions while simultaneously masking the violence that structures it. Space's role as a generative medium and modality, on the other hand, is not only the reason that violent sociopolitical projects have historically been invested in spatial intervention and reorganization but also the opportunity that any proponent and project of social justice must seize by exploiting this generativity to upend violence and its reverberations. Where this book's political analysis deprioritizes the question of the undoubtedly diverse experiences and modes of being and belonging found among its interlocutors and instead amplifies how they think through space, what they do to space and what it does to them, my intention is not to flatten differences between individuals or essentialize communities but to contribute, if modestly, to such a project of social justice.

Part One
Nationalizing Victimhood

Introduction

On the 14th anniversary of the *exogenously focused* scenario that constituted the painful events of July 2, 1993, we don't want to see *outsiders* in Sivas. . . . We shall lay flowers in memory of the dead. There's no
need for *outsiders* to participate.

Thus read the press statement released by a number of NGOs in Sivas ahead
of the 2007 episode of the annual commemoration held in the city since
1994 by those wishing to remember the victims of the 1993 arson attack.[1]
Delivered nearly a decade and a half after the blaze, the statement epitomizes the conviction that the atrocity has not been fully investigated; only
some thirty assailants caught on camera have received sentences, although
a crime of such scale most likely involved the backing of a much larger network that has yet to be revealed. While this conviction is widespread across
different social groups in Turkey, not as commonly shared is the answer
to the question of exactly whom the network in question comprises. For
those upholding the legacy of the festival participants killed in the blaze, the
answer lies in the inaction of the governing authorities and that of the thousands of onlookers: it is they who encouraged the assailants (Tüleylioğlu
2010). For mainstream politicians, journalists, and various other influential
figures in Sivas, however, the arson was but one part of a larger plot orchestrated by foreign powers (Ünsal 1995; Doğan 2007). Hence the opening
statement's reference to the atrocity as "exogenously focused" (*dış odaklı*):
an event whose origins remain outside the field of vision.

---

1. Italics added. For the full statement, see "Dışarıdan Kimsenin Gelmesini İstemi-
yoruz" [We Do Not Want Any Outsiders Coming Here], *Anadolu*, June 27, 2007, 1.

The decade in which the statement was uttered culminated in a state-sponsored project of what senior figures like the then prime minister, Tayyip Erdoğan, called "democratization" (*demokratikleşme*) and "transparentization" (*şeffaflaşma*) (T.C. Devlet Bakanlığı 2010, 5).[2] In 2011 these developments yielded practical outcomes at two sites of state-endorsed violence, Ankara's Ulucanlar Prison and Sivas's Madımak Hotel, whose conversion into a memorial museum had long been the subject of memory activism. Following a series of workshops and an architectural competition run by the Ankara chapter of Turkey's Chamber of Architects, the Ulucanlar Prison was turned into a museum. In Sivas, following a series of meetings with the city's "notables" and representatives of its "civil society" (ibid., 12–13), the state transformed the Madımak Hotel into a commemorative-cum-educational institution. If these projects signaled the becoming-mainstream of discourses and practices of "confronting the past" throughout the late 2000s and early 2010s in Turkey, then the statement that opened part 1 indicates how this development unfolded not only simultaneously but also in entanglement with the proliferation of understandings of histories of state-endorsed violence as "exogenously focused" conspiracies against the entire nation.[3]

2. This state-sponsored project of "democratization" and "transparentization" developed simultaneously with a government-backed criminal investigation and subsequent court proceedings that purported "to purge patterns of corruption and illegality within the state" or "what has come to be known as the deep state" (Ertür 2016, 178). Those put on trial included Turkey's "prominent conspiracy theorists" whom progovernment circles associated with the country's ultranationalist and ultrasecularist establishment (185), thereby setting the image of a democratizing and transparentizing Turkey against the background of one dominated by conspiracy-theoretical approaches to politics.

3. The roots of this understanding lie in the early twentieth century when the Ottoman Empire gave way to the Republic of Turkey, and more specifically in two events that marked this transition and over time became the stuff of conspiracy theories. The first is the 1908 constitutional revolution led by the Young Turks, which climaxed in the toppling of Abdülhamid II—the last Ottoman monarch to reign not just on paper but also in practice over the crumbling empire—and which laid the groundwork for the secular republic founded in the early 1920s. That the Young Turk movement was based in Salonika (today's Thessaloniki), then still a predominantly Jewish-inhabited city and antecedently the epicenter of a seventeenth-century wave of conversions from Judaism to Islam, was made by antisecularists

The notions of inside versus outside and visual clarity versus obscurity, which characterize the above-mentioned references to *exogenously focused* scenarios, are among the most prominent tropes employed in both conspiracy theory and its treatment in scholarly discussions (Fortun and Fortun 1999; Stewart 1999; Dean 2000; Bastian 2003; Marcus

---

into the stuff of the anti-Semitic conspiracy theory that its members were crypto Jews acting in the interests of the global Jewry—a theory later extended to the modern-day republic's Salonika-born founder, Mustafa Kemal Atatürk (Baer 2013). The second relevant event is the post–World War I Treaty of Sèvres, which partitioned much of today's Turkey into Allied-controlled territories. Although the Turkish National Campaign of 1919–22, which enabled the founding of the modern republic, was largely successful in overturning Sèvres, over time the treaty became the stuff of what is now known as the "Sèvres paranoia" (Göçek 2011, 98–184) or "the conviction that the external world is conspiring to weaken and carve up Turkey" (Kirişçi 1999, 258). Often working in tandem with the anti-Semitic conspiracy theories (Nefes 2015), the Sèvres paranoia became especially prevalent in the post–Cold War era when the preceding decades' symmetrical political alignments among states began to complexify (Taşpınar 2005, 214n1). The Sèvres paranoia has continued to thrive in the new millennium, as previously peripheral conspiracy theories permeated the mainstream. This was first because the immediate aftermath of the Cold War rejuvenated the popularity of conspiracy theories in geographies like Turkey "where cold-war [sic] disciplines and interventions shaped the experience of civil society" (Marcus 1999, 3). It was then that conspiracy theory began to function increasingly as a practice that draws from "actual experience" rather than as a merely discursive representation of affairs (Navaro-Yashin 2002, 182). In many ways, the AKP's electoral success in 2002 and subsequent consolidation of its grip through consecutive majority governments (Guida 2008) constituted the rise of a political movement with religious conservative origins that have historically been among the proponents of the aforementioned conspiracy theories, as it was largely excluded from the secularist republican project for the better part of the twentieth century (Gürpınar 2013, 425–26; cf. Navaro-Yashin 2002, 191)—an evolving story that is about to complete its eighteenth year at the time of writing. The second reason behind the Sèvres paranoia's ongoing significance to contemporary politics in Turkey concerns ultrasecularist nationalists. Having found themselves in the margins of the 2000s new political mainstream and facing ideological bottleneck, they sought to regain influence by resorting to populism, the prime pillars of which in Turkey comprise conspiracy theories of the above-mentioned sort (Baer 2013, 554–55; Nefes 2013). Indeed, recent shifts in Turkish politics following the rekindling of war in Kurdistan (2015-16) and the failed coup attempt (2016) have led some of these ultrasecularist nationalists to ally with Erdoğan's AKP, leading the conspiracy theories that constitute the common ground of both these political movements' proponents to become ever more prominent.

and Powell 2003; Comaroff and Comaroff 2003; West and Sanders 2003; Fenster 2008). Yet their significance here transcends mere figuration. The conspiracy theory, which implies that those who started the fire and those killed in it are both legitimate victims, inspires a state-sponsored on-site memorial. Conjointly, a change of attitude among mainstream politicians and media gives the arson attack greater visibility through live broadcasts and high-profile visits. But, on the ground, various law enforcement apparatuses are introduced to isolate the commemoration, physically reinforcing the inside-outside delineation that characterizes related conspiracy theories. If these developments establish conspiracy theory's role in negotiating violent events, they also demonstrate that it hinges on a constant interplay between the figurative and the physical. Understanding this role, therefore, requires that the physical underpinnings and consequences of the visual and spatial tropes involved in conspiracy theory be considered seriously.[4]

How might this consideration contribute to analyses of the work conspiracy theory does with respect to histories of state-endorsed violence? Part 1 explores this question through the cases of the Madımak Hotel in Sivas and the Ulucanlar Prison Museum in Ankara.

4. Here, in approaching conspiracy theory as a material and spatial practice, I echo human geographer Barry's (2013) exploration of physical infrastructures as constitutive of the politics of transparency and public knowledge.

1

Commemoration as Conspiracy in Sivas

As seen in the quote that opened part 1, practices of "confronting the past" and the avowed steps toward transparentization and democratization— renowned as hallmarks of globalization and cosmopolitanization in post– Cold War contexts—did not forestall conspiratorial thinking; if anything, they proliferated alongside each other.[1] The proliferation is evident in

1. The conventional understanding of the relationship between conspiracy and transparency being an antithesis (Hunt 1999, 22, 25; Fenster 2008, ix) has increasingly been subjected to criticism in the aftermath of the Cold War (Marcus 1999), a historical period marked by not only the collapse of a physical wall preventing visual and spatial access to the political Other (West and Sanders 2003, 2, 7) but also transparency's becoming the mainstay of liberal democracies (Dean 2000). Rather than take transparency at face value "in a world where varied institutions claim to give structure to the 'rational' and 'transparent' operation of power," conspiracy theorists in the post–Cold War period have maintained that power continues to operate "in realms normally concealed from view" (West and Sanders 2003, 7). Conspiracy theory has continued to proliferate despite liberal projects of transparency, because it "religiously set[s] up two separate worlds, this one of appearances and that other one of secrets" (Fortun and Fortun 1999, 159) and is driven by "a desire for an Other order of a true US and THEM coming from someplace outside our control" (K. Stewart 1999, 13) or for "a surface to power" that conceals the space from which power operates (West and Sanders 2003, 16). In associating conspiracy theory with transparency, the appearance of its surfaces and the spaces it is taken to conceal, these discussions have revealed the importance of spatiality and visuality to conspiratorial thinking. Consider, alongside these invocations of a delineation separating the space of power's formulations from that of its operations, the fact that optic improvements between the seventeenth and nineteenth centuries shaped epistemological notions

37

how the mainstream press in Sivas and the city's "notables" mentioned in the opening quote espoused the sort of conspiracy theorizing that sees the culture festival in 1993 whose guests were attacked in the arson, the arson attack itself, and subsequent initiatives of commemorating it on site all as the work of outside forces. This raises the question: Outside of what, or of where? To explore this question, consider, alongside the opening quote, the below excerpt, also from the local press in Sivas, which is especially significant in this respect as its coverage of the culture festival in late June and early July 1993 is known to have aggravated the atmosphere that culminated in the arson attack (Coşkun 1995, 355n1). Written by the longtime chair of the Sivas journalists association, who also authored a monograph on the arson attack, the excerpt was published as the editorial of one of the city's best-selling newspapers a couple of days before the atrocity's tenth anniversary, when the commemorations had begun to draw thousands of participants instead of the hundreds they had until then managed to attract (Ünsal 1995).

> Neither the murderers of ASALA [the Beirut-based Armenian militant organization active between the late 1970s and the early 1990s], who were behind the events [the arson attack], nor the festival participants were invited to Sivas by its people. . . . These plotters are the same hitmen of ASALA who insist on keeping the events on the agenda. Let's all be level-headed and vigilant tomorrow [during the commemoration] and avoid falling into ASALA's trap. . . . Tomorrow, the perpetrators will likely mourn alongside them [those who claim the legacy of the festival participants]. . . . They first kill, and then weep at graves. (Ünsal 2003)

---

of both transparency and its "obverse: a concern with refraction, distortion, concealment, collusion," accompanied by metaphors such as "the camera obscura" and "the hidden hand" (Comaroff and Comaroff 2003, 292). More recent cases evidencing spatiality's and visuality's significance to conspiracy theory include how surveillance technologies used in the post-9/11 United States and United Kingdom have produced the opposite of their purported aim of social discipline (Holm 2009, 37, 42) and how the proliferation of the live broadcasting of socially infuriating events has fueled rather than quelled unrest (Bastian 2003, 85). These instances all show that, far from serving as a passive backdrop or conduit to discourses and practices of transparency and/or conspiracy theory, physical spaces and objects may well be shaping them actively.

As epitomized by both the editorial above and the quote that opened part 1, conspiratorial readings of the arson attack blame it on actors from outside Turkey. While in the above quote these actors are said to consist of ASALA, this has proved interchangeable with any other group considered "exogenous" at a given time; for instance, the same writer cited above has elsewhere blamed the arson attack on the PKK—the guerrilla organization active since the mid-1980s in eastern and southeastern Turkey or northern Kurdistan.[2] Such placing of blame therefore imagines Turkey as an immaculate and peaceful inside threatened by a hostile and polluted outside.

The editorial quoted above moreover indicates that the imaginary of the national inside versus outside has involved scales much smaller than that of countries or nations, including the city of Sivas and the eponymous province of which it is the center. Conspiracy theories premised on this imaginary have at times also mapped it onto the city and the province. The origins of this mapping stretch back to the immediate aftermath of the arson attack when mainstream politicians and the media pointed the finger at two groups.[3] The first group was the alleged ringleaders of the

2. See "Sivas Olaylarındaki PKK İzi" [The PKK Imprint on the Sivas Incidents], *Akşam*, June 1, 2011, http://www.aksam.com.tr/guncel/sivas-olaylarindaki-pkk-izi--444 83h/haber-44483.

3. In speaking of "mapping" here, I have in mind Fredric Jameson's understanding of conspiracy theory as "the poor person's cognitive mapping" in the late capitalist age (1988, 356). Leaving aside momentarily the question of whether conspiracy theories are necessarily the preserve of "the poor person," here I reconsider Jameson's "mapping" as not just a cognitive but also a physical spatial practice. This reconsideration recalls West and Sanders's framing of transparency within Arjun Appadurai's (1990) notion of "ideoscapes"—a means of condensing larger sets of ideas and facilitating their export to and superimposition on "geographical landscapes" (2003, 10). But it differs from the way they place heavy emphasis on the first half of Appadurai's notion (that is, ideas) while neglecting its "scape-ness." My methodology here prioritizes the latter and, as such, contributes to analyses of conspiracy theory as a "search for the missing plot" rather than "a rigid, all too clear plot"—as "practice" rather than just "theory" or "prefabricated ideology" (K. Stewart 1999, 16). Put simply, I attend not just to the actors involved in conspiracy theory but also to the settings in which it unfolds. While anthropological work on the topic has often focused sharply on actors that produce, promulgate, and/or subscribe

arsonist crowd, blamed on the basis that they were entirely unknown to the people of Sivas and have not reappeared since, whether as suspects in court or as residents of the city (T.C. Devlet Bakanlığı 2010, 52). Second, conspiracy theories labeled as outsiders the organizers of the cultural festival whose participants died in the blaze, accusing them of both conducting an event many of whose aspects were allegedly foreign to the city's way of life and refusing to cancel it despite the likelihood of a violent backlash becoming increasingly apparent in the run-up to the arson (67).

These accusations drew on certain organizational and historical aspects of the festival. Organized in central Sivas by an Alevi association headquartered in Ankara, the festival was not the first but the fourth of its kind. The inaugural event had taken place in summer 1978 in Banaz in provincial Sivas, which is famously the native village of Pir Sultan Abdal, a sixteenth-century minstrel revered in Alevism after whom the festival was named (Koerbin 2011, 191n3). Although the festival had been intended as an annual event, it was interrupted owing to sociopolitical unrest across Turkey in the late 1970s, which partly also targeted Alevis in the country's central and eastern cities such as Malatya, Çorum, Sivas, and Maraş and led many to flee for metropolises like Istanbul, Ankara, and Izmir or even beyond, for Europe (Eral 1995). Then followed the 1980 military coup, whose drastic restrictions on social rights precluded events like this festival. Therefore, the organizers had to wait another decade to repeat the event. Like the inaugural festival, its second and third episodes in 1991 and 1992 were held in Banaz and appealed mainly to Alevis. But in 1993, the festival board made the unprecedented decision of partly relocating to central Sivas and composing a two-day program that was not only Alevism related. They thus facilitated what was for many an organizer

---

to conspiracy theories, "[w]hat distinguishes conspiracy theories from other theories is the precise manner in which such theories are embedded in sociopolitical fields" and the various and often unforeseeable "use values" they acquire as a result (Pelkmans and Machold 2011, 68). I advocate a shift of focus from actors to fields as it helps complicate the notion that conspiratorial thinking is the preserve of one set of actors or another, à la Jameson's "poor person," and take seriously the materiality and spatiality—the "fieldness"—of conspiracy theory.

and participant a return to the center of the geography that they or their parents had been forced to flee in the 1970s and 1980s. Part of a wider phenomenon called the "Alevi Revival" (Van Bruinessen 1996; Çamuroğlu 1998), it is this aspect of an outreach or return to the city that has been repurposed to substantiate allegations regarding the festival's being the work of outsiders infiltrating Sivas (Deliktaş 2000; Akbulut 2006).

Gradually throughout the 1990s and 2000s, the mapping of the national inside onto the urban inside (that is, the city of Sivas) engulfed the organizers and participants of the commemorations held annually in Sivas. As the 2000s saw these commemorations attract increasing numbers of participants each year, mainstream press and politicians in Sivas labeled them the work of outsiders based on the significant role of the Cologne-based European Alevi Unions Confederation in organizing these events and drawing large crowds to them—an example of the financial and ideological support Alevis in Europe have provided to those in Turkey (Özyürek 2009, 240). In fact, the main reason such an organization exists in Germany in the first place is that, for members of marginalized social groups like the Alevis who left Turkey in the 1970s, '80s, and '90s, escaping political violence was as significant a motivation as better economic prospects (Ögelman, Money, and Martin 2002). Indeed, several individuals with such a migration background were among the Sivas arson-attack victims (Aksoy 2014, 13). Conspiracy theories perceive the fact that Europe-based Alevis, many of whom are indeed originally from Sivas, continue to engage with Turkey as an intervention by the European Union and specifically by Germany, where in the 1980s they were given the opportunity for the first time to legally organize under their ethnic and religious identities and where many of them continue to reside (Wilpert 1990). So mainstream has this perception become as to repeatedly feature in statements made by Erdoğan (Taştekin 2014).

In sum, the spatial imaginary of the national inside versus outside at work in conspiratorial readings of the arson attack has involved both Turkey as the sociospatial national interior and Sivas as a material-spatial microcosm onto which to map the latter. How might this imaginary have shaped and been shaped by the reorganization and use of space during commemorations at Turkey's sites of state-endorsed violence? This chapter explores this question through my fieldwork in Sivas, which consisted of two components. The first was an ethnography of the site of atrocity within the daily life of Sivas. This involved spending entire work-days inside the building, whose recent state-sponsored transformation has opened it to free-of-charge visits between 8:30 a.m. and 5:00 p.m. during the workweek, and in-depth conversations with a group of Sivas residents. The second component was to participant-observe the site's significance within the annual commemoration, which I attended twice (in 2011 and 2012) with groups coming from outside central Sivas.

The site's recent transformation has introduced a "Memory Corner," a 70-square-meter room whose centerpiece is a 3-by-4.5-meter stainless-steel structure complete with a victims' name list, an electrically operated set of fountains, and a couple of statements (figure 1). There are as many fountains as there are names commemorated: thirty-seven. As previously mentioned, the number includes not only the thirty-three participants of the culture festival and the two hotel workers killed inside the hotel but also the two members of the crowd outside, a decision that state authori-ties have defended as "a human-centric" refusal "to discriminate between the dead" (Yalçınkaya and Ceylan 2011). Of the two statements, one is more relevant to my discussion here than the other (the latter will be dis-cussed in chapter 3). The statement is unsigned and reads, "In the painful incident that took place on July 2, 1993, thirty-seven of our people have lost their lives. With the wish that such pains do not recur . . ." This is effectively a synopsis of the following speech that Minister of State Faruk Çelik delivered in 2010 when he became the first government representa-tive to visit the site:

> July 2, 1993 is one of the painful days in our history. . . . On this day, insidious foci sought to stage their dark scenarios. . . . [This] is the pain of the whole of Turkey. There can be no sides in this incident; to take a side in this incident means to not extinguish the fire. . . . The screen of fog surrounding this incident has not yet been lifted. . . . It is no other person than yet again us, the people of Sivas, who have the remedy for our problems. . . . I remember with grace and respect our thirty-seven citizens who lost their lives on July 2, 1993. (Aytekin et al. 2010)

1. The Memory Corner inside the Science and Culture Center, 2012.

These emphases on "the people of Sivas" and/or "the whole of Turkey" as sufferers, on "our thirty-seven citizens" as victims, on the "dark scenarios" that constituted the arson, and on the "screen of fog" surrounding it echo conspiracy theories that have placed the blame on "exogenous foci" (*dış odaklar* or *dış mihraklar*). The echo is discernible not only textually (in the statements) but also numerically (in the thirty-seven names and fountains). This has led those upholding the legacy of the thirty-three festival participants to refuse to enter the building that now hosts the Memory Corner, as they believe doing so would be to legitimize it.

But there are also various others who pass by the building without ever setting foot inside and do so owing to certain assumptions they have about it. As some of these assumptions concern the building's exterior, the latter merits further exploration. The recent transformation preserved the facade's structural composition but reclad it entirely (figure 2). The fenestration now consists of one-way mirrored windows that render interiors invisible from the outside. The rest of the facade is clad in composite panels in the pastel shades of dark red and beige characteristic of state buildings. There are no signs outside the building regarding the services provided or the operating hours. The only sign, except the one bearing the institution's name, is a plaque that reads, "This building is monitored twenty-four hours by CCTV." Made of glossy brass, the plaque is much more ostentatious than the usual CCTV disclaimer; I observed that it misled potential visitors who were confusedly drawn to it in the absence of any other sign. The confusion was most evident during lunch breaks when the institution closes its doors for an hour. Potential visitors would come, see the closed doors, and search for a sign, only to notice the CCTV disclaimer and turn away perplexedly. All these features led the building to exude an appearance that potential visitors found inaccessible at best and intimidating at worst.

In 2011 and 2012 these issues were compounded by the way the institution was staffed. In fall 2011, four people—a director, a kindergarten teacher, and two primary school teachers—were employed here by the Ministry of National Education. When I returned the following summer, the time of year when the building's visitor numbers are at their highest because of visits to the city by people with migration backgrounds who originally hail from Sivas, the director was still in place, but the teachers had left; each visiting class was now asked to bring along its own teacher, I was told. In their stead, there were four new staff members: two men in their late twenties, a man in his midthirties, and a woman in her early twenties. They were all unskilled workers hired through the state's employment agency on contracts ranging from six to twelve months. There was no training scheme in place regarding the site's historical significance or anything else, for that matter. Not much was expected of the employees except, in the words of the man in his midthirties, "to keep this place clean, tidy and orderly, as the director likes it that way." The director's occasional admonitions also included, according to the man in his late twenties, reminders about how "we should never speak with any visitors about the incident."

If in its institutional inconspicuousness the building sought to downplay the contested legacy of the arson attack, this in effect exacerbated

2. The Science and Culture Center as seen from the outside, 2012.

speculation regarding whose "side" its occupants were on vis-à-vis the atrocity. Consider the case of a couple of women (one in her midtwenties and the other her early fifties) who in the summer of 2012 passed by the entrance back and forth several times without entering. The female employee noticed them and went out to welcome them in. The younger woman explained that "we were here last year, too, but hesitated to enter. You see; my mom is covered, and although I'm not, we thought her head scarf could cause eyebrows to raise."[4] The employee replied that they wel-

4. The secular reforms of the 1920s that inaugurated the Republic of Turkey prevented state employees from wearing head scarves at work. In the 1990s this culminated in a full-fledged ban affecting the recipients as well as providers of state services (Elver

come all members of the public indiscriminately. Standing at the doorstep, the women explained why they had second thoughts about entering the building. The mother said: "I chair the AKP women's branch in my hometown. Plus, I am covered. Hence my belonging to the opposite camp. Nevertheless, I condemn this terrible atrocity. Being human is enough to condemn it, although you and I might not be of the same opinion." The staff member interrupted the woman's comments: "What do you mean by the opposite camp? To whom did you think this place belongs? The Alevis?" The women both nodded in affirmation. The employee corrected them: "No, no, no; not at all. This place belongs to the state." Only after having received this clarification did the women go inside.

Many residents of Sivas have also yet to visit the revamped building. I observed this not only during my research inside the building, when I found out that only about one in ten visitors was a resident of Sivas, but also during the regular and lengthy evening conversations I had with men in their late twenties and early thirties at what is one of the oldest and most popular coffeehouses in the city.[5] Described by my interlocutors as "the local intellectual hangout," this is an alcohol-free establishment whose clientele consists virtually solely of men. My interlocutors here included several outspoken supporters of the BBP (Great Union Party), whose ideology synthesizes Sunni Islamism and Turkish nationalism (De Tapia 2011, 309). Sivas is famously the BBP stronghold and, at the time of my fieldwork, was the only municipality governed by one of its members. The party is immensely pertinent to the arson attack, owing to how some thirty survivors fled the blaze: through the air well to an adjacent building then occupied by the BBP. BBP supporters take pride in this story and present it as proof that they have done their utmost to mitigate the consequences of what was a dark plot orchestrated by external powers (Doğan 2007, 189–92). The survivors, however, have recounted that they had to force their way into the

---

2012). The ban was lifted gradually in the late 2000s and early 2010s except for judges, prosecutors, and military personnel (Asimovic Akyol 2016).

    5. Coffeehouses have held immense sociopolitical significance in Turkey throughout the late Ottoman (Kırlı 2004), early republican (Özkoçak 2007), and Cold War (Beeley 1970) periods.

building; at first, they were cursed at and chased away by those inside the party's offices (Günbulut 1994, 205–6). BBP supporters believe that such claims have unjustly stigmatized them as perpetrators and caused innocent onlookers to receive heavy court sentences (Öztürk 2011).

Hence the interest my research stimulated among the members of my coffeehouse circle, whose numbers ranged from five to twelve per night. Many of them not only openly condemned the arson attack as the work of "exogenous foci" but also maintained that the AKP "government do not want July 2 to be elucidated," as evinced by the continuing lack of a comprehensive investigation that could "reveal the actual plotters." Regarding the recent transformation of the site of the blaze, my interlocutors were unanimous that it is not a project that speaks, or would be of interest, to "the people of Sivas": "The ordinary resident of Sivas will never go there. They would say, 'What's going on behind those mirrored windows?' and think that the place is being sacralized and that the Culture Center is the penultimate stage before it becomes a *cemevi* [place of Alevi worship; literally, house of gathering]. Yes; many think that the place will soon become a house of worship in which to perform *semah* [an Alevi ritual]. I personally have not been there to this day, and neither have any of the people I know." Such reactions demonstrate that the architectural banality and institutional ambiguity resulting from the site's recent transformation have led to its being disowned by not just those upholding the legacy of the thirty-three festival participants but also various others. This banality and ambiguity, therefore, are not merely a consequence of conspiracy theory— the theory that the arson attack was an "exogenously focused" event—but also its instigator. If the project's implicit subscription to the conspiratorial reading of the arson attack as the work of "exogenous foci" is packaged in a refusal "to discriminate between the dead," the architectural banality and ambiguity embodying it have caused conspiracy theories to ramify rather than subside. The extent of this ramification is such that the project itself has triggered new conspiracy theoretical rumors regarding how certain Alevis are collaborating with the authorities to hijack the building.[6]

6. In speaking of "rumor" here, I take my cue from Veena Das's work on civilian unrest in post-Partition India. In a way that recalls George Marcus and Michael Powell's

The physical implications of conspiracy theories involving the building extend beyond its walls. Consider the commemorative procession held in Sivas annually by those upholding the legacy of the festival participants killed in the arson. Over the past decade, this event has drawn increasingly larger crowds to Sivas from across Turkey and beyond. Following the hotel's commemorative-cum-educational transformation in 2011 amid state-endorsed discourses of "confronting the past," the commemoration

---

argument that post–Cold War conspiracy theorizing is characterized by the reversal of "cause and effect" as it seeks to reckon with "the invisible, unpredictable and incalculable risks of our contemporary world" (2003, 332), Das understands rumor as a practice that is less about representing a preexisting reality than about precipitating a new one. As such, rumor does not merely communicate but produces events "in the very act of telling" by authorizing them (Das 2007, 108). The authorization involves reanimating particular "regions" of the past, which are the stuff of collective consciousness, and the "regionality" of which is defined not by chronological proximity but by affinity to the "affective qualities of the present moment" (100). Rumor produces new events—in this case, violent events—by sociohistorically anchoring them in these regions (121). Moreover, rumor's productive capabilities concern space as well as time; its materializations are not uniform across geography. Certain physical environments across which rumor circulates significantly shape its consequences in degree, if not always in kind (135–61). Rumor, therefore, is a means of spatial production as well as a sociopolitical one. There are glimpses of an understanding of conspiratorial thinking as just such a production in Carol Delaney's ethnography of a village in central Turkey, which discerns the spatial demarcation of an inside from its outside as a trope villagers employ frequently vis-à-vis adverse events or the likelihood thereof. "Bad and threatening things," they believe, "come from outside . . . the body, the family, the village, or the nation" (Delaney 1991, 206–7). Tangible implications of this trope are discernible in how villagers inhabit the village and their houses. The village's topographical positioning enables a clear view of those approaching it, giving "villagers the sense that they have some control over who enters" (206). New roads connecting the village to the world outside are met with skepticism by the villagers: if roads mean better logistics, they also expose the village "to polluting influences from town" (207). On an architectural level, villagers' perception of their houses as clean and streets as dirty has physical underpinnings: "Houses are swept several times a day," whereas rubbish "is dumped outside the house onto the street" and remains untended except by passing animals that eat the organic bits (237). Unlike Das's, however, Delaney's account does not feature a particular event or set of events and is therefore somewhat historically unspecific. It is this sort of specificity that my analysis here aims to offer.

3. Remnants from flowers laid by victims' relatives, survivors, and memory activists at the site of the blaze, 2013.

was unprecedentedly broadcast live and nationwide by a popular TV channel. The event proceeds along a two-kilometer route starting in Alibaba, the reputed "Alevi neighborhood" of central Sivas and one of the scenes of the late 1970s wave of violence against Alevis and leftists. It ends at the site of the blaze with the laying of flowers (figure 3). Most commemoration participants then return to Alibaba in groups, albeit not in the shape of a single collective that they take during the procession.

4. Police checkpoint at the border of central Sivas on commemoration day, 2011.

There are numerous ways this annual event is shaped by the insinuation that it is the work of outside forces. In both 2011 and 2012 the police conducted checkpoints at the border of central Sivas to stop and search those traveling to the city for the commemoration (figure 4). Police officers invariably greeted people here by saying, "Good morning, our guests, welcome to Sivas." One of my interlocutors, a civil servant in his midfifties who indeed originally hails from Sivas but moved to Ankara in the early 1980s for sociopolitical as well as economic reasons, challenged the police: "Guests? Who says we're guests? I'm from Sivas. You may be stationed here now, but who knows where you're originally from!" He later told me that, while these checkpoints have always been conducted, they used to be more technical than social affairs of the sort the officers' remarks now sought to render them. My interlocutor therefore exposed the function implicit in what otherwise seemed a benign gesture of hospitality: to demarcate the space of the commemorations as the "outside" of Sivas.

Such attempts at delineation continued throughout the day and became much more overtly physical, as streets leading to the route of the procession were double barricaded. An interlocutor in his early thirties, who is a non-Alevi resident of central Sivas and lives in a building situated about halfway along the route, remarked that in 2011 he had left home to participate in the commemoration, only to run right into barricades. Police officers told him that if he wanted to join the procession, he ought to go up to Alibaba, the reputed "Alevi neighborhood" where the procession starts. My interlocutor "didn't feel like doing so, as I don't know anyone there," and gave up on the idea.

Nearer the site of the blaze, the distance between the double barricades expanded to constitute a buffer zone across which commemoration participants and residents of Sivas gazed at one another (figure 5). At times this spatial separation took forms less peaceful than the exchange of gazes. Disapproving gestures coming from some balconies along the route were met with a group of young commemoration participants who chanted "Sivas's arsonists: watching from balconies."[7] Finally, the procession itself became subject to an obstacle in what was perhaps the least technically justifiable "security" measure by the police. Whereas commemoration participants were formerly able to walk right up to the doorstep of the hotel and lay flowers, from 2011 onward—following the site's transformation—the authorities began to try to obstruct the procession as it approached the building. In 2011 they mounted barricades about fifteen meters ahead of the building, blocking off the street where it is located (figure 6). When the participants insisted on laying flowers at the building's doorstep as per tradition, the scuffle between them and the police resulted in the latter's use of tear gas. The following year, the police moved the barricades about four hundred meters farther up along the route, only to pull them back to where they were in 2011 after an hour-long sit-in by commemoration participants. Even then, once the procession reached the street of the building targeted in the blaze, it emerged that the barricades had morphed from simple police shields into a steel

7. *"Sivas'ı yakanlar: balkonlardan bakanlar."* For accounts of similar instances from past commemorations, see Başkaya 2006; and Kaçmaz 2009.

5. Double police barricades separating locals from activists on commemoration day, 2011.

6. Police barricades blocking access to the Science and Culture Center on commemoration day, 2011.

7. Police barricades blocking access to the Science and Culture Center on commemoration day, 2012.

wall, which has since then become a standard architectural feature of the site on commemoration day (figure 7).

Rather than serve their purported purpose of providing safety and security for the commemoration, the barricades therefore functioned as an instigator of aggression. They did so not only by isolating the procession and thus rendering it the outside of downtown Sivas, but also by enabling the conditions for the portrayal of commemoration participants as troublemakers aiming to provoke the city's residents. The portrayal continued to reverberate after the procession, as scenes of teargassing captured by the press and especially by the mainstream TV channel that live broadcast the event circulated in news reports and national dailies the following day under such headlines as "18 years on, and yet another provocation."[8]

8. "18 Yıl Sonra Yine Tahrik," as the front-page headline of the newspaper *Türkiye* read on July 3, 2011.

2

Depoliticization of Violence at Ulucanlar Prison Museum

This chapter further explores how commemoration at Turkey's sites of state-endorsed violence has shaped and been shaped by the spatial imaginary of the national inside versus outside central to conspiracy theoretical approaches to "confronting the past." It does so by focusing on the Ulucanlar Prison's transformation into a memorial museum. Having hosted inmates since 1925, Ulucanlar was modern Turkey's oldest prison when it was shut down in 2006. During the three years following its evacuation, the site remained abandoned and inaccessible except for a few special occasions. This period saw Ulucanlar's fate twist dramatically as it was first saved from demolition and then renovated from 2009 to 2010 to become what is today called the Prison Museum. Although the refurbishment had been declared complete when my fieldwork began in April 2011, the museum was still not open to the public. I had to book an appointment with the museum administration in order to access the site and was guided by a senior administrator throughout my visit.

The main building, which now hosts offices of the museum administration, was key to Ulucanlar's recent transformation (figure 8). Designed in what architectural historians of Turkey have come to call the First National Style, the building dates from 1925 and was constructed as part of Ankara's first urban plan, dated 1924—also known, after its designer, as the Lörcher Plan (Cengizkan 2004, 157). It was this architectural historical significance that saved the prison complex from wholesale demolition following its evacuation in 2006. This was a time when the metropolitan municipality, then run by a member of the ruling AKP, had set its sights on Ulucanlar as part of its plans to open the part of central Ankara where the prison was located to speculative development. The municipality's plan, more specifically, was to use the site of Ulucanlar Prison for a new shopping mall. As rumors regarding these plans began to circulate in Ankara, the Chamber of Architects' local chapter appealed to the Council of Preservation with an official letter demanding that Ulucanlar Prison be listed as a heritage site. The council's positive reply paved the way for a consortium of four that was put in charge of the listed prison. This consortium comprised the Ministry of Justice, the Bar, the Chamber of Architects, and the local Altındağ Municipality run by a member of the ruling party. While ownership was handed over to the municipality, the remaining three institutions were given inspection rights. Therefore, all four became legal stakeholders in the renovation phase launched soon after the council's decision against wholesale demolition.

Ulucanlar's architectural transformation followed from a series of events and initiatives organized between 2006 and 2009 by the Chamber of Architects, where the idea to turn it into a museum was first aired (Ünalın 2010, 86–87). These events, which included workshops, festivals, preplanned group visits, and an architecture competition, will be discussed at length in chapter 5. But suffice it to say here that they foregrounded Turkey's political Left as the primary victims of Ulucanlar's past and therefore the main interlocutors for deciding on its present and future. The past in question, more specifically, involved three episodes of state-endorsed violence. The first took place in May 1972 when Deniz Gezmiş, Yusuf Aslan, and Hüseyin İnan, three leading figures of Turkey's revolutionary youth, were sentenced to death under the influence of the military and hanged in Ulucanlar's courtyard. The second was the immediate aftermath of the 1980 coup that saw the imprisonment and torture of thousands of left-wing activists. The third concerned the state's violent and countrywide crackdown between September 1999 and December 2000 on political (revolutionary leftist) prisoners fasting unto death in protest against the introduction of solitary confinement (Robinson and Baktir 2000). Halit Çelenk, the veteran lawyer who represented the 1970s revolutionary youth leaders in the process that resulted in their

8. Ulucanlar Prison main building, 2007 (*top*; courtesy of Turkey's Chamber of Architects, Ankara Chapter) and 2011 (*bottom*).

being hanged, was a prominent contributor to the series of events and initiatives organized by the Architects' Chamber, where he time and again brought up the unjust harshness of the death sentence that the three were delivered (Ünalın 2010, 24–25). Other contributors included veteran leftists who served time in the prison in the 1980s and underwent torture as part of the violent methods the junta sanctioned to fight the country's political Left; indeed, they constituted the majority among audience members (85–87). Alongside some of these veteran leftists, victims and survivors of the violent crackdown on prisons in 1999–2000 served as tour guides when the Architects' Chamber organized group visits to the prison (Gündoğdu 2011).

The outcome of the transformation, however, reflects little to none of this left-wing past, as evidenced by what parts of the former prison complex have been demolished and how those that still stand have been refurbished. Although activism between 2006 and 2009 resulted in the prison's being saved from wholesale demolition, it failed to secure the preservation of the entire complex. Sections made exempt from preservation included extensions built in the 1980s when the prison's capacity was stretched owing to an exponential rise in political (mainly leftist) inmates following the junta government that inaugurated the decade. These extensions, which were demolished by the local municipality immediately upon their takeover of the prison complex, included the ward where renowned Turkish director Tunç Başaran filmed his cult movie *Don't Let Them Shoot the Kite* (1989), based on a story by veteran leftist Feride Çiçekoğlu, who served time in Ulucanlar in the wake of the September 12 coup. The prison's transformation into a museum has replaced the ward with an ornamental garden (figure 9).

Another relevant section of the former prison whose physicality has been fundamentally altered comprises the wards numbered from 1 to 6, each known among former Ulucanlar inmates as a "coffin house" (*tabuthane*) (figure 10). The museum administration mentions this colloquialism in its communications with the public but also alleges that it originates in the architectural quality of the wards—or, according to a senior staff member I interviewed in April 2011, in "the unique geometry of the rooftops, which resemble a coffin." In fact, the association of these parts of

9. The garden laid out at the former site of a ward built in the 1980s that, until its demolition in 2010, was central to Ulucanlar-related left-wing culture, 2011.

the prison with coffins has to do with much more than mere architectural form, as some of them, especially the fourth ward, are infamous for having witnessed the highest number of casualties and fatalities during the state's violent crackdown in 1999–2000 on death fasters protesting against the introduction of solitary confinement (Şimşek 2000).[1] The crackdown is not at all mentioned in what the museum has chosen to exhibit in this part of the former prison. When I inquired with the museum administration about this absence, I was taken to the fourth ward and shown bullet holes from the crackdown that were still visible, albeit without any accompanying information or signage. If anything, a door with bullet holes, each the size of a fingertip, had been freshly painted.

1. The deadliest episode of this crackdown took place between December 19 and 26, 2000, when a total of ten thousand soldiers raided forty-eight prisons and killed more than thirty prisoners, wounded more than four hundred, and disappeared eight. The crackdown resulted in the transfer of more than one thousand prisoners to solitary confinement cells, but also in hundreds more joining the fast unto death (Anderson 2004).

10. Wards 1–6 at Ulucanlar, 2007 (*top*; courtesy of Turkey's Chamber of Architects, Ankara Chapter) and 2011 (*bottom*).

Former Ulucanlar inmate Murat Özçelik's documentary film Ölü-canlar (2010) is a work of cultural production that seeks to reveal what the Prison Museum erases regarding the crackdown in 1999–2000. While serving time in the fourth ward, Özçelik witnessed the crackdown first-hand. The title of his film translates into English as "Dead Souls" and is a play on the compound word that makes up the prison's name (ulu-canlar is Turkish for "sublime-souls"). Özçelik's documentary combines archival media footage, interviews with survivors of the operation, his own testimonies, and views from the abandoned prison shot in the late 2000s. The film is striking not only for the attention it draws to the crackdown but also for its documentation of how Ulucanlar used to look prior to its transformation into a museum. The barbed wire surrounding the prison grounds and the iron mesh over the courtyards shown in the film are now absent from the museum. Also absent are wall writings of the following sort, which the crackdown's victims left behind and which Özçelik encounters as he takes viewers through the abandoned wards: "I was tortured until 10.11.2000." The filmmaker himself recounts that "during the operation, we had to use the kitchen counter to store our dead," and adds, "The bathroom evokes very different sentiments in me. Here they beat us with iron planks. That's how a friend died. My own thumb and head were also smashed." Another former inmate shares her own recollection of the crackdown: "The clothes of our friends who were killed and whose bodies were taken away were stored here. All the way from the infirmary up to here, the hallway was covered with bloody clothes, shirts, and jackets."

Presences speak as much about the version of history the museum seeks to promote as do the absences. Fitted with brand-new taps and basins, clad in marble and stone, and neatly sprinkled with loincloths characteristic of the traditional Turkish bath, the bathroom where the most violent episodes of the 1999–2000 crackdown took place now looks like one in a commercial establishment (figure 11).[2] The kitchen that inmates repurposed

---

2. Another work of cultural production worthy of mention here as evidence of Ulucanlar's significance within Turkey's revolutionary Left is the late leftist filmmaker Yılmaz Güney's renowned film Duvar (The Wall) (1983). The film is based on a story Güney wrote during his imprisonment in Ulucanlar in the 1970s, which is titled Soba,

11. Bathroom at Ulucanlar, 2011.

as a morgue during the crackdown as well as the several toilets found across the complex have been similarly revamped. The sixth ward hosts an exhibition of personal objects that used to belong to famous former inmates, including some who in fact did not serve time in the prison, such as Erdoğan. In the fifth ward there is special emphasis on the intellectuals who served time in Ulucanlar. In these two sections, short biographies and photographs of poets, journalists, filmmakers, and writers are juxtaposed regardless of the fundamental differences in their political views, although

---

Pencere Camı ve İki Ekmek İstiyoruz (We Want a Stove, a Windowpane and Two Loaves of Bread) (1977). The story and the film depict a law-enforcement crackdown on juvenile inmates protesting for better prison conditions. The crackdown results in the inmates' being subjected to tear gas, torture, and humiliation. Although when Güney was imprisoned at Ulucanlar the juvenile ward was in a different section of the prison, the sign atop the entrance to the ward where the crackdown takes place in the movie reads "The 4th Ward," likely because this was where the filmmaker served his sentence. As such, the movie suggests a spatial continuity regarding where left-wing inmates are made to serve time within the prison complex.

12. Ward 4 at Ulucanlar, 2011.

it was precisely these views that had resulted in their detention—and, in some cases, their death—during periods of military repression. The fourth ward is decorated with wax sculptures imported from China depicting inmates along with random artifacts mostly associated with masculine culture, including soccer pictures, hometown postcards, and film posters (figure 12). More wax sculptures fill up the isolation cells in the below-ground level. These cells are also equipped with sound installations meant as reenactions of exchanges between inmates and wardens that used to take place here, none of whose content is made to bear a political character. In the courtyards, photographs of former left-wing inmates like the three revolutionary youth leaders hanged here in 1972 are placed inside filmstrip-shaped frames, and popular songs about prison life by renowned left-wing or Kurdish singers such as Selda Bağcan and Ahmet Kaya are played on a loop, albeit with no reference to the sociopolitical biographies in which they are grounded.

Among the museum's various erasures through presence, the isolation cell stands out as the best-known one (figure 13). It received wide

13. Isolation cell at Ulucanlar, 2011.

media coverage in December 2010 when the then nascent museum administration embarked on a public relations offensive and invited members of the press and high-ranking politicians for a preview. The visit resulted in wide coverage based on a press release circulated by the state's news agency that praised the museum for being "true to the original" and "an opportunity to experience imprisonment."[3] The latter aspect of the museum was most evident, the press release said, in the solitary confinement cells where visitors would be able to be temporarily locked up for an additional fee. Visitors to the museum access the section that houses these cells by walking, upon entry, through the pink-washed walls of a

3. For the full press release, see "Ulucanlar İşkence Müzesi Oldu" [Ulucanlar Has Become a Torture Museum], *TRT*, Dec. 29, 2010, http://www.trt.net.tr/haber/HaberDetay .aspx?HaberKodu=d462d3f2-b932-43b1-aa66-e58d3e40ff04; and "Ulucanlar Cezaevi Müze Oldu" [Ulucanlar Prison Has Become a Museum], *Hürriyet*, Dec. 28, 2010, http:// www.hurriyet.com.tr/gundem/ulucanlar-cezaevi-muze-oldu-16632650.

narrow but long passage. The section is half underground and is sign-posted *DİSİPLİN HÜCRESİ—ZİNDAN* (Discipline Cell—Dungeon) in brand-new steel. The idea to use solitary confinement cells as a visitor attraction was dropped by the time the museum opened to the public, owing mainly to reservations of the Cultural and Tourism Ministry, which licenses museums, be they public or private, as in the case of Ulu-canlar. But the idea continued to fascinate the staff members during my visit. A senior staff member recalled that their plan was to charge visitors for this attraction in inverse proportion to duration: "The longer the visi-tor could bear the experience, the lower the fee would be." The disturb-ing fact, of course, is that solitary confinement is precisely the form of imprisonment against which prisoners carried out the protest the state quashed violently in 1999–2000.

Facing the isolation section are the ninth and tenth wards, known together as the Hilton Ward. The colloquialism originates in the fact that high-ranking politicians jailed by juntas were lodged in this section. The walls of the tiny hall that separates the Hilton's two halves are decorated with clippings from mainstream newspapers where emphasis is placed on the run-up to the September 12 coup and its immediate aftermath (figure 14). Little to no historical contextualization is given alongside the clippings, and thus visitors are left with the mainstream media coverage that records the most spectacular outbursts of violence, such as shoot-outs and assassinations. This orients the exhibition affectively rather than epistemically, charging it with anxiety, worry, fear, and even ter-ror. The exhibition continues inside the two identical wards to either side of the hall, where pictures and biographies of some of the former Hilton inmates are installed vertically on self-standing units. Similar to the curatorial approach used in collating the newspaper clippings, the pictures and biographies chosen for display are those of late leaders from across the political spectrum, ranging from the far-right former member of Parliament Osman Bölükbaşı to the center-left former prime minister Bülent Ecevit.

This chapter has shown that the Ulucanlar Prison Museum's represen-tation of episodes of state-endorsed violence has been one of depoliticizing

14. Wards 9 and 10 at Ulucanlar, 2011.

and/or decontextualizing them. If the museum gives a platform to victims of state-endorsed violence, it does so only by detaching them from their ideologies and the political projects they pursued. Here everyone from revolutionary youth leaders through center-left prime ministers to far-right backbenchers is made to peacefully coexist as apolitical individuals devoid of agency. The museum has, moreover, used the possibilities afforded by architectural preservation to turn away from rather than engage directly with the task of confronting the past that it promised to facilitate. As buildings that are older and canonically more important have been deemed worthier of preservation, others have been condemned to erasure despite their association with some of the best-known episodes of state-endorsed violence and oppression targeting the Left. The latter includes those sections of the prison that have become positively memorable through cultural production by veteran leftists as well as those associated with the deadliest episodes of violence perpetrated under the authorities' watch, such as the 1999–2000 crackdown on prisons. Even in cases where material traces of such episodes remain, they are unkempt and unincorporated into the museum's exhibitions. Putting aside the necessarily complicated task of narrating political history, Ulucanlar's representation of the victims of state-endorsed violence as ideologically undifferentiated entails a co-optation of the political work done by the Left in securing the prison's preservation and its transformation into a museum.

Conclusion

In part 1, I have discussed conspiracy theoretical approaches to Turkey's histories of state-endorsed violence, which have pointed the finger at "exogenous foci." I have shown that these interpretations not only continued to circulate unabated but also ramified in the early 2010s when discourses and practices of "confronting the past" moved into the country's political mainstream and the government's project of "democratization" and "transparentization" was in full swing. In Sivas—the case that pioneered memory activist campaigns for commemorating violence on site—conspiracy theoretical approaches erased in both discursive and material ways the sociopolitical specificity of the victimhood that resulted from the arson attack. In Ulucanlar—Turkey's first site of state-endorsed violence transformed into a museum proper as part of the government's discourses and practices of "confronting the past"—not only was victimhood depoliticized as it was in Sivas; this depoliticization also erased the ideological specificity of those who carried out the political work that saved the prison from demolition and enabled it to become a museum.

Contrary to what has been rightly suggested with respect to various other contexts, however, conspiracy theoretical interpretations of histories of state-endorsed violence thrived in 2010s Turkey not as an adverse reaction to the promises of transparentization and democratization that featured prominently the government's approach to "confronting the past" but rather as a direct outcome of them (cf. Fortun and Fortun 1999; K. Stewart 1999; and West and Sanders 2003). Two aspects of the government's approach worked in tandem to enable this outcome. First, the government produced its own account of who the victims of violence were: virtually the entire nation. By implication, this meant that, alongside the few dozen individuals sentenced in court, the perpetrators included anyone unable to fit in this national imaginary. Most important, such an implication excluded state officials with varying degrees of culpability from the category of perpetrators. Unlike many of the examples discussed in relevant scholarship, however, conspiracy theorizing in this case was no mere backlash to the transparency of the official account. Instead, conspiracy theorizing was largely in agreement with and indeed underpinned officials' understanding of the victims as comprising virtually the entire nation. The only disagreement was that adherents of conspiracy theory found this understanding only partially satisfactory even as they welcomed it, as they wanted the few dozen individuals sentenced in court to also be considered among the victims. This created an axis of dissensus that overwhelmed the one pursued by memory activists, who called for recognition of the victims' sociopolitical specificity and for the extension of culpability to the authorities. Because this axis was successfully created and indeed established as the main divide that framed the debate around the histories of violence involved, the memory activists' work could be effectively undermined without necessarily being altogether censored or outlawed. If anything, that they *were able* to carry out their work was repurposed to provide substance to the government's promise of "democratization" and "transparentization." If this substance was a merely cosmetic one involving making visible and platforming plurality, the spatial way in which this cosmetics was managed at sites of violence worked to expose those communities made visible and the ones platformed to the risk of being antagonized by continually ramifying conspiracy theories.

In Sivas, securitization of urban space during commemorations held by memory activists rendered tangible the central conspiracy theoretical trope of "exogenous foci" and did so on a scale much more accessible to the ordinary eye than that of the national interior/exterior imaginary that underpins it. Checkpoints and barricades blurred the lines separating security from provocation, hospitality from hostility, and aggressee from aggressor. The architectural transformation of the site of the arson attack resulted in an aura of bureaucratic anonymity and a sweeping approach to remembrance that echoed understandings of the arson attack as outsiders infiltrating the inside. If these developments may appear to have been aimed at curbing the contestation surrounding the atrocity, they produced the exact opposite effect. And they did so not only among those upholding the legacy of the thirty-three festival participants but also among those who began to embroil the architectural transformation of the site of atrocity itself, and the actors behind it, in their theorization of the arson attack as conspiracy.

In Ulucanlar, violence's sociopolitically differentiated production of victimhood was flattened by equating all former political prisoners to one another—even those who did not serve time in this prison complex. If the aim was to use the 1980 coup as an authoritarian backdrop against which to distinguish the early 2010s administration as democratic and in so doing depoliticize both the democracy and the authoritarianism in question, this depoliticization was soon revealed as itself an extension of the past it purportedly aimed to confront. The erasure of the political work carried out by the Left soon gave way to nationalist ideology's creeping into the museum. In its first months as a publicly accessible museum, Ulucanlar saw a far-right gathering in memory of a former nationalist inmate hanged in the prison in the wake of the 1980 coup. When a few participants of the gathering cursed at the late general Kenan Evren, who had led the 1980 coup, an altercation arose among the group and the cursers were silenced. The incident thereby unmasked the continuities between the politics of the 1980 coup and the politics of contemporary nationalists who claim to be among the heirs of the period's supposedly sociopolitically undifferentiated victims.[1] In the late 2010s, the museum's initial efforts to distance itself from ideological difference gave way to a gradual alignment with nationalism. In 2017 the administration announced that a section dedicated to nationalists—or "idealists" (*Ülkücüler*), as the movement is known in Turkey after the nationalist "ideal" they have upheld—was in the works as they were preparing to open to the public the second ward, where nationalist prisoners were known to have been lodged in the

1. For a detailed news report of the incident, see "Evren'e küfür kavga çıkarttı" [Swearing at Evren Started a Fight], *Milliyet*, Oct. 7, 2011, http://www.milliyet.com.tr/gundem/evrene-kufur-kavga-cikartti-1448124.

past (Boynueğri 2017). In 2019, pro-Kurdish member of Parliament and filmmaker Sırrı Süreyya Önder's name was removed from Ulucanlar's exhibitions, where it had enjoyed a place since the museum's inauguration, while he was eight months into serving the three-and-a-half-year sentence delivered to him under the state of emergency introduced in 2016 on the grounds of "terrorist propaganda" (Alan 2019).

In 2010s Turkey, conspiracy theory permeated not only "society" but also the "state," as it underpinned the authorities' approach to confronting histories of state-endorsed violence by promoting a sociopolitically undifferentiated—a *nationalized*—notion of victimhood. This permeation not only reiterates that the categories of "society" and "state" are empirically much less distinct from each other than is often assumed by those who assume that civil society and publicness are inherently and context-independently emancipatory forces (Navaro-Yashin 2002, 152). It also demonstrates that conspiracy theory operated in this context less as a challenge posed by "society" to the "state" than as a prominent mechanism through which to forge the former as distinct from, and at times even antagonistic to, the latter. The effectiveness of this operation, moreover, hinged on its spatiality. The conspiracy theoretical approach to histories of state-endorsed violence promulgated the imaginary of "society" being the national "inside." This promulgation sought to flatten various other empirically grounded distinctions produced by state-endorsed violence (that is, distinctions between victim, perpetrator, bystander, and survivor) and its sociopolitically differentiated effects. Seeking physical evidence for its imaginary of society as the national interior, conspiracy theory turned to the very environments where histories of state-endorsed violence took place and, in so doing, naturalized the political legacy of this violence by making it the basis of the contemporary spatial order. Part 2 focuses on "public space" as the stuff of various and often conflicting notions and experiences that threw into sharp relief both the spatial order in question and the significant challenges posed to it by those communities seeking to underscore the sociopolitical specificity of victimhood.

Part Two
Protesting Victimhood

Introduction

In the aftermath of violence, the object with which the verb *protest* is employed tends to be innocence or guilt. In the context of 2010s Turkey, however, one of the most significant strands of activism was oriented toward protesting victimhood. This activism developed in response to the growing attempts at nationalizing victimhood discussed in part 1. To foreground the sociopolitical specificity of violence and its victims, the activists organized commemorations in the manner of protests. The etymology of the verb *protest* indicates the act of testifying *publicly* (Hightower and East 2018). It is not coincidental, then, that notions and experiences of public space, as detailed below, were central to memory activism around the Sivas arson attack, the Ulucanlar Prison in Ankara, and the Diyarbakır Prison as activists sought to protest victimhood in the sense mentioned above. But mainstream discourses and practices of "confronting the past" also invoked certain notions of public space to invalidate the activist work of protesting victimhood. Part 2 discusses these various and often conflicting notions and experiences of public space.

Just as this book considers commemoration and violence entangled in one another, part 2 approaches public space as the stuff of that entanglement. Doing so echoes Giorgio Agamben's notion of "the camp" that for him conditions the conventional "models by which social sciences, sociology, urban studies, and architecture today are trying to conceive and organize the public space of the world's cities" (1998, 181). He developed this notion by redrawing the arc of biopolitical history from the ancient Roman *homo sacer*, whose murder lacked legal definition as it was categorized neither as sacrifice nor as crime, to the twentieth-century concentration camp—a period that, for Agamben, rendered the sort of semantic ambiguation facing *homo sacer* increasingly prevalent. Agamben's history is problematic for overlooking the questions of racism and patriarchy; he disregards racialized and gendered power structures that render biopolitics' operations uneven across populaces and, more broadly, seeks to condemn biopolitical subjects to disempowerment (Butler 2004, 68; Weheliye 2014). But it is useful for attending to semantics' importance to the entanglement between public space and violence; indeed, this attention helps address the very question of power Agamben overlooks.[1] "Often it is only by being 'violent' that excluded groups have gained access to the public spaces of democracy" and "forced the liberalization of public space laws" (Mitchell 2003, 52). Don Mitchell's use of the scare quotes and reference to laws here highlight not only the role of semantics and legislation in negotiating the relationship between violence and public space but also power's centrality to this negotiation. The authorities' tendency to identify challenges to sociospatial marginalization as "violent" depoliticizes both those challenges and the concept of violence; it flattens the uneven power relations that underpin both (Dikeç 2017). Countering this tendency, then, requires that the "publicness" of public space be understood not as "preordained" but rather as shaped and continually reshaped through "the struggle for rights" and "social justice" (Mitchell 2003, 35–36). If resolving violence's semantic ambiguity is part of this struggle, precisely what sorts of spatial imaginaries might it involve, and how might these relate to conventional models of public space?

Recent scholarly responses to this question echo Michael Warner's theory of publics and counterpublics. Counterpublics, for Warner, operate

---

1. The prominent way semantics features in Agamben, moreover, speaks directly to this book's approach to violence outlined in the introduction and does so for two reasons. To recall, the first reason is his attention to not only readily visible manifestations of bodily violation but also systemic and symbolic structures that institutionalize violence, including semantic and constitutional ones. The second reason concerns Agamben's indication that these bodily, systemic, and symbolic registers of violence operated in interlinked ways rather than discretely. For instance, the semantic ambiguation of death, this ambiguity's being instituted into law, and the same legal system's permitting further such semantically ambiguous deaths all cooperate to propagate each other.

against "not just a general or wider public, but a dominant one," where the dominance concerns "speech genres," "modes of address," and "media" as opposed to simply "ideas or policy" (2005, 119; cf. Negt and Kluge 2002). He considers rational-critical hermeneutics a foremost medium used by dominant publics and argues that (counter)publics challenge it by preferring "embodied sociability" over "the ideology of reading" or "performance" over "print" (Warner 2005, 123).[2] Mirroring Warner's emphasis on medium, contemporary scholarship on violence's relationship to public space has considered "spontaneous action and performance" and "unscripted interaction" conducive to contrarian positions, categorizing the latter as "nonviolent" while associating "violence," in Arendtian fashion, with the annihilation of politics or with cyclical mechanisms of domination and submission that foreclose any possibility of emancipation

2. Warner's theory of counterpublics therefore differs from Nancy Fraser's, which is based on a critique of Jürgen Habermas's idealization of the bourgeois public sphere as civil, accessible, rational, and *the only* public sphere at that (Fraser 1990). For Fraser, Habermas's "sharp separation of (associational) civil society and the state" allowed only for "weak publics"—publics that engage merely in "opinion-formation" while leaving other essential business such as "decision-making," "self-management," "inter-public coordination," and "political accountability" to states (75–76). Conversely, counterpublics are strong publics; they facilitate not only "withdrawal and regroupment" but also "agitational activities directed toward wider publics" (68). That counterpublics are conceptualized in contradistinction to neither privacy nor the state but to other publics and that they continually aspire to become publics warrant parenthesizing the concept's adjectival prefix, as in (counter)publicness. Theorists of radical democracy since the millennial turn have criticized Fraser for paradoxically reproducing the very theoretical sway on which she challenged Habermas: the idealization of full integration, reasoned deliberation, and harmonious convergence as the ultimate aspirations of publicness (Deutsche 1996, 286). I follow this critique in its wariness of the celebration of absolute convergence implicit in Fraser. However, as I hope will become clear throughout part 2, I also prioritize a certain contextual specificity and empirical sensibility that require attention to how power structures publicness and counterpublicness. Put simply, my analysis privileges a focus on how power shapes and wields publicness and how it is challenged as such in concrete circumstances, which requires me to refrain from dismissing the political agency involved in any aspiring counterpublic's pursuit of reasoned deliberation, full integration, and harmonious convergence.

(Springer 2011, 526; Mustafa, Brown, and Tillotson 2013, 1111, 1121). Such arguments and analyses have insightfully avoided reproducing rationality and civility as preconditions for (counter)publicness. But they have largely evaded questions such as precisely how the boundary between the rational-critical and its other is probed and constituted and how violence bears upon this process as a phenomenon whose meaning is not necessarily always unambiguously determined prior to its occurrence. This is the question that guides my empirical analysis in part 2.

Before proceeding with empirical analysis, however, some context and background are necessary. "The birth of [Habermasian] public space" in what is now Turkey dates from the late Ottoman era when it took place under the influence of western European–style consumerism, replacing various other already existing sites of socialization (Göçek and Özyüksel 2012). This systemic transformation not only continued unabated but also assumed a new facet in the early twentieth century as ethnically driven nationalisms gained prominence. Between 1913 and 1950, various ethnic homogenization policies such as the Armenian genocide prevented citizens from performing difference and in so doing established Turkish nationalism's hegemony in and over "public space" (Üngör 2011, 212–34). This had implications for all three sites discussed in this book. Sivas and Diyarbakır were among the genocide's epicenters; prior to it, a third of Sivas's population and nearly half of Diyarbakır's were non-Muslim, and Armenians were the majority within that demographic (Marchand and Perrier 2015, 26; Aydın and Verheij 2012, 21). Some of the most symbolic sites that today constitute the publicly owned institutional heart of Turkey in the capital, Ankara, where Ulucanlar Prison Museum is located, were in fact confiscated during the Armenian genocide (Kezer 2012). Squares were a major public-spatial medium of ethnic homogenization in the early republican era, a prototypical example being Ankara's Ulus (Nation) Square built in the 1930s in lieu of an already existing site of political demonstration, commercial activity, and socialization called Taşhan Square (Sargın 2004). If, physically, interventions of the sort that transformed Taşhan into Ulus were government-led and premised on west-central European urban planning (Bozdoğan 2001, 67–77), social substance was forged through collective performances of national homogeneity. In Ulus this took the form of a citizen-led campaign for a monument around which to focalize the square and that aimed to perform the citizenry's absolute coalescence with the emergent nation-state (Sargın 2004, 665; Akgün Yüksekli and Akalın 2011, 651). The radicalness of such interventions was tempered with nominal continuity; the word *meydan*, long employed to denote sites like Taşhan whose identification as "public space" owed more to historical habituality than to prescription by design, was adopted as the official descriptor for the "new" squares.

In the second half of the twentieth century, violence began to feature increasingly conspicuously in these squares. Non-Muslim populations identified as minorities under the 1923 Lausanne Treaty, which had secured international legal recognition for the then nascent Republic of Turkey, were assaulted in episodes of "civil violence organized and/or overlooked by the government" such as the mid-1950s pogroms in central Istanbul (Batuman 2015, 892). Mainstream politicians and journalists identified these episodes not as "violence" but as "the people's reaction" to some other contemporaneous event. That official "public" spaces played a central role in many of these "people's reactions"—for instance, Istanbul's central Taksim Square in the mid-1950s pogroms—amplified violence's centrality to the spatial ways the people and the publicness in question co-constituted each other. As the century progressed, such "reactions" turned inward to engulf the constitutional majority, an example being the assault on an anti-imperialist rally that communist students held in Taksim Square in 1969. The intensification of ideological conflict in the 1970s turned spaces like Taksim Square into "a symbolic battlefield" over which mutually conflicting publics competed (892–93). The September 12, 1980, military coup brought this process to an end and did so not only by restricting social rights but also by using squares like Taksim for state rallies where the "popularity" of restrictive policies was performed (Baykan and Hatuka 2010).

The mid-1980s saw the restoration of electoral democracy and the neoliberal curtailment of the state's socioeconomic presence, inaugurating a period Habermasian accounts have associated with "the expansion of the public sphere" (Göle 1994; M. Yavuz 2009, 58). But these accounts overlooked "martial law and war in the southeast" and other "repressive"

measures the political and the economic establishment employed throughout the same period to shape that which is public (Navaro-Yashin 2002,
132). Indeed, operating in entanglement with "free-market" forces, the
state continued to influence "public life" so significantly as to empirically
invalidate distinctions between it and civil society or notions of publicness based on such a distinction (Özyürek 2006, 7–8). Evidencing this
influence is the term *kamusal alan*, which has come to serve as the primary Turkish-language rendition of "public space." While the adjective
kamusal is intended to convey publicness, *alan* can mean both "space" and
"sphere." *Kamusal* suffixes the noun *kamu* with -*sal*, which implies relation. *Kamu* can mean "the state" as well as "the people," or even "public"
with markedly libertarian undertones, as evidenced in the word *kamuoyu*
(public opinion) (Özbek 2005). Despite these ambiguities, the late 1980s
and early 1990s—the very period that Habermasian accounts have associated with the expansion of the public sphere in Turkey—saw *kamusal alan*
rise to prominence, especially among scholars of urbanism and architecture, as the Turkish rendition of "public space" (Açıkgöz 2004). However,
as the etymology and the history provided above show, any expansion that
kamusal alan is alleged to have undergone necessarily entails a risk of sub-
jugation to, rather than just emancipation from, such dominant forces as
the state and/or the market (Çınar 2005, 38). The same risk has inhered in
the conventional models of public space that have featured in mainstream
approaches to "confronting the past" in 2010s Turkey and their attitude
toward sites of state-endorsed violence.

If the fragments constituting the background and context outlined
above are not entirely spatially focused, the claim to publicness that characterizes each makes them pertinent to part 2: "If the publicly accessible
spaces of the city are easy to understand as 'locations' for the public sphere,
it is important to remember that they are not the only locations" (Staeheli 2010, 72; cf. Mitchell 2003, 35). Indeed, few sites are further from the
conventional image of public space than the former Madımak Hotel—a
building located on a side street that long served as a private hotel before
becoming host to a nine-to-five state institution—not to mention the cases
of Ulucanlar and Diyarbakır, both of which are prisons and thus are pro-
grammatically the very antonym of public accessibility. But this has not

prevented all three sites from becoming subject to spatial imaginaries of publicness; as discussed below, the episode of violence each witnessed led to that development. This is not to say that each site's physicality is irrelevant to these imaginaries. That "publics have no proper location . . . does not mean that all kinds of space are equivalent or equally available for those engaged in struggles to make publics." The physicality of each location through which imaginaries of publicness become manifest bears upon their political potentials and limitations. Assessing these potentials and limitations therefore requires that such locations be subjected to "empirical analysis" rather than being celebrated as ideal public spaces or dismissed as failed ones (Iveson 2007, 13). Part 2 offers just this sort of an analysis of spatial notions and experiences of publicness that have been constitutive of and constituted by the commemoration of state-endorsed violence in Sivas (chapter 3), Diyarbakır (chapter 4), and Ankara (chapter 5).[3]

3. Analyzing the publicness of commemoration in such a way dovetails with this book's broader critical analytical contribution to the literature on commemorative practices. Publicness features prominently in this literature, as memorials and monuments are appraised in terms of their ability to trigger "public discourses" (Carrier 2005, 228; Huyssen 1995, 254; Linenthal 2001, 117; Stevens and Franck 2016, 236; Wagner-Pacifici and Schwartz 1991; Young 2016, 16), to enhance the public-spatial quality of their surroundings (Aguilera 2014, 110), and to engage the "publics" that cross paths with them (Wagner-Pacifici and Schwartz 1991, 416). Appraising commemoration in this way has been useful in considering its "publicness" not just a matter of content and production but also of form, medium, method, and reception. But doing so has treated "public" as a descriptive rather than analytical concept and as one that describes political progress or emancipation, at that. And this has reproduced commemoration's presumed antitheticality to violence, which this book problematizes through and through.

3

Spatial Entanglements between Violence and Publicness in Sivas

The Sivas arson attack took place on July 2, 1993, at a time when debates on *kamusal alan* in Turkey were in full swing. Rather than a sudden assault, it was the culmination of an entire afternoon of unrest in central Sivas instigated by tens of individuals, ultimately attracting thousands. Judging by the slogans they chanted, the ringleaders were antisecularists and Islamic fundamentalists protesting certain aspects of the Pir Sultan Abdal Culture Festival (Tüleylioğlu 2010, 47–51). As explained in chapter 1, the festival was being held in 1993 for the third time in a row after more than a decade of hiatus owing to sociopolitical unrest, episodes of violence whose targets included Alevis, and a military coup, and for the fourth time overall since its inauguration in 1978. Still, it had the quality of a debut. For the first time, the festival's venues included those in central Sivas. In its first three iterations, the event had been confined to a remote location in the city's hinterland, Banaz, known as the sixteenth-century minstrel Pir Sultan Abdal's native village. Moreover, contrary to precedent, the 1993 festival was programmed as not just an Alevism-related event but a broader one. It involved writers, performers, and musicians who were not necessarily Alevis but were renowned in Turkey's left-leaning circles. In other words, the festival organizers' aspiration to reach—and, in so doing, constitute—publics wider than their fellow Alevis mobilized both space and programming. In that respect, the festival indexed Alevis' return to the geography that state-endorsed violence throughout the 1970s had forced them to flee. But this return would not simply entail the restoration of the previous status quo marked by the commonplace opposition of public to private life

82

and by faith's strict association with the latter. It would endeavor to ensure that Alevism "is no longer confined to secrecy and has entered the public space" (Sökefeld 2002, 169).

The chain of events that culminated in the arson attack, however, would reiterate that the "public space" being "entered" was less a socio-politically neutral container than one whose publicness is entangled in the question of violence. First, with only days until the festival, an anonymous leaflet addressed to "the Muslim public" and posted through mailboxes in central Sivas incited violence against the festival's key-note speaker, Aziz Nesin, the pretext being his recent declaration that he might commission a Turkish translation of Salman Rushdie's *Satanic Verses* (Tüleylioğlu 2010, 38–39). The night before the arson attack, another such leaflet appeared; this time, the addressee was "our people," and a postscript requested that "readers reproduce this text and circulate it further" (Aşut 1994, 323). Meanwhile, right-leaning local newspapers agitated against the festival, questioning especially the "public" funding it received through the Cultural Ministry held by the left-wing partner of the then-governing grand coalition. The agitation centered on a "Minstrels Monument," which the ministry had funded and placed outside the cultural center that was the festival's main venue to mark the occasion. The newspapers speculated that the monument did not honor all minstrels as per its official name but clandestinely commemorated Pir Sultan Abdal—the sixteenth-century minstrel venerated in Alevism, after whom the festival was named—which infuriated them, as they considered him "one of the foremost rebels in Anatolia's history" (Bozgeyik 1993). "Why, how, and by whom" taxes were dedicated to such a project kept secret from "the public" was posed as a question that ought to preoccupy "the people of Sivas." The local ministerial representative released a statement to quell the speculations targeting the monument, but also pledged to "tear it down if necessary."[1]

---

1. For a record of this back-and-forth between the local press and the authorities, see "Kültür Merkezi Önüne Pir Sultan" [Pir Sultan to the Culture Center's Forecourt], *Hürdoğan*, July 1, 1993, 1; and "Bu Anıt 'Ozanlar Anıtı'" [This Monument Is 'the Minstrels Monument'], *Hürdoğan*, July 2, 1993, 1.

The claims to and mobilizations of publicness that marked these incendiary reactions to various aspects of the festival would assume an overtly spatial character on the day of the arson attack. Present in Sivas throughout the festival was a group of reporters from a conservative-leaning national network launched just half a year before the arson attack, when the state's monopoly on radio and television broadcasting had ended—a development Habermasian accounts of this period in Turkey often feature as symptomatic of the expansion of the public sphere. At a book exhibition held in the courtyard of a public museum (located in a historic building called the Buruciye Madrassa) on the morning of the festival's second day, one of the reporters from this network challenged Nesin on his plans to translate the *Satanic Verses*. Embarking on an ad hominem attack, the reporter brought up the author's atheism and produced newspapers and leaflets from the past few days that berated him and his participation in the festival. Nesin's response that "I don't believe Allah's word; I would need to lose my mind if I were to do so" was met with attempts by some members of the small crowd watching the encounter to lunge at him (Tüleylioğlu 2010, 46). This encounter was something of an omen, not only as the first instance of physical hostility toward a festival guest, but also for what it foreshadowed about the press's role in the arson attack: that this role was not limited to reporting on violence but actually served to incite it (cf. Chalfont et al. 1980). The demonopolization of broadcasting in the 1990s that some, as mentioned in the introduction to part 2, have categorically celebrated for its contribution to "the expansion of the public sphere" was therefore thrown into sharp relief as having expanded not simply the range of publics allowed into this sphere, but rather, conventional imaginaries of publicness that were underpinned by decades of violent homogenization.

About an hour later, a small crowd gathered outside a nearby mosque after Friday prayers to head to the culture center hosting one of the festival's events. Chanting slogans reminiscent of the above-mentioned anonymous leaflets, the crowd defaced the Minstrels Monument located in the building's forecourt (figure 15). This constituted the threshold where the previous days' mutually constitutive calls to publicness and to violence translated from discourse into practice. The assailants then turned to the

15. The Minstrels Monument as seen after its defacement outside the main festival venue, 1993. Courtesy of photographer Cevat Üstün.

offices of the governor to protest the state's providing the festival with public funding. Having shuttled once more between the culture center and the governor's office and having been pushed back by the police in both locations, they went on to surround the nearby hotel hosting many of the festival's guests. As the number of assailants grew to hundreds, members of the local government and law enforcement arrived on the scene.

Their calls for dispersal were met by the crowd with three prerequisites, among which was the removal of the Minstrels Monument (Tüleylioğlu 2010, 488–92). The authorities complied and brought the toppled monument to the crowd as proof of their compliance. But this only further encouraged the assailants, who seized the monument and dragged it to the forecourt of the hotel where they burned it, constituting the penultimate stage before the building itself was set ablaze (186–87).

The broadcasting network continued reporting from Sivas in the run-up to the arson. This meant that the festival guests sheltering inside the hotel from the assailants outside were able to watch TV reports on the events unfolding around them. While the crowd grew in number, chanting inflammatory slogans and attacking the building with stones, the reports periodically and misleadingly announced that "there has been unrest in Sivas, but the situation is now under control" (Özbakır 2010). It was not until the building was set alight that they reflected a more up-to-date account of the events. The way the events were reported therefore had a twofold contribution to the violence. Not only did it hinder various attempts to alert the authorities to the urgency of the situation when the arson attack was still preventable, including those by victims-to-be who made phone calls from inside the hotel to dignitaries they personally knew, albeit to no avail (Tüleylioğlu 2010, 50). Choosing to broadcast images of the event at its most visually sensational moment—an inhabited building set ablaze before the eyes of thousands of spectators—amplified the marginalization of those identifying with the victims and the legitimacy of those outside the hotel as constitutive of "the people." Hence the president's remarks the following day: the arson attack was "an isolated incident" where "the public was agitated" owing to "severe provocation" and the law enforcements' inaction was only right in refusing to "pit the public and the security forces against each other" (61–62). Similarly, when asked about the casualties, the prime minister referred to the victims and survivors as "individuals," while highlighting that "thankfully our people outside the hotel were unharmed" (59). These remarks recalled the "popular reaction" descriptor to which members of various administrations in Turkey throughout the twentieth century resorted when referring to certain episodes of state-endorsed violence. In so doing, they demonstrated from day one that the stakes involved in the arson attack included not just what had occurred but also how it would both define and be defined by notions of publicness.

If the state representatives' response to the arson attack followed this tradition of seeing in violence an opportunity to reinvigorate the sociopolitical homogenization underpinning conventional imaginaries of publicness, it was nevertheless particular in its spatiality—in its mapping of "the people" onto the hotel's "outside." Those upholding the victims' legacy have since challenged this by reclaiming the space as a site for commemoration. Their very first defiance of the ban on commemorative gatherings at the site, which had been instituted the day after the arson attack, occurred on September 4, the locally celebrated anniversary of the "1919 Sivas Congress," an official historiographical milestone in the Turkish National Campaign (1919–22). Three associations founded by Alevis originally hailing from Sivas but headquartered in Istanbul and Ankara brought three hundred of their members to Sivas to attend the official public ceremony marking the anniversary. Halfway through the event, they performed an act of *détournement* by suddenly marching to the hotel to commemorate the arson attack's victims.[2] This set the tone for the annual commemoration that memory activists have since then held on site.

Challenges to the spatiality characterizing the authorities' response to the arson attack involved not only reclaiming the space outside the hotel but also obliging them to affiliate with its inside. This is evident in the most significant commemorative campaign mounted by those claiming the victims' legacy. Launched just days after July 2, 1993, by representatives of various left-leaning political parties and professional organizations, this ongoing campaign demands that the site of the arson attack be turned into a public memorial museum. Although, following the attack, the site was fast repaired and returned to business as a hotel, the campaign has continued unabated over the years while also placing increasing

2. Not unexpectedly, prominent local newspapers portrayed this impromptu commemoration as a provocation; see "Kim İzin Verdi" [Who Gave the Permission], *Hakikat*, Sept. 5, 1993, 1.

emphasis on precisely who the addressee is—the state. The emphasis was thrown into sharp relief in the mid-2000s when Europe-based Alevi associations had amassed enough funds to purchase the hotel and transform it in whatever manner they saw fit but decided otherwise. A senior member of these associations explained the decision thus: "To accept a memorial museum that is not supported by state officials means also to unjustly claim responsibility for the Sivas massacre. The state authorities, both past and present, are responsible for and guilty of the Sivas massacre—both because they were negligent and because they have since then portrayed it as an ordinary event" (Kaplan 2008). Framed as such, the campaign grew in popularity throughout the 2000s and inspired additional campaigns regarding numerous other sites of state-endorsed violence in which activists have considered the authorities culpable. These campaigns dovetailed with various intellectuals' calls for Turkey to "reckon with" its violent past (Sancar 2007). The decade culminated in the government initiative known popularly as Demokratik Açılım (Democratic Opening), as part of which the authorities held a series of workshops with nongovernmental actors and representatives of historically underrepresented groups, including Alevis. That the state convert the site of the arson attack into a memorial museum was among the five demands raised during the so-called Alevi workshops. This kick-started a process in which the site hosted the first ministerial-level commemorative visit, was expropriated in late 2010, and underwent a state-sponsored architectural transformation project in spring 2011. I began my fieldwork in Sivas just days after a press preview held in June 2011 revealed that the building had become a commemorative-cum-educational institution named the Science and Culture Center and open to the public for visits throughout the working week.

Spatializing (Counter)publicness through Commemoration

The Memory Corner, which is the commemorative centerpiece of the Science and Culture Center, displays two statements. One of these statements as well as the overall Memory Corner was discussed in chapter 3. It is the second statement to which I now turn: "Regardless of the different ideas, different beliefs in society, there is no unachievable task, no unsurpassable obstacle for a nation that knows how to act in national unity and togetherness." The Memory Corner attributes this statement to Mustafa Kemal Atatürk, who famously led the Turkish National Campaign and served as the founding president of the Republic of Turkey until his death in 1938. The attribution is conveyed through Kemal's iconic signature and a gilded mask portraying his face, which accompany the statement. Use of Kemalist iconography has led the Memory Corner to resemble the so-called "Atatürk corners" that have long populated the lobbies of Turkey's official institutions, public buildings, and schools (Navaro-Yashin 2002, 188–203). The rest of the Science and Culture Center is geared toward schoolchildren between the ages of seven and fourteen who are expected to visit the site with their teachers. The educational spaces look markedly different from the building's commemorative section; they are brightly lit; furnished in curvaceous lines and vibrant shades of red, blue, and yellow; and sporadically decorated with Olympic rings.

According to the construction engineer in his late thirties who ran the transformation project, the building's various functions were determined by senior government representatives, who "concurred that this place should become a common [ortak] one." For him, even the building's name embodied this objective: rather than reference certain events or people upheld by nationalist historiography as per standard practice in Turkey, the name reads "Science and Culture Center—a thoroughly neutral, kamu name" befitting a building "identified with kamu." Indeed, the term kamu (public, the state, the people) had figured prominently in the hotel's transformation even before construction began. It is the root of kamulaştırma (literally, making kamu), the Turkish word for "expropriation," which constituted the first step toward the building's transformation. The term was also central to the way the architect commissioned for the project reflected on it. "Like all kamu buildings around the world, this, too, is a heavy, oppressive and serious building," he admitted. The term indicated neutrality for the architect just as it did for the engineer. That the building was redesigned with an awareness of its "belonging to kamu," he suggested, has helped accommodate future scenarios in which the authorities may decide to use parts of it for various other purposes. For him, the decorative use of Olympic rings—a world-renowned motif of national and/or political impartiality (Lennartz 2001–2, 29–61)—and the alphabetical ordering of the name list were also evidence of the building's alleged neutrality.

My research inside the building revealed that the architectural elements employed in substantiating its alleged neutrality also included the upper four floors that constitute the bulk of the building and remain empty to this day. When faced with visitors' criticism, employees invoked the emptiness of these floors. When a couple in their midthirties lambasted the Memory Corner's inclusion of "assailants' names," the employee tending them admitted to the "imperfection" of the Science and Culture Center. But he stressed that this was just a well-intentioned start; in fact, the bulk of the building remained empty, and feedback of the sort provided by the couple could well influence what might later become of it. When a father and his teenage son complained that the building had become a Science and Culture Center rather than a memorial museum proper, the employee tending them pointed yet again to the upper floors. Presuming that the father and son were Alevis as per the affiliation of the organizations that have campaigned most ardently for an on-site memorial museum, the employee mentioned the possibility of handing the upper levels over to an Alevi association, which could then use them as it sees fit: "turn them into a museum, or perhaps even into a *cemevi*."

The idle upper floors also proved useful in dealing with antimuseum stances. When faced with visitors who found even the Memory Corner too significant a concession granted to those campaigning for an on-site memorial museum, the employee highlighted that the building had after all been expropriated (*kamulaştırıldı*); it now belonged to *kamu*, who, "if necessary, might turn it into a post office or a bank." The likelihood of change, according to the employee, was evident in two facts. An official opening ceremony had yet to take place; until the authorities' blessing is secured, one could never be sure that the building's current state was here to stay.[3] But a sign of incompletion clearer than the latter, suggested the

3. Prime Minister Erdoğan was scheduled to visit Sivas on June 9, 2011, as part of his general election campaign. In the run-up to his visit, it was rumored that he would inaugurate the Science and Culture Center with an official ceremony. Such an inauguration, however, never took place, Erdoğan's pretext being "election campaign restrictions." See

employee, was the emptiness of the upper floors. Emptiness—an architectural quality that has elsewhere been seen as enabling greater "publicness" by allowing "interpretation" (Spector 2014, 183–84)—was therefore being repurposed here to substantiate the alleged neutrality of the Science and Culture Center through a performance of openness to participation and willingness to adapt.

Larger implications of such performances of and claims to neutrality enacted through various aspects of the Science and Culture Center became evident during the 2011 episode of the annual memory activist commemorations in Sivas. Held in the immediate aftermath of the building's relaunch as the Science and Culture Center, the commemoration was declared illegal by the local authorities for the first time in its eighteen-year history. The event's organizers, representatives of various left-leaning organizations and Alevi associations, met with the governor of Sivas a week before the anniversary as usual to inform him of the commemoration, only to be told that the building is now "*kamusal alan* and therefore no longer available for such gatherings" (Yıldız 2011). Although the commemoration eventually went ahead, the attempted ban materialized in police barricades mounted fifteen meters ahead of the building, which prevented flower laying at its doorstep except by a handful of victims' relatives and senior Alevi figures. The police also barricaded every side street leading to the spot except the procession route. Ironically, the organizers had already decided that commemoration participants would refuse to enter the building in order to demonstrate their disapproval of various aspects of the Science and Culture Center, including its general failure to deliver a museum proper but more specifically its all-encompassing name list, against which victims' relatives had also filed a lawsuit (Benli 2016). Still, flower laying at the doorstep was a gesture that hundreds of commemoration participants tended to perform every year. When more than

---

"Madımak'ın yeni yüzüyle açılışı seçim yasaklarına takıldı" [Madımak's Inauguration with Its New Face Is Prevented by Election Restrictions], *Beyaz Gazete*, May 24, 2011, http://beyazgazete.com/haber/2011/5/24/madimak-in-yeni-yuzuyle-acilisi-secim-yasak larina-takildi-844787.html. As of October 2020, the site has yet to host an official opening ceremony.

just the handful allowed past the barricade insisted on reaching the build-ing's doorstep to lay flowers there, the police reacted by using tear gas. This triggered a brief scuffle between approximately twenty young activ-ists and the police, snapshots of which were featured in front-page news the next morning, fueling allegations regarding the violent tendencies of commemoration participants.

The 2012 commemoration was heavily influenced by a court decision delivered in March that year, when one of the lawsuits related to the arson attack lapsed because of the statute of limitations (Tanyeri-Erdemir 2012). Hundreds gathered outside the courthouse in Ankara during the hearing to insist that, had the judiciary treated the arson attack as a crime against humanity rather than a simple case of homicide, the case would not have been subject to the statute of limitations (Ziflioğlu 2012b). When the out-come of the hearing was declared, the gathering spontaneously became a sit-in. It was soon dispersed by the police with tear gas and water cannons.

A few months later, the commemoration in Sivas saw the barricades move farther up along the route of the procession by about a half kilome-ter and therefore closer to the predominantly Alevi-inhabited neighbor-hood whence the event departs every year. A sit-in ensued, which led the police to move the barricades back to where they had been in 2011. Virtu-ally all side streets leading to the site were also sealed, as they had been the previous year. What was different was the type of barricade erected in the building's forecourt. The simple plastic shields employed previously were replaced with a two-meter-high steel barrier, which the police have since continued to mount at the site on commemoration day. Also dif-ferent from 2011 was the proactivity with which the commemoration's organizing committee responded to the provocative potential of these instruments of "public safety." The bus that had just led the procession was now parked sideways to obscure the steel barrier (figure 16). This was significant not only because it reduced the likelihood of confronta-tion with the police but also because it created a spatial arrangement that helped orient the entire body of activists toward the Science and Cul-ture Center. Each speaker addressing the event was therefore able to use the building as the object of their successive denunciations of the arson attack, the authorities' and the media's roles in it, the failure of the site's

16. Forecourt of the site of the Sivas arson attack as seen on commemoration day, 2011.

architectural transformation to deliver a museum, and the recent lapsing of the court case owing to the statute of limitations. The building was also mobilized as a reference point against which to articulate alternatives regarding how the arson attack ought to be condemned both architecturally and judicially. The speeches culminated in the following remarks by the chairperson of the Alevi association that leads the commemoration's organizing committee: "The court case on this massacre is not held in palaces of justice; it is held here in this *meydan!*"

The chairperson's use of the term *meydan* in reference to the otherwise nondescript space occupied by the commemoration is significant for at least two reasons. First, *meydan* denotes the sociojudicial and spiritual platform in Alevism where grievances are raised, disputes are resolved, and misdoings are penalized (Shankland 2003, 127–28). Second, as explained in the introduction to part 2, *meydan* is the Turkish word for "public square." Its variants are employed across the geographical triangle demarcated by and inclusive of Libya, Ukraine, and India to convey the same meaning. The word, moreover, has recently acquired an overtly political significance across this geography owing to the numerous waves of mass protest that have taken place in its metropolises and that were named after the central square in each metropolis, including Istanbul. A direct link between the latter and the Sivas arson attack materialized in mid-June 2013 when the police's crackdown on activists occupying Istanbul's Taksim Square and the adjacent Gezi Park sparked a new wave of antiviolence protest in the form of individuals standing motionless in Turkey's cities. Among the venues of this protest was the forecourt of the Science and Culture Center, providing further substance to its association with the concept of *meydan* (Verstraete 2013, 8).[4]

In sum, associating the site of the arson attack with the concept of *meydan* is irreducible to a repudiation of the *kamusal*-ness that the Science and Culture Center project has attributed to the building. Rather, it is a means of repurposing the site toward the collective expression of dissent and the pursuit of social justice.

4. The distinct sense of confrontationality that inheres in the concept of *meydan* echoes in such Turkish idioms as *meydan okumak* (to challenge; literally, to read meydan) and *hodri meydan* (I dare you).

4

Commemorating Diyarbakır Prison Victims in Public

This chapter extends the empirical analysis offered thus far in part 2 to the case of Diyarbakır—the largest predominantly Kurdish-inhabited city in southeastern Turkey and the unofficial capital of northern Kurdistan. It explores how spatially charged notions and experiences of publicness and counterpublicness have been formed by and formative of attempts to commemorate torture at 1980s Diyarbakır Prison as an episode of state-endorsed violence central to the political history of the city and the pro-Kurdish movement.

> *July 13, 2012, Diyarbakır. On this early Friday afternoon, I follow tens of Kurdish-speaking Sunni Muslim men heading toward Dağkapı Square to attend the week's communal Islamic prayers. The prayer is part of a wave of collective civil disobedience known popularly as "Civilian Friday" and performed across Turkey's Kurdistan. Their disobedience is against state-sponsored prayers; whereas the latter are conducted only in Turkish, Civilian Fridays are held in Kurdish.[1] Dağkapı Square*

1. Friday prayers in Turkey are conducted by the Directorate of Religious Affairs (in Turkish: Diyanet İşleri Başkanlığı), a state institution established in 1924 in the wake of the nascent republic's abolition of the caliphate. It is considered the country's highest Islamic religious authority whose remit includes "carrying out affairs concerning Islamic belief, worship and ethics," and "issuing permits for and administrating mosques and masjids." See "Kurumsal," *T.C. Cumhurbaşkanlığı Diyanet İşleri Başkanlığı*, May 28, 2013, http://www.diyanet.gov.tr/tr-TR/Kurumsal/Detay//1/diyanet-isleri-baskanligi-kurulus -ve-tarihcesi. This means that all mosques in Turkey and the activities they host, including Friday prayers, are under the directorate's control.

(figure 17) serves as Diyarbakır's Civilian Friday venue because this was where Sheikh Said was hanged by the state in 1925 after leading a failed rebellion against the nascent Republic of Turkey (Üngör 2011, 122–48).[2] Civilian Fridays were launched in March 2011 as a response to the government's failure to resolve long-standing issues plaguing Turkey's Kurds despite its repeated promises to do so through recent initiatives such as the Democratic Opening and semiofficial peace talks with the PKK. The popular appeal Civilian Fridays gradually came to enjoy throughout the spring and summer of 2011 dissipated toward the end of that year.[3] But, more than a year after their first iteration, they seem to have returned with vehemence, not least because this weekend marks the thirtieth anniversary of an episode significant for Kurdish political history. On July 14, 1982, pro-Kurdish political inmates in Diyarbakır Prison began fasting unto death in protest against their penitentiary conditions under the junta government. The pro-Kurdish political movement has scheduled a mass protest for Saturday, calling for a "Democratic Solution to

2. Throughout my fieldwork in Diyarbakır, Civilian Fridays were performed at the underground arcade below the square in order to avoid the adverse effects of summer heat as opposed to aboveground, where they were held otherwise. Also at this time, there was a campaign led by a pro-Kurdish Islamist association to replace the name Dağkapı with Sheikh Said, to excavate a site overlooking the square where they believed the Kurdish leader and his forty-six men were buried upon being hanged, and to mark the spot with a tomb (İnan 2012). I encountered varying beliefs on precisely where Sheikh Said was hanged in Dağkapı Square. Some believed he was hanged right by where a solar clock was placed in 2006 as part of the municipality's refurbishment of the square. In June 2012, on the anniversary of Sheikh Said's execution, a political organization claiming his legacy, called *İnîsiyatîfa Azadî* (Freedom Initiative; after the 1920s armed organization *Azadî* led by Sheikh Said) chose the solar clock to deliver their commemorative press statement. But the clock's designer, Babek Sobhi, denied his work's having anything to do with Sheikh Said when I spoke with him on October 28, 2012. Another spot in the square subject to unconfirmed Sheikh Said-related interpretations has been the Mustafa Kemal monument planned in 1934 and built in 1964 (Dalkılıç and Halifeoğlu 2011).

3. Other reasons that contributed to the revival of Civilian Fridays at this time included an attempt by the Directorate of Religious Affairs to curtail their sociopolitical influence by appointing around a thousand Kurdish-speaking imams (in Kurdish: *mele*) to work in the region (Konuralp 2012).

17. Dağkapı Square, 2011.

the Kurdish Question" as a way of honoring the memory of those who lost their lives fasting unto death.[4]

Diyarbakır Prison has always been central to pro-Kurdish politics in Turkey but, as this introductory vignette indicates, the early 2010s saw

4. Those being commemorated are Akif Yılmaz, Kemal Pir, Mehmet Hayri Durmuş, and Ali Çiçek. They reputedly decided to begin their death fast on July 14 owing to the date's international significance as the anniversary of Storming of the Bastille in 1789 (Tanboğa and Yetkin 2011, 200). The reason I use the term *pro-Kurdish* here instead of *Kurdish* is because not all death fasters identified as ethnic Kurds. Nevertheless, they all consciously stood up against the junta's oppression of Kurds and the Kurdish language in Turkey. For instance, Kemal Pir is known to have identified as Turkish but also to have resisted the prison administration's Turkification-by-torture strategies: he is reported to have continuously refused to pronounce his Turkishness whenever he, like many of his fellow Kurdish inmates, was asked, "Tell me, are you Kurdish or Turkish?" and would be severely beaten for his refusal (Aydınkaya 2011, 87). By the time a prison reform was introduced in 1984, sixty-five people had lost their lives in Diyarbakır Prison (Zeydanlıoğlu 2009).

its public-spatial significance soar.[5] This was a period when an activist campaign launched in 2009 to turn the prison into a museum drew purportedly favorable commentary from the government's ranks, albeit without any practical outcome. The longer that outcome took to materialize, the more Diyarbakır Prison grew out of its spatial confines and became a site for not only remembering the past but also expressing collective dissidence vis-à-vis present-day developments such as the lack of official status for Kurdish and a constitutionally binding peace process. Throughout this period, prison-as-date, July 14, came to stand in for prison-as-space.[6] Not only did the pro-Kurdish political movement schedule important initiatives for the date, but the authorities repurposed it as an excuse to ban expressions of collective dissent, the 2012 protest being an example of both. What might this temporalization of space have meant for the role Diyarbakır Prison played in discourses and practices of "confronting the past" that centered on campaigns for and promises of transforming sites of state-endorsed violence into memorial museums? In this chapter, I show how the temporalization of space at work here was accompanied by a spatialization of sociopolitical temporality as a perpetually processual, carceral experience.

The origins of the campaign to transform Diyarbakır Prison into a memorial museum lie in 2007, when the "Commission for Research and Truth about Diyarbakır Prison" was launched on September 12 to coincide with the anniversary of the 1980 coup (Karaköse 2007). Members of the commission, who included representatives from pro-Kurdish and/or left-wing political parties and former political convicts organized under the '78ers Federation and '78ers Foundation, were the first to demand the

---

5. A well-known example of Diyarbakır Prison's centrality to pro-Kurdish politics is the prominent Turkish journalist Hasan Cemal's book on the Kurdish question. It begins with an extensive interview with Felat Cemiloğlu, a former inmate of coup-era Diyarbakır Prison (Cemal 2003, 15–34). "If I were young when I had been out of the prison," admits Cemiloğlu in the sentence that opens the book, "I would have gone up to the mountain," where "going up to the mountain" means joining the PKK whose operations have been mainly based from the mountains of northern Iraq, or southern Kurdistan.

6. On the importance of dates in memory activism, see Zerubavel 2003.

prison's transformation into a museum. But, while the commission was founded in 2007, the demand for a memorial museum was not raised until 2009, when the government's Democratic Opening, which purported to address grievances affecting historically marginalized communities such as Kurds, Alevis, and non-Muslims, was in full swing. In August that year, a senior minister from the AKP government, who is himself from Diyarbakır, paid an official visit to the city and announced that the prison would be moved to a new location and that a school would be built in its stead.[7] In the wake of his remarks, a plethora of responses by pro-Kurdish political figures and former convicts appeared in mainstream media that criticized him and suggested the prison's transformation into a memorial museum as the better alternative (Korkmaz and Kaçar 2009; Çakır 2009; Altan 2009; Muradoğlu 2009; M. Yavuz 2009). They stressed that the minister's idea to turn the prison into a school echoed, troublingly, the coup-era administration's discourse. Many a former political convict's memoir records that the infamous lieutenant Esat Oktay Yıldıran, who was put in charge of Diyarbakır Prison by the junta, referred to the penitentiary as a school (Aydınkaya 2011, 1–11, 181–82; Welat 2010, 120). He often lectured prisoners with remarks of the following sort, attempting to rationalize the torture he oversaw: "This is a school. Your brain, your soul has been contaminated outside. In this school, you will be cleansed of the dirt in your brain, your blood will be purified, the dirty blood which has taken over your body will be replaced by fresh blood coming from the pure Turkish blood, and only then will you be a dutiful child for the country" (Welat 2010, 37). In fact, the troubling education-themed analogy had already materialized in a beautification project at Diyarbakır Prison in November 2007, when a group of students from the art education department in the local Dicle University collaborated with the prison's administration to decorate two of the penitentiary's outer walls. The collaboration saw the students paint murals based on the works of modernist painters such as

---

7. For the minister's full speech, see "Diyarbakır Cezaevi taşınıyor" [Diyarbakır Prison Is Moving], *Hürriyet*, Aug. 22, 2009, http://www.hurriyet.com.tr/gundem/diyarbakir -cezaevi-tasiniyor-12323563.

18. An example of education-themed quotes painted on outer walls of the Diyarbakır Prison compound, 2011.

Joan Miró and Pablo Picasso and quotations attributed to famous intellectuals associated with the history of European modernity (figure 18). One
of the quotations was attributed to Honoré de Balzac and read, "In order to
master knowledge, one has to be enslaved by work." Another was quoted
as Henry Brougham's and read, "Education does not make one a dictator
but leads to one's becoming a leader." Accompanying these quotations was
the anonymous dictum "One school shuts down ten prisons."[8] Speaking of
the decision to visually reference Miró, Art Education Department head
Mustafa Diğler said that the painter "is known to have represented the
world of children in his works." The prison's director, İsmail Gül, stated
that their intention in displaying the quotations was to provide daily pass-
ersby "with educational messages and a nice image" at such a site as this

8. The Turkish originals of these quotations, respectively, are as follows: "Bilginin
efendisi olmak için çalışmanın kölesi olmak gerek"; "Eğitim, bir insanın diktatör olmasına değil önder olmasına yarar"; and "Bir okul on cezaevi kapattırır."

one whose visibility had become undeniable owing to the then recent and ongoing expansion of Diyarbakır's urban center.[9] At the time of my field-work in summer 2012, these quotations were still intact on the prison's outer walls. They were frequently referred to during my conversations with former political convicts and human rights activists in the city, who saw them as evidence that the relationship between the 2010s government and 1980s junta was one of continuity rather than rupture.

This sort of a rupture was indeed the very bedrock of the government's political identity at the turn of the decade, and the Diyarbakır Prison fig-ured heavily in their attempts to consolidate it. Central to these attempts was the 2010 referendum on constitutional amendments. The referendum was held on September 12 to coincide with the coup's thirtieth anniver-sary, and the government campaigned for a yes vote on account of redress-ing historical grievances dating from 1980. During a rally in Diyarbakır on the campaign trail, the then prime minister, Erdoğan, spoke at length about the prison, promising that his government would shut it down and demolish it.[10] In response, a group of former political convicts took to the press on the day of the referendum to not only reiterate the demand for the prison's transformation into a museum but also propose that a monument be placed at Dağkapı Square in memory of the death fasters who lost their lives inside the penitentiary in 1982 (Eskin and Aslan 2010). However, as of my fieldwork in summer 2012, a monument to coup-era atrocities inside the Diyarbakır Prison had yet to be built on site or elsewhere in the city—an absence that remains today.

---

9. See "Cezaevi Duvarına Picasso Makyajı" [Picasso Makeup on Prison Wall], *Yapı. com.tr*, Nov. 22, 2007, http://www.yapi.com.tr/haberler/cezaevi-duvarina-picasso-makyaji _57569.html. Such beautification attempts as well as the broader incentive to relocate Diyarbakır Prison should be seen in light of changes affecting the Bağlar neighborhood where the penitentiary is located. The expansion of urbanization in Diyarbakır from the mid-2000s onward has seen Bağlar transform from a leafy village to a midtown district, and land value in the neighborhood has soared as a result (Yılmaz and Yiğitler 2019).

10. For Erdoğan's full speech, see "Diyarbakır'da herşeyi cevapladı" [He Answered It All in Diyarbakır], *Sabah*, Sept. 3, 2010, http://www.sabah.com.tr/Gundem/2010/09/03 /basbakan_erdogan_diyarbakirda.

If the idea to commemorate the victims of torture in coup-era Diyarbakır Prison had emerged simultaneously with the late 2000s apparent sea change in the state's attitude toward the Kurds, its failure to materialize in the early 2010s not only symbolized the stagnation of the peace process and the Democratic Opening but also contributed to the demise of these government initiatives. The mass protest scheduled for July 14, 2012, was a most evident case in point. When the governor of Diyarbakır—the highest-ranking state representative on the local level—was asked why he had banned the protest, he pointed not only to his concern for "public safety" but also to the date for which the event had been scheduled: "Had they asked permission for the 15th," suggested the governor, "we might have allowed it" (E. Karaca 2012).[11] The protest's organizers, the pro-Kurdish political party Barış ve Demokrasi Partisi (BDP; Peace and Democracy Party), defied the governor's ban. The authorities confronted activists with a complete lockdown not only of Diyarbakır but also of neighboring provinces in the region, each of whose residents were banned from leaving their province lest they join the protest (Şulul 2012). In Diyarbakır anyone daring to gather at the designated protest venue faced a violent crackdown by around ten thousand riot police who had descended on the city. Eighty-seven activists were arrested, and scores more suffered injuries, including senior members of the pro-Kurdish party.

A press conference that representatives from the Human Rights Association held the following day detailed these facts and figures from the attempted protest while also offering qualitative analysis of the violence

11. In Turkey the mayor (in Turkish: *belediye başkanı*; literally, municipal president) is distinct from the governor (in Turkish: *vali*); mayors are elected by popular vote, while governors are appointed by the central government (throughout the 2000s and the first half of the 2010s, Diyarbakır had a mayor from the pro-Kurdish party, as did many other predominantly Kurdish-inhabited cities in Turkey). The date of July 14 has also been used by the PKK to conduct offensives, demonstrating the importance they attach to this anniversary. The most recent and notable example include their attack on the Turkish Armed Forces in 2011 in Diyarbakır's Silvan district where thirteen soldiers were killed. The authorities' rationale for outlawing the 2012 demonstration referenced such attacks to imply that for them, too, July 14 is not just any date but indeed a time of mourning.

that protesters faced.[12] The association's regional director suggested that what the city had experienced was of a kind not seen even in the 1980s. The experience, said the director, reminded Diyarbakır's residents of the state of emergency that had been instituted across Turkey's Kurdistan during the purported transition from the junta to democracy and that remained in effect until 2002.[13] Many organizers and activists as well as representatives from the pro-Kurdish party spoke of the police violence as "torture on the street" and as tantamount to rendering the city a "war zone" (Oral 2012; Bozarslan, Bulut, and Sunar 2012; Bozarslan and Sunar 2012). Several of my interlocutors involved in the campaign around Diyarbakır Prison suggested that torture was made "public" on July 14; the police's attitude was not only reminiscent of the torture inflicted on pro-Kurdish political inmates in the 1980s but also signaled the expansion of this form of violence from within the confines of penitentiaries into "public space."

Taking place at a time when the pro-Kurdish political movement was losing patience with the authorities' repeated promises to improve the

12. For the full transcript of this press conference, see "İHD: Diyarbakır 14 Temmuz'da Sıkıyönetimi Yaşadı" [Human Rights Association: Diyarbakır Experienced Martial Rule on July 14], *İnsan Hakları Derneği Diyarbakır Şubesi*, July 16, 2012, http://www.ihddiyarbakir.org/tr/post/13988/ihd-diyarbakir-14-temmuz8217da-sikiyonetimi-y.

13. Although Turkey has seen various periods of emergency rule, what I am referring to here is a process that affected the country's predominantly Kurdish-inhabited east and southeast and that started with a piece of legislation on July 19, 1987, to then be extended (and in some cases geographically expanded) forty-six times, for four months each, until November 30, 2002, when it was shelved. The years between these two dates witnessed vast human rights violations across the region. The official human toll of emergency rule is as follows (Türkiye İnsan Hakları Vakfı 2004, 30–32). A total of 5,105 civilians, 3,541 security personnel, and 25,344 guerrilla fighters died; 371 members of the armed forces and 572 civilians lost their lives owing to mine or bomb explosions; and 1,248 activists or politicians were extrajudicially killed. Perpetrators of 421 of the latter remain unidentified; 18 died while in custody, and 194 were disappeared. Some of the latter were found in prison, either still serving their time or having lost their lives therein, but 132 remain missing. There were 1,275 complaints of torture recorded, 1,177 of which were investigated. In total, 296 cases against civil servants were brought to court. Although 60 of these court cases resulted in convictions, only 4 sentences have been carried out, while the rest have been suspended.

state's attitude toward its Kurdish citizens, the developments surrounding July 14 are noteworthy for three reasons. First, the scheduling of a mass protest for this date shows that, for the pro-Kurdish political movement, commemorating Diyarbakır Prison was never just that; it was also about seeking sociopolitical progress in the present by demanding equal rights and an end to the state's antagonization of its Kurdish citizens. Second, the authorities' simultaneous acknowledgment of coup-era torture in the prison and crackdown on collective expressions of dissent such as the 2012 rally, and the way that this was interpreted by activists, indicate that commemoration no longer served merely to represent the relationship between the past and the present. Instead, commemoration now served to *present* this relationship—to bring it before a public—thus tying in with the practice of *"protesting* victimhood" that I aim to develop in this part of the book. More specifically, I use this notion to convey a practice that not only publicly reclaims the victims of past violence and their sociopolitical specificity but also rejects the authorities' bestowing victimhood upon a people as a disempowering identity. Third, and following from the first two points, the violence with which commemoration as such a protest was met not only evidenced the lack of sociopolitical progress but also exacerbated it. As indicated by how activists and human rights defenders compared 2012 to the 1980s and 90s, the exacerbation was from stagnation to regression.

(Counter)public Responses to Carceralization of Sociopolitical Temporality

How might commemorative practice have broken out of the cycle of violence that confronted early 2010s attempts at protesting victimhood in the above-mentioned sense? Materially and spatially charged works that Kurdish artists produced throughout the same period speak directly to this question. I would like to conclude this chapter by discussing three such works. Consider, first, Miraz Bezar's 2010 movie *Min Dît* (literally, I Have Seen; official English-language titles of the movie include *The Children of Diyarbakır* and *Before Your Eyes*), which is set in 1990s emergency-ruled Diyarbakır. The movie revolves around two siblings whose dad was killed by JİTEM (in Turkish: Jandarma İstihbarat ve Terörle Mücadele; Gendarmerie Intelligence and Fight against Terrorism), the nonofficial but state-sponsored paramilitary organization whose undercover forces were extrajudicially deployed in the 1980s and 1990s against pro-Kurdish activists and politicians. The plot resolves when one of the siblings blows the cover of the former JİTEM member who killed their dad. Following the discovery, the siblings publish leaflets and graffiti the streets, informing the killer's neighbors that he lives among them (figure 19). The approach to publicizing violence that the movie promotes, then, focuses on the everyday rather than the spectacular. Bezar's decision to resolve the plot in this manner is a significant intervention into a sociopolitical context characterized both by heightened discussions on spatial memorialization and by the authorities' deferred promises on issues affecting the Kurds. This artistic decision operates tactically rather than strategically; it prioritizes time over space—or, upends the routinization of the lack of political settlement by unsettling that which is routine—rather than privileging permanence and staticity as does many a conventional commemorative artifact and practice.[14]

14. Here I echo de Certeau's (1984, 35–39) distinction between strategies and tactics. *Min Dît*'s director, Miraz Bezar, confirmed to me that the way the film's plot resolves is inspired by an Argentinian memory-activist practice: "The idea came to me after watching a documentary from Argentina. The film showed a group of civil activists that found out . . . where former junta members/torturers live and started to organize demonstrations in front of their houses/neighborhoods where they, for example, distributed flyers to their neighbors. It was that kind of empowerment that I wanted my film to end with, especially knowing that this kind of civil disobedience does not take place very often in Kurdistan" (email conversation, Aug. 23, 2012). The practice invoked here by the director is called *escrache* and has been developed by groups such as GAC (El Grupo de Arte Callejero; The Group of Art-in-the-Street) and HIJOS (Hijos por la Identidad contra el Olvido y el Silencio; Children for the Identity against the Oblivion and the Silence—an organization formed by the children of the disappeared). Operating in a country where thousands were tortured, executed, kidnapped, and disappeared under military rule between 1976 and 1983, these groups employ *escrache* to link the everyday to histories of state-endorsed violence. Named after the slang word *escrachar*, which means "to uncover," the practice of *escrache* exposes the junta's collaborators by signposting where they live or work in the present (Kaiser 2002). On the broader question of West-centric modernity's linearization of temporality and subaltern responses to it, see Chakrabarty 1998; Hirsch and Stewart 2005; and C. Stewart 2012.

19. Still from the film *Min Dît* (2010). Courtesy of the director Miraz Bezar.

The second work of cultural production is the play *Disko 5 No'lu* (Disco No. 5), which was launched in late 2011 and staged regularly throughout 2012.[15] Set in Diyarbakır Prison in the 1980s, *Disko 5 No'lu* is a solo act where Mirza Metin plays different human and nonhuman characters from the penitentiary, including its director Lieutenant Esat Oktay Yıldıran, a political inmate, and a spider trapped in the inmate's cell. Out of the three, it is the spider that features most prominently in the plot, helping the play capitalize on the powerful Kafkaesque effect widely associated with such vermin-like characters. The spider's prominence is evident in not only the length of stage time the character is allocated but also in the set design; a gigantic cobweb placed in the background looms over the performance and the audience (figure 20). The play's pursuit of a Kafkaesque effect is reflected in its spiral temporality. Flashbacks and flash-forwards occur

15. This title includes a wordplay, as *disko* is both the Turkish word for "disco," and ironically the colloquial abbreviation of *Disiplin Koğuşu* (discipline ward), the ward with the harshest conditions.

20. Scene from the play *Disko 5 No'lu* (2011), photographed by Nazım Serhat Fırat. Courtesy of the directors Mirza Metin and Berfin Zenderlioğlu (Şermola Performans).

frequently throughout the performance. The play eventually ends where it started, with the actor playing the spider throughout this ending. As the play's actor and playwright, Mirza Metin, and its director, Berfin Zenderlioğlu, told me, these aspects of the work derived from a conscious dramaturgical decision to convey the sort of sociopolitical temporality that the duo and others around them experienced in "real life" throughout the late 2000s and early 2010s: "Things have not really changed, and the political climate of the 1980 coup is in many ways still in place."[16]

The third and final example is also marked by a foregrounding of temporality but less intentionally so than the two works mentioned above. It concerns a series of charcoal drawings by Zülfikar Tak, who served time at Diyarbakır Prison as a political convict in the 1980s. The drawings, which Tak began to make in 1989 following his transfer to another penitentiary, depict scenes of torture from the prison (figure 21). Of what motivated

16. In-person interview, Istanbul, Aug. 29, 2012.

21. A selection of Zülfikar Tak's drawings (1989–2007) depicting torture at Diyarbakır Prison. Courtesy of the artist.

him to make the drawings, Tak said, "I drew them not because I wanted to but because I had to and, from now on, do not want to draw such scenes."[17] Underpinning the artist's motivation, then, was a testimonial urge to record and, in so doing, process the experience of subjection to violence, rather than an artistic one to make statements about victimhood or historiography. In other words, Tak pursued a sense of progress and did so on a rather private, if still a decisively sociopolitical, level.[18] However, amid late 2000s and early 2010s discourses and practices of "confronting the past," his work spawned situations that publicly deprived him and his audiences of the sense of progress that the artist was after. The opening of one of Tak's exhibitions in Diyarbakır was just such a situation. Many of the artist's fellow former inmates were in attendance, as was, unexpectedly, a retired military prosecutor who served under the junta but was known

17. In-person interview, Diyarbakır, July 12, 2012.

18. For an excellent discussion of further examples of cultural production and activity that political convicts were able to undertake following the mid-1980s relative relaxation of violent measures in the Diyarbakır Prison, see Hakyemez 2017, 122–31.

to have been among the very few prosecutors who strove to observe legal norms throughout the period. Coup-era roles were reversed as the former political convicts began to question the retired prosecutor about his role in the junta's operations throughout the 1980s, about the period's ripple effects, and about the possibility of redress. "The gallery transformed into a courtroom—a public court where the coup was put on trial," the artist said afterward, quavering as many attending the opening had done when confronting the retired prosecutor, which evidenced the intensity of the confrontation. But the transformation of which the artist spoke was not necessarily a politically emancipatory experience. The fact that truth and redress were being pursued in an art gallery as opposed to courts of justice did not compensate for but rather exacerbated the stalled sociopolitical temporality that marked the citizenship experience of many of Turkey's Kurds in the early 2010s, including those persons attending the opening.

These three works of art show how in cases such as Diyarbakır Prison where protracted promises of peace and reconciliation entangle commemoration in the very violence it seeks to commemorate, temporality rather than memorialization's conventional claims on permanence animates contrarian imaginaries of public space. In such cases, temporality becomes a foremost medium through which to "protest victimhood" in the sense developed in this part of the book and to do so not simply to claim suffering as the crux of one's identity but rather to use it as the basis of one's sociopolitical agency.

5

Ulucanlar Prison as Public Space

In this chapter, I further the empirical analysis developed in the last two, as I discuss the ways in which conventional and contrarian notions of spatial publicness have been formed by and formative of commemorative initiatives at the Ulucanlar Prison Museum. Central to the process that led to Ulucanlar's transformation into a museum was a series of events that the Ankara chapter of Turkey's Chamber of Architects organized throughout 2007. The event series was titled "Ulucanlar Prison Opens to the Public." This was one of the few occasions between 2006 and 2009—a period during which Ulucanlar had ceased to serve as a penitentiary but had not yet assumed a new function—that the prison was publicly accessible. Members of the audience at these events, the majority of whom were former political inmates of a left-wing persuasion, were given access to the prison buildings and invited to share their thoughts and experiences on site.

"Ulucanlar Prison Opens to the Public" was the first platform where the idea to turn the prison complex into a museum was aired, not least by veteran lawyer Halit Çelenk, who had represented the three revolutionary youth leaders at the 1972 trial that resulted in capital punishment under the political influence of the military (Ünalın 2010, 24–25, 86–87). Indeed, the event series marked the finale of a design competition called "Urban Dreams," also sponsored by the Architects' Chamber. The competition called for proposals to "transform the prison toward a public end" vis-à-vis the threat of its being purchased by the metropolitan municipality and turned into a shopping mall.[1] A protocol cosigned in February 2007 by

1. For the full terms and conditions of this competition, see "Kent Düşleri: 'Ulucanlar Merkez Kapalı Cezaevi Değerlendirme Projesi' Ulusal Fikir Yarışması Şartnamesi"

the local (district) municipality of Altındağ, the Ministry of Justice (the site's proprietors), the Architects' Chamber, and the Bar Association guaranteed that the winning design would be implemented.[2] The results were announced on May 6, 2007, coinciding with the thirty-fifth anniversary of the three revolutionary youth leaders' execution. The winning entry was coauthored by Zeynep Kutlu, Figen Kıvılcım, and Gürem Özbayar, who led the team (figure 22). Among its main principles was the preservation of not only the officially listed parts of the prison complex but also others that are of architectural significance in the broadest sense of the term (Özbayar, Kutlu, and Kıvılcım 2008). Having seen in person that the outcome of the prison's transformation was, as outlined in chapter 2, almost completely inconsistent with this principle, I spoke with Gürem Özbayar on June 6, 2011, to find out why.

Özbayar began by confirming that their proposals regarding what to preserve of the prison complex were intended to reflect the full range of "politically significant" events Ulucanlar had witnessed until its closure in 2006. However, in late 2008, when the architects embarked on implementing the project, they realized that both the local municipality and the Council of Preservation—the official body that regulates architectural heritage—were keen on preserving only those parts of the prison complex that date from 1925 and that the authorities called "original facilities." The council's rejection of the architects' proposal to preserve more than these "originals" started a ten-month process of negotiation and revision that lasted until late 2009, when implementation finally began (Özbayar and Kutlu 2010). Throughout this process, the architects not only had to compromise on their initial preservation proposals but also were confronted with fresh demands from the municipality and were obliged to continually tweak the project to meet them.

[Urban Dreams: "Ulucanlar Central Closed Prison Evaluation Project" National Idea Competition Specifications], *TMMOB Mimarlar Odası Ankara Şubesi*, Feb. 1, 2007, http://www.mimarlarodasiankara.org/ulucanlar/sart.html.

2. For more on this protocol, see "Ulucanlar Cezaevi'nde Proje Tartışması" [Project Debate at Ulucanlar Prison], *Evrensel*, June 5, 2008, http://www.evrensel.net/haber /223208/ulucanlar-cezaevi-nde-proje-tartismasi.

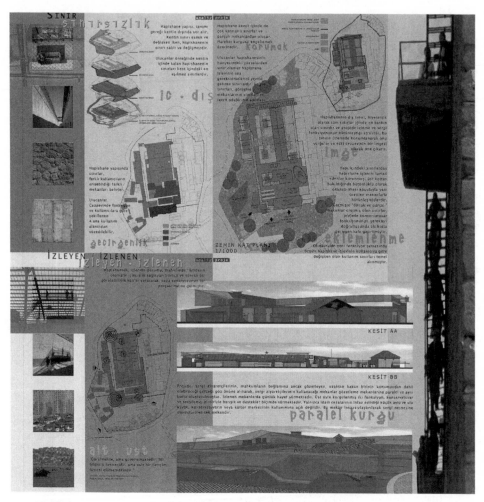

22. The winning entry in the architectural competition for the transformation of Ulucanlar Prison, 2007. Courtesy of the architect Gürem Özbayar Sargın (K.Ö.K. ARCHITECTS).

Revisions to the project soon became much more than just the stuff of verbal negotiations. "One day when we visited Ulucanlar to pay what ought to have been one of our regular construction site visits," recalled Özbayar, "we encountered a couple of bulldozers in front of the inmates' entrance," which were there to demolish the outer walls. This was contrary to what all parties involved in the project had agreed to. The agreement had been "that no outer walls surrounding the wards would be interfered with" and that demolition would be limited to interior walls, as this would help expand usable space. "The outer walls were to be left as they were," stressed the architect. "They teemed with prisoners' stashes which we had planned to preserve and exhibit in their original state and which included notebooks, rolled cigarettes, and pieces of paper with messages or drawings on them" (figure 23). This was only the first of many instances when implementation, overseen by the municipality, strayed radically from the approved project. The final straw was when the architects went to the site to supervise "the work being done on the interiors," only to encounter "brand-new ceramic washbasins and radiators" installed without their prior knowledge or authorization. The architects inquired into the matter with the municipality, "who told us they might consider turning the whole place into a hotel." As a last resort, they requested a meeting with the district mayor, during which they cited various violations of their project that were under way at the construction site. The only substantial gain from the meeting was the removal of the radiators. "Following this meeting, our relationship gradually dissipated; when we last went to Ulucanlar about a year and a half ago, we were not even allowed in," concluded the architect.

If the architects were not in charge of the process behind the outcome that visitors now encounter at the Ulucanlar Prison Museum, then who was? This was one of the questions to which I sought an answer when I met with the museum's administration. Who decided which wall to paint in what color; whose pictures, biographies, and personal objects to exhibit; and where and how to place them? The senior administrative staff member replied that, while a team had been set up to prepare a detailed report intended to guide the transformation, "eventually all detailed decisions were taken by the mayor himself." Hence my meeting and interview on June 10, 2011, with the mayor of Altındağ, the district municipality responsible for implementing the project. He began by referring to the museum as an "open-ended process," one that was continually open to "feedback and contributions from the public." A recent case in point, according to the mayor, was "the rector of Gazi University, who told me he was among the 'thought criminals' imprisoned here in the '70s." This meant that the mayor was now considering adding the rector's name and biography to

23. Outer walls of the Ulucanlar Prison compound, 2007 (*top*; courtesy of Turkey's Chamber of Architects, Ankara Chapter) and 2011 (*bottom*).

those of the intellectuals on view at Ulucanlar. Indeed, just as he finished his sentence, the mayor picked up the phone to instruct a staff member to "find the rector's contact for me, please; we should add his profile to the fifth ward." While the mayor may have intended to demonstrate Ulucanlar's principle of openness to the public, he effectively evidenced his own virtually single-handed sway over the museum.

An article by the mayor in the Prison Museum's inaugural publication suggests that Ulucanlar "will be a living museum and a living memory of Turkish political life" and that it "must be visited in order to avoid reliving what we have witnessed and experienced in the past" (D. Yavuz 2010, 5). I raised these remarks with the mayor during our interview, as I found them exceptionally significant at a time when a number of dissident politicians had just been denied candidacy in the run-up to the general election (Arsu 2011), a graduate student had been in prison for more than a year on trumped-up charges, and a prominent dissident journalist remained in jail owing to the censoring of a yet-to-be-published book he had written (Perrier 2011).[3] Citing the mayor's remarks in the book, I asked him precisely what "past" and "memory" he was referring to. "Why have we turned this place into a Prison Museum? The reason is that today no one is convicted of the sort of crimes that, in the past, put people in Ulucanlar," he replied, and continued thus: "Back then it would be enough for people to read certain books—recently, I visited someone who told me he went in and out [of prison] so many times in the 1960s and the '70s. You ask him

3. The imprisoned student himself wrote about the Ulucanlar Prison Museum. Following the wide coverage that the museum enjoyed across mainstream media in mid-2011, he penned a letter from his cell to plead for justice by highlighting the contradiction between his condition and Ulucanlar's much-celebrated transformation: "I know that prisons are being turned into museums, opening for visits in the name of human dignity. Past conditions and convicts are being rediscovered. But, for some reason, the current prison conditions receive little attention. No one cares to look into today's prisons, no one sees us. Or people turn a blind eye, who knows? I do not want to be remembered in museumifed wards. Now is the right time. I want to be remembered while I am still, flesh and blood, in those wards" (Alpar 2011).

why, and he says it all had to do with writing and publishing books—even those that were not illegal to publish." At this point the mayor's assistant interjected to clarify that "even only the possession of books was enough" to get one into trouble. "Yes," wrapped up the mayor. "That is why we have turned Ulucanlar into a museum." If the museum's avowed openness to change endorsed an idea of historiography as a continually open-ended process, the endorsement was in fact premised on the present's being categorically seen as not only distinct from the past temporally but also an improvement on it sociopolitically.

I asked the mayor if he was satisfied with the outcome of the prison's transformation into a museum. "We have been considerate," he said. "Others would have demolished this building in order to profit from it." The mayor followed by admitting, "[We are] not professional curators and renovators, but we have done these things in a rather amateur spirit—with passion." He then returned to the theme of publicness as openness to feedback and change: "There may be deficiencies; if the public inform us about these, then we will do our best to make the necessary changes." Following my meeting with the mayor, I raised some of my outstanding questions with a senior museum administrator. I asked if she knew anything "about the architecture competition on Ulucanlar organized by the Chamber of Architects," adding that "I read in the press a while ago that the winning entry has been announced and that it would soon be implemented." She replied that the museum's administration was not concerned with "the architectural side of the project; the kind of work we do has, rather, to do with content." Echoing the mayor, she stressed that this content would be continually open to "participation and contribution" from the public. The fact that an official opening ceremony had neither taken place nor been scheduled yet, for her, was evidence of this openness to the public's feedback.[4]

4. Days after this interview, the museum declared itself open to the public with a press release. See "Ulucanlar Cezaevi Müzesi halka açıldı" [Ulucanlar Prison Museum Opened to the Public], *Milliyet*, June 16, 2011, http://www.milliyet.com.tr/gundem/ulu canlar-cezaevi-muzesi-halka-acildi-1403184. The museum's official inauguration, however, did not take place until late 2013 when it hosted a ceremony involving dignitaries.

Reclaiming the Publicness of Ulucanlar Prison

If, in the mayor's and the senior administrator's remarks, publicness was conceived as a future-oriented quality—a willingness to adapt—and limited to the material being exhibited rather than applied to the entire space of the prison complex, for veteran leftists who had served time in the prison, it carried overtly spatial import. This was already evident at the time of the design competition. Jury members who were also veteran leftists and former inmates spoke of the competition's imperative as "ensuring that Ulucanlar *remains* a public space" (Ünalın 2010, 21, 24–25, 113; D. Yavuz 2010, 5; Alkan 2007). Note how public space is conceived here as not only the desired outcome of the prison's future transformation but also a characteristic deriving from its penitentiary past. In other words, the extent to which the prison is public space is understood here as a question that concerns not only ownership or use but also the state-endorsed violence that it witnessed in the past and that targeted those who fought in the name of the people.

The part of the prison complex where this idea of publicness became most manifest was the courtyard where the three revolutionary youth leaders had been executed. Some former political inmates suggested that the execution spot could be rearranged as "a place to leave flowers," others wanted a monument to be built there, and still others referred to it as "public space" (Ünalın 2010, 85–86, 113). Take the following words by veteran leftist and former Ulucanlar inmate Halil Çelimli:

> For us revolutionaries, the most important place in Turkey is this courtyard where you have the gallows and the poplar tree where Denizler [the three revolutionary youth leaders] were hanged. I don't think that the state will allow us to organize and control this place in its entirety. But the small place—the exact place where Denizler had been hanged—is

---

Even then the inauguration was rather low-key, attended by only two former AKP ministers sidelined from the cabinet. See "TBMM Başkanı Çiçek Ulucanlar Cezaevi Müzesi Açılış Törenine Katıldı" [Head of Parliament Çiçek Attends Ulucanlar Prison Museum's Opening Ceremony], *Meclis Haber*, Sept. 26, 2013, http://meclishaber.tbmm.gov.tr/develop/owa/haber_portal.aciklama?p1=126323.

ours; no one can take it from us. I believe we need to be really serious and insistent on this issue. We have our blood and life in this small courtyard. That's what we call public space. We must definitely keep it, retain it. (129)

The gallows is indeed given a prominent role in the museum. It remains in the courtyard, where it is exhibited behind bars and together with a sign that reads, "According to Act 5218 issued on 14.07.2004, the death penalty was completely abolished in Turkey" (figure 24). The gallows also features prominently in the museum's promotional booklets, where it is accompanied by the slogan, "The gallows sentenced to life" (Altındağ Belediyesi 2010, 31). The notorious poplar tree still stands near the imprisoned gallows, now decorated with tiny pictures of those whose executions it witnessed framed as filmstrips.[5]

While the museum sought to foreground the gallows' historical significance by exhibiting it in a rather spectacular fashion, former left-wing Ulucanlar inmates continued to stress that this was incompatible with their requests and expectations. The incompatibility became most strikingly

5. The manner of display at work here must be seen in the context of the late 2000s and early 2010s. This context was marked by various works of popular cultural production that prominently featured similar representations of imprisonment. A case in point is the soap opera *Bu Kalp Seni Unutur Mu?* (Would This Heart Forget You?), which was produced in 2009 and aired during primetime on one of Turkey's most popular TV channels. The show's story line covered a time span that stretched from the September 12 coup to November 2002, the month when the Justice and Development Party first rose to power. The show's opening credits comprised footage—some archival, others based on reenactment—of various events subject to discourses and practices of confronting the past in Turkey. The first episode began allegorically in the female protagonist's visit to a male therapist who took her into the past, interweaving the biographical with the national. One of the series' first episodes had a dramatic scene set in early 1980s Diyarbakır Prison. The scene reminded viewers of the September 12 junta's ban on public use of the Kurdish language. Other less overtly political examples include a TV show titled *Kadere Mahkumlar* (Prisoners to Fate), where the experience of imprisonment is turned into a spectacle. This weekly show hosts guests who sing popular songs about life in prison, while viewers are provided a particular gaze that almost always positions them outside the bars, epitomizing the show's exhibitionist and objectifying approach.

24. The gallows at Ulucanlar Prison Museum, 2011.

evident in a controversy that erupted in September 2010, ahead of the constitutional referendum scheduled for the twelfth of the same month. Recall
that this was a referendum that senior cabinet members, including Prime
Minister Erdoğan, portrayed as an invaluable opportunity to "confront"
the coup of September 12, 1980, and "remove the shield of immunity surrounding it" (Hamsici 2017). Indeed, the prime minister's campaign for
a yes vote had featured photographs and memoirs of well-known leftist
figures who had been hanged or spent their youth behind bars as political
prisoners during and after the coup. Just weeks before the referendum, the
Revolutionary '78ers Federation—a civil society organization membered
by veteran leftists and victims of the 1980 coup—announced their plans to
launch an exhibition they named the "September 12 Museum of Shame"
in central Ankara. As part of this exhibition, they requested the gallows
that municipal staff involved in Ulucanlar's then ongoing transformation
into a museum had discovered in the prison's storage and placed in the
courtyard. Upon negotiations with the municipality, the '78ers were told
that the gallows would be lent to them in exchange for personal belongings
of famous left-wing victims of the coup, which the veteran leftists held in

store and which the authorities wanted to exhibit in the prison museum (Tahincioğlu 2010). Despite fulfilling the municipality's request, the veteran leftists were not given the gallows.[6] This denial led them to produce and exhibit a replica instead (figure 25), accompanied by a sign that read thus: "AKP member and Altındağ mayor Veysel Tiryaki promised that he would allow the Revolutionary 78'ers Federation to exhibit Ulucanlar's gallows. He changed his mind when this made the headlines. So much for the AKP's being against coups."[7]

A year later, when the museum had finally opened for visits and the '78ers were preparing to organize another episode of their exhibition to mark the coup's thirty-first anniversary, they repeated their request for the gallows but were once again denied by the municipality. Their renewed criticism of the municipality's attitude emphasized the manner in which the gallows was now being exhibited at the museum: in a prison cage. While the museum has sought to present this form of display as a commitment to condemning capital punishment to obsolescence, the veteran leftists saw it as a measure to prevent them from seizing the gallows. As a leading member of the federation said during the opening of the 2012 episode of their exhibition: "The gallows belongs to us—to the people [halk]. It has cost [and/or become the property of; mal olmak] the public [kamu]. Where it is located is public [kamusal] space. They may have put the gallows in a cage for now, hoping to prevent us from reclaiming it. Either they return it to us for the duration of our exhibition or we will steal it. And, if need be, we are ready to serve another prison sentence for this."

The veteran leftist's words capture the essence of how he and his political kin perceive the relationship between publicness, commemoration, and histories of state-endorsed violence. The architects' idea of publicness involved expanding the notion of preservation worthiness to include both

6. For the activists' account of this communication between them and the municipality, see "12 Eylül Utanç Müzesi Açıldı" [September 12 Museum of Shame Opens], Radikal, Sept. 9, 2010, http://www.radikal.com.tr/turkiye/12-eylul-utanc-muzesi-acildi-1017257.

7. See "Darbe Karşıtlığı Daracağına [sic] Takıldı" [The Gallows Limits Anti-coup Stance], Evrensel, Sept. 5, 2010, http://www.evrensel.net/haber/182604/darbe-karsitligi-daracagina-takildi.

25. Replica of the gallows at "September 12 Museum of Shame" as seen during the exhibition's 2013 Istanbul run. Courtesy of photographer Berfu Arslan Ağırsoy.

canonical architectural value and politico-historical significance, but assumed a shared understanding of the latter. The mayor and the museum administration employed publicness as a self-fulfilling meta-ideology: for them, it entailed continual openness to the public's participation and con-tribution but only insofar as they pertained strictly to the past so that the present could be politically legitimized as a categorical improvement on the latter. For the veteran leftists, however, publicness was not only distinctly political but also required collective work to become political. They saw the political economy of what makes space (including the objects that constitute it) public as deriving both from monetary contribution (that is, taxes) or ownership and from the politically motivated work put into making it public in a *specific* way and not in other ways.

Conclusion

Part 2 has worked from the axiom that, if violence and conventional models of public space are inextricably linked, the untangling of this link is less an ontological question than a semantic one. In other words, there is no single spatial form or method that defines the link between violence and publicness. The link is made, unmade, and continually remade through context-specific political work; the spaces in and on which this sort of work is undertaken offer, at each turn, a spatial imaginary for the legal and cultural systematization of certain notions and experiences of publicness. The making of the link between violence and publicness and its legal and cultural systematization are, therefore, causal processes rather than teleological ones. Each such process is an opportunity to expose and, in so doing, challenge the conventional model of public space preceding it. In protesting victimhood or testifying to it publicly, Turkey's memory activists have therefore mounted just such a challenge and developed their own contrarian models of public space, as well as underlining the victims' sociopolitical specificity.

In Sivas the authorities spatially mobilized a concept of publicness characterized by a double homogenization, one that involved the state's absolute coalescence with a citizenry conceived as a sociopolitically uniform entity. In so doing they aimed to, first, incite violence; second, give violence physical visibility; and, finally, obscure the uneven power relations structuring the varying degrees of culpability for violence. If memory activists were aware of this threefold mobilization, they sought to challenge it not just by condemning it but also by precipitating its architectural materialization. Hence their campaign for a state-sponsored memorial museum on site, to which the authorities responded with the Science and Culture Center—a project that mobilized various spatial imaginaries rooted in the concept of *kamu* (public, the state, the people), including *kamulaştırma* (expropriation; literally, making *kamu*) and *kamusal alan* (public space/sphere). This architectural materialization gave the activists a reference point against which to demonstrate their own spatial imaginaries of publicness by way of performance and direct action. In Sivas, such performance and direct action involved relating to the site of violence as *meydan* (public square and the sociojudicially charged space of Alevi ritual) and refusing to enter the building unless its "neutral" attitude toward the arson attack was rectified. In Ulucanlar, former inmates put together their own "museum" and pursued the return of the gallows in order to exhibit it in their own way. The pursuit involved paying the museum a surprise visit and threatening to steal the gallows if necessary.[1] In Diyarbakır, activists used an anniversary that has come to encompass the various episodes of state-endorsed violence at Diyarbakır Prison from the 1980s onward as a platform to not only draw attention to outstanding issues plaguing state-citizen relations from a pro-Kurdish vantage point but also perform potential solutions, such as the delivery of publicly funded services in Kurdish as well as Turkish.

The significance of performance and direct action in Sivas, Ankara, and Diyarbakır notwithstanding, these modes of political work constituted only one way of spatializing contrarian imaginaries of publicness. They were combined with rational-critical hermeneutics. In Sivas this was evident in the activists' legal challenge against the name list. In the case of Ulucanlar, it was evident in ex-convicts' making formal requests to the municipality and setting up a conventional museum display. In the case of Diyarbakır, rational-critical hermeneutics' importance for contrarian imaginaries of spatial publicness became manifest through temporality. The works of cultural production that advanced such imaginaries were characterized by a desire for progressively linear sociopolitical temporality

---

1. On the surprise visit in question, see Gökçer Tahincioğlu, "'Üç Fidan'ın Darağacı Sergilenecek" [The Three Saplings' Gallows to Be Exhibited], *Milliyet*, Aug. 31, 2010, http://www.milliyet.com.tr/gundem/uc-fidan-in-daragaci-sergilenecek-1283072.

that anticathartic performance and direct action might otherwise be praised for interrupting and throwing into disarray. To be sure, these contrarian mobilizations of rational-critical hermeneutics contrasted with the sociopolitically homogenizing rational criticality characterizing the model of public space that became manifest through the Science and Culture Center's self-proclaimed neutrality, Ulucanlar Museum's depoliticization of history as accessible through architecture, and the authorities' violent securitization of central Diyarbakır in July 2012.

Therefore, it is through the combination of performance and direct action with rational-critical hermeneutics that provictim activism and cultural production have subverted conventional imaginaries of publicness by compelling the spatial crystallization of these imaginaries' semantic and systemic entanglement in violence. It is also through this combination that memory activists and cultural producers have brought forth contrarian imaginaries of publicness by protesting victimhood in a site-specific manner. In Ulucanlar as well as in Sivas, the authorities overseeing the transformation of sites of violence professed an idea of publicness as continual openness to participation and to contribution of ideas, albeit on terms strictly framed by them and oblivious to the imperative of empowering victims and survivors. In both cases, moreover, formal inauguration—otherwise considered in relevant scholarship a prominent means through which states imbue infrastructures with "public recognition" and "monumentality" (Harvey and Knox 2015, 188–94)—was made to endow the authorities' transformation of sites of violence with political power not as an event that takes place but rather as one that is perpetually postponed. In Diyarbakır, the prison's inaccessibility to the wider public led memory activists and cultural producers to take to other spaces in the city, ranging from its main square to ordinary neighborhoods and art galleries. Doing so has helped bring the histories of those sites into direct relation with the history of the Diyarbakır Prison.

The commemorative practices discussed in part 2, which have developed contrarian models of public space dialectically with conventional ones and have combined the methods of rational criticality with those of embodied sociability, are therefore far from unscripted or spontaneous. Nor might they be rigidly formalized as bottom-up or direct versus top-down or legislation-facing. Still, there is a distinguishing characteristic of the (counter)public-spatial imaginaries that these processes indicate. This characteristic concerns an awareness that the context-independent acceptance of such formal methodological oppositions might itself contribute to the semantic means through which violence is legally and culturally systematized into conventional models of public space. In part 2, I have aimed to bolster this awareness through my conceptualization of the activism of those who seek to develop contrarian imaginaries of spatial publicness. Specifically, I have refused to confine this activism to a single mode, such as performance and direct action. Breaking out of such confines, I argue, might help to illuminate the question of power at the interface of commemoration and violence and do justice to the empowerment those upholding the victims' legacy pursue. In part 3, I turn to how this pursuit unfolds at sites of violence.

Part Three

Self-Reflexive Victimhood

Introduction

The first campaign to turn one of Turkey's sites of state-endorsed violence into a memorial museum was premised on spatially charged notions of testimony and its cognates. On July 9, 1993, a group of activists in Turkey launched a campaign for the authorities to preserve the Madımak Hotel's charred remains as "a witness" to the arson attack that had unfolded there the week before and to declare it a "museum of shame" (Ekinci 1993). A mass funeral held a few days after the attack had seen mourners commemorate each of the thirty-three victims as *şehit*—Turkish for martyr and cognate of *şehadet*, which denotes the act of testifying as well as the status of martyrdom.

What might be the political and analytical implications of mobilizing testimony and its cognates as spatial mechanisms for condemning state-endorsed violence? Literatures exploring this question across the fields of architecture, anthropology, archaeology, and media studies have grown since the early 2000s for both empirical and theoretical reasons. First, since the millennial turn, sites of violence and/or their images have featured increasingly prominently in the documentation, communication, and litigation of human rights violations in which states are implicated. Second, the early 2000s was when the post-Holocaust "era of testimony" (Felman 1991) or "era of the witness" (Wieviorka 2006) became subject to criticism for relying on individual witnesses in the production of historical truth. The criticism, more specifically, was that this reliance conflated the personal and psychological with the collective and sociopolitical (Douglass and Vogler 2003), overshadowed numerous other resources through which to piece together historical truth (Sarlo 2005, 9–26), cast the witness as a sweeping category that overlooks significant subject-positional differences between various witnesses (Givoni 2011), and treated survivors as self-evident embodiments of veracity and thus obscured the politically charged processes of exclusion, selection, validation, and analysis that in fact govern truth production (Fassin 2008).[1] Eyal Weizman has suggested that the post-Holocaust paradigm deprived testimony of its epistemic function by employing it "primarily as an 'ethical' resource" whose "function was in being delivered in the first place" rather than in "revealing knowledge or authenticating claims of historical injustice." Against the grain of this paradigm, Weizman has heralded a decisively object-centric one termed "forensic architecture" where, thanks to recent technological and legal developments, artifacts serve as "object-witnesses" on a near par with their human counterparts (Weizman 2010, 14). Whereas "the era of the witness" prioritized ethics over epistemics and thus engendered an "anti-universalist" notion of truth as an "inherently relative, contingent, multiple, or non-existent" category of knowledge, "forensic architecture" promises to reclaim "truth as a common project" by mobilizing the epistemic potential of artifacts toward registering and conveying violent histories in collectively palpable ways (Weizman 2014, 29).

However, such mobilization has not been uncontested. Consider architectural historian Andrew Herscher's discussion of how human rights advocacy's increasing reliance on surveillance transforms space "from a target of violence to a witness to violence" (Herscher 2011, 130–41). He criticizes this reliance for assuming truth to be readily locatable in violence's spatial effects rather than in its markedly human causes, driving forces, aims, and intentions. In fact, the human continues to significantly shape the summoning of artifacts as witnesses, as evidenced in the work of experts both before and during court hearings. Before hearings, experts manipulate the materiality of objects so that they can serve as witnesses

1. The context of early 2010s Turkey saw witnessing's cognate martyrdom reach new heights as such a sociopolitically sweeping category and with legislative implications. The government announced preparations for an act of Parliament that would expand the legislative definition of martyrdom (hitherto granted only to officers killed on duty) to include civilians murdered in yet-to-be-solved acts of violence (Tosun 2012).

(Schuppli 2014), and, in court, it is the expert's illocutionary acts that help artifacts "speak of" violence (Schuppli 2013, 165). The expertise at work here is also worthy of scrutiny for its entanglement in knowledge-based power structures. Contributors to a recent forum on "archaeology as bearing witness" have problematized archaeologists' claiming center stage in the condemnation of violence for exacerbating the disempowerment of victims, survivors, and their descendants (Hauser et al. 2018, 537–40, 542–44). Herscher hints at a similar problem; he argues that "looking," or visually mediated encounter with spatial testimony, ought to be approached neither as a neutral means of verification nor as an inherently emancipatory act but with an awareness of the "distribution of power and knowledge" in which it is entangled (Herscher 2014b, 496).

The problem here concerns not only looking as such but also the registers through which violence is looked at. Rather than just problematize the assumption that seeing violence means acting upon it, Joshua Ewalt's work on contemporary humanitarianism's reliance on real-time satellite mapping questions why an intervention from outside is at all necessary or legitimate (Ewalt 2011). To associate activism with such intervention, for him, is to reproduce the colonialist and imperialist gaze as the only possible register through which to approach contemporary conflict. Similarly, for anthropologist and media theorist Allen Feldman, imperial power increasingly relies on the mimetic hollowing out of forensic procedures and methods; it exploits their symbolic capital for reducing victims' and survivors' "bodies, topography, and demography" to "raw material" and thus furthering the violent dehistoricization to which they were subjected in the first place (Feldman 2015, 82). Invoking filmmaker Jean-Luc Godard's aphorism that, gradually throughout the second half of the twentieth century, "the Jews became the stuff of fiction; the Palestinians of documentary," Feldman problematizes humanitarian projects for remaining permeated by imperial power as such to the extent they adhere to the way it compartmentalizes peoples into separate "media regimes" and "geographies" of epistemic "sensibility and insensibility" (137). Historian Marc Nichanian's work on the Armenian genocide elucidates how such a shuffling and assignment has affected discourses and practices of testimony. Nichanian argues that the predominant approach to testimony in "the era of the witness" debilitated itself by subscribing to the logic of the archive in the modern mode. The debilitation, for him, is owing to the homology between the logic of the modern archive and that of the very "genocidal will" testimony sought to challenge: both equate truthfulness with institutional authority and archival existence (2009, 11). Terming this self-debilitating approach "testimony as document," Nichanian contra-distinguishes it from "testimony as monument": testimony that aspires to develop new "categories" of truth outside the archival logic by exploiting perspective, imagery, and interpretation instead of accuracy, authenticity, and factuality; by operating emblematically rather than realistically; and by engaging with the task of historicization as an infinitely divergent one contrarily to the archival mode's tendency for convergence (3–4, 10, 94).

The politics of the role of space (including its images) in witnessing state-endorsed violence must therefore attend not just to content, or to what is being witnessed. It must also attend to agency, or to the ways in which what is being witnessed is historicized and the extent to which these historicizations challenge the dehistoricization resulting from the violence. In employing historicization here and throughout part 3 as an operative concept, I follow anthropologists Eric Hirsch and Charles Stewart. According to them, whereas "history" is characterized by West-centric modernity's divorcing of the present from the past, "historic-ity" conveys the way historical time is experienced and "historicization" entails the process of negotiating historicity (Hirsch and Stewart 2005).[2] Hirsch and Stewart's formulation therefore helps not only problematize the hegemony of established narratives over experiences—that is, history's hegemony over historicity. It also helps reverse that hegemony by granting

---

2. Hirsch and Stewart's tripartite formulation has been influenced by Chakrabarty's (2000) critique of West-centric modernity's approach to history. Charles Stewart has fur-ther developed this formulation in his study of dreams in Island Greece as "unconscious historicization," arguing that "Western historicism is, however, but one specific and recently developed principle of historicization . . . with peculiar ideas about linear tem-poral succession, homogeneous time units (days, weeks, minutes), causation, and anach-ronism . . . [and] must not be allowed to exclude alternative modes of thinking about and representing the past as forms of 'history'" (2012, 197).

the experiencers the agency to process and render meaningful—that is, to historicize—their experience as opposed to just being subjected to it, such that the meanings and narratives produced as a result can contest established ones. It is this attention to the agency involved in the right to make sense of and promulgate one's own experience of history that guides the analysis I offer in chapters 6 and 7.

6

Spatial Testimony in Sivas

This chapter details the spatial discourses and practices of witnessing and martyrdom at work in the case of the Sivas arson attack. This book through and through has treated what purport to be postviolence representations as entangled in the violence they represent. Therefore, a theme-specific recapping of the arson attack itself is in order before moving on to empirical analysis of spatial discourses and practices of witnessing and martyrdom in 2010s Sivas. Pir Sultan Abdal (the sixteenth-century minstrel after whom the culture festival targeted in the arson was named) is venerated in Alevism as a martyr hanged by the governor of Sivas for refusing to submit to his authority. Pir Sultan is a prominent figure in Alevi "martyrology," a sacred lineage based not on birth but on tragic death during nonviolent resistance against tyranny (Hess 2007). This lineage originates in a series of mid-seventh-century events known to have engendered the schism between Sunnism and the rest of Islam. Such events include the assassination of Ali—prophet Muhammad's son-in-law and the fourth caliph (651–61), whose name many Alevis consider the origin of the term *Alevi*, that is, "pertaining to Ali" (Dressler 2013). They also include the Battle of Karbala (680), where Ali's son and his six dozen supporters were killed by the larger forces of the second Umayyad caliph, whose dynasty's claim to the caliphate they repudiated as based on tyranny rather than on rightful heirdom (Zırh 2016).[1]

---

1. Crucially, that Alevism has sided with Ali's descendants in the Karbala affair does not make it a subset of Shia Islam. For many Alevis, this stance has less to do with an ethnic or genealogical obligation than it does with the sociopolitically motivated principle of siding with the underpowered, the righteous, and the unjustly treated—a stance

As recounted in chapter 3, in the lead-up to the Sivas arson attack, Pir Sultan's name became embroiled in a controversy surrounding the state-funded "Minstrels Monument" placed just outside the main festival venue to mark the occasion (albeit without prior knowledge of the organizers). The local press flagged certain features of the monument to speculate that it honored Pir Sultan rather than all "minstrels" (as the authorities argued), labeling the minstrel "a foremost rebel in Anatolian history" (Bozgeyik 1993).[2] Portrayals of the festival as rebellious embroiled the Minstrels Monument in the arson attack in physical ways, too. The monument was defaced by assailants as they surrounded the main festival venue around noon on July 2. The assailants then shuttled between various buildings associated with the festival and its sponsors, including the governor's office, and reached the thousands in the process. They ultimately surrounded the hotel where the festival's guests had sought refuge. When the authorities demanded that the assailants peacefully disperse, the latter reportedly presented three prerequisites, one of which was the removal of the Minstrels Monument (Tüleylioğlu 2010, 488–92). The authorities complied and brought the toppled monument to the crowd outside the hotel. This proved to only encourage the assailants; they seized the statue and burned it on the spot, moments before setting fire to the hotel itself (Tüleylioğlu 2010, 86–87).

The media's involvement in this chain of events was not limited to local newspapers; it also included the conservative-leaning national network launched just six months earlier thanks to the privatization of TV broadcasting. Recall from chapter 3 that the network's continuous reporting from Sivas throughout the day of the arson attack ostensibly amounted to a live broadcast, albeit a selective and monitored one. Shortly before the attack, "the unrest in Sivas" was reported as having been "brought under control," to the utter dismay of those trapped inside the hotel who watched some of this reporting on their TVs while also witnessing the crowd

best captured by Zırh (2016), who terms it "transhistorical" in his analysis of Karbala's importance to Alevism.

2. See also "Bu Anıt 'Ozanlar Anıtı'" [This Monument Is 'the Minstrels Monument'], *Hürdoğan*, July 2, 1993, 1.

outside grow both larger and more aggressive (Özbakır 2010). Once the building was set ablaze, near-live footage of it surrounded by thousands of onlookers arrived on screens. The resulting sociopolitical impact was such that many children born in the 1980s to Alevi families discovered their connection to the faith while watching this footage live: hearing their parents cry, "They're burning us!" the children learned that "us" meant Alevis (Özer 2015). The collective televisual witnessing soon informed the thirty-three victims' incorporation into Alevi martyrology regardless of their confessional affiliations (Yildiz and Verkuyten 2011). In speaking of the thirty-three as martyrs, many Alevi activists and intellectuals have emphasized their having testified to values central to the faith "before the eyes of the whole world" (Öz 2012; K. Demir 2015).

Scholars have tended to approach the Sivas victims' being remembered as martyrs in light of the opposition between Alevi and Orthodox Islamic—in Turkey's case, Sunni—notions of martyrdom, associating it squarely with the former (Hess 2007; Yildiz and Verkuyten 2011; Zırh 2016). Some (Yildiz and Verkuyten 2011) have been readier than others (Hess 2007; Zırh 2016) to acknowledge that the arson attack did not merely dovetail with a preexisting notion of Alevi martyrdom but also shaped it significantly, owing mainly to its inclusion of non-Alevis. Still, their explanation for why memory activism around the arson attack and Alevi martyrology have so decisively influenced each other has been virtually identical. The explanation is ontologically oriented in that it emphasizes certain qualities as having characterized both the historical Alevi martyrs' and the Sivas martyrs' ways of inhabiting the world at the time of death: "passive" subjection instead of "active" aggression (Hess 2007), unawareness of the likelihood of death as opposed to clear awareness of it (Yildiz and Verkuyten 2011), and sociopolitically motivated resistance against majoritarian tyranny rather than ethnically driven combat against the religious other (Zırh 2016).

The genealogical validity of this explanation notwithstanding, another one that considers the events of July 2, 1993, as generative rather than simply derivative and does so for spatially charged reasons surfaced during my ethnography among experienced memory activists. What justifies an amalgamation of the thoughts of these otherwise distinct individuals is not limited to their sustained engagement in commemorating the Sivas victims and includes two other biographical similarities. First, all have long identified personally with Alevi Sivas martyrs owing not only to shared values (religious or otherwise) but also to generational affiliation, as most of these victims, like the activists in question, were young adults at the time of the arson attack. Second, they all hail originally from Sivas province but have lived in Ankara since the late 1970s, to which they or their families migrated owing partly to the period's wave of violence that targeted central and eastern Turkey's Alevis, including a pogrom in Sivas's reputed "Alevi neighborhood" of Alibaba (Jongerden 2003, 83). It is worth quoting at length an activist in his late forties as emblematic of how this generation of Alevi activists recalls learning of the arson attack:

> Although we were not in Sivas at the time, I can say we experienced the massacre minute by minute. Word was out already in the afternoon that reactionaries had begun to harass our dear ones. Soon news emerged about things starting to get physical. But then the situation seemed to be calming down, or at least was not worsening, according to the news. Toward the evening, though, we were confronted with images of the hotel being besieged, stoned, and set on fire. Hundreds, maybe thousands, holding a handful of people—the country's best and brightest—captive and then setting them on fire. . . . This is not something you can easily get over. Of course, first you place blame for what the martyrs went through where blame is due: the state, the law enforcement, the arsonists. But then you begin to introspect. Could we have done something? Why did we just sit and watch? In fact, some of us were in touch with Alibaba, which is just a twenty-minute walk from the hotel. While the news kept fluctuating, Alibaba's residents were on tenterhooks—naturally so, given the neighborhood's recent history. Some even tried to convene and march to the city center. But they were stopped in their tracks by the gendarmerie who went up to the neighborhood to quell the reactions. Meanwhile, the assailants were given a free hand. Still, you ask yourself, could more have been done to prevent what happened?[3]

3. These remarks were made during a conversation I had with the activist on July 6, 2011, in Ankara.

Reiterating that the material and the visual co-constitute the experience of urban space (Wells 2007), these remarks render televisual mediation a factor that needs consideration in spatially focused analyses of witnessing and martyrdom in the Sivas case. Consider the spatially charged way that footage of the attack was broadcast. As the activist indicates, two features made spatiality central to this footage. The first was the extensive use of long shots, through which the vastness of the crowds surrounding the hotel was foregrounded. The second was how unevenly the footage was experienced across the viewership, where the unevenness derived from spatial knowledge of central Sivas and its history.

What, then, might be the relationship between this twofold spatiality and the need for introspection regarding the events? Here it is useful to think with John Ellis, the prominent theorist of media witnessing. Writing in the immediate aftermath of the rise to prominence of live-from-the-scene news, he suggested thus: "The feeling of witness that comes with the audio-visual media is one of separation and powerlessness: the events unfold, like it or not. . . . At once distanced and involving, it implies a necessary relationship with what is seen. The relationship is one of complicity; [that] you know about an event . . . implies a degree of consent to it" (2000, 11). Ellis's repeated use of the verb *imply* to convey a certain sense of complicity recalls Michael Rothberg's term *the implicated subject*. The term refers to "various modes of relation" involved in many contemporary contexts of violence that are unassimilable into the categories of victim, perpetrator, and bystander and that therefore "move us away from overt questions of guilt and innocence and leave us in a more complex and uncertain moral and ethical terrain" (Rothberg 2013, 40). Indeed, the truth that testimony produces necessarily involves not just an epistemic but also an ethical component. The first establishes guilt or innocence based on "witnessing" an event at a specific time and place and communicating this experience to others, whereas the second concerns "bearing witness . . . to that which cannot be seen" (Oliver 2000, 31). While witnessing orientates one's "subject position" in space and time, bearing witness constitutes "subjectivity"—one's sense of agency and "response-ability" (Oliver 2003, 137). It does so by continually encouraging one's "encounter with otherness" or one's quest to address others and receive their response (Oliver 2001, 85–106). This quest intensifies for implicated subjects who are left continually oscillating between the two extremes of guilt and innocence.

The arson attack's televisual mediation has produced just such implicated subjects through both form and content. Formally, the extensive use of long shots that foregrounded the crowd outside the hotel sought to portray the arson attack as based on popular dissent, bolstered periodically throughout the footage by supportive commentary from anonymous individuals near the camera. The reporting's near-live feel—still a novelty for Turkey at the time insofar as breaking news was concerned—engendered the popular assumption that millions knew what was happening yet failed to intervene. In fact, its content was selective. As recalled by the above-quoted activist, some, like those in Alibaba, did indeed attempt to intervene but were suppressed both physically (by the very law enforcement that was missing from the hotel's forecourt) and epistemically (by way of exclusion from televisual reporting). Therefore, spatial knowledge of both the suppression of counterassailants and Sivas's previous violent histories such as the 1978 episode served to further exacerbate the helplessness felt by those identifying with the thirty-three victims. This is how televisual mediation amplified violence's sociopolitical impact: by turning the very individuals who remember the victims as martyrs into "implicated subjects" haunted by continual introspection regarding what more might have been done.

I would like to suggest that the affective focus of the memory activist campaign for an on-site "museum of *shame*" is informed by such an "implicated" subjectivity that derives from a sociopolitically specific, spatially charged, and televisually mediated experience of witnessing the arson attack. There is cause to argue that the affective focus on shame is underpinned by this experience rather than one assumed to be sociopolitically uniform and to dovetail with preexisting and universally shared notions of innocence and guilt. According to Thomas Keenan, global and live transmission of human rights violations was central to shame's rise to prominence in late twentieth-century humanitarianism, whose approach to putting sociopolitical pressure on violators was marked by a shift from reason to affect (Keenan 2004). But, in mobilizing shame as such a televisually driven mechanism, the humanitarianism of the period overlooked that the very human rights violators it sought to bring to account were often also relying on the same televisibility, as they committed violations consciously for the cameras (446). If Keenan casts doubt on the sort of outward mobilization of shame that figures prominently in pithy depictions of the arson attack as an atrocity that unfolded "before the eyes of the whole world," Agamben considers it a catalyst for self-reflection. "Shame," Agamben argues in his analysis of Primo Levi's eponymous essay, is not easily framable within the guilt-innocence binary, therefore resonating with Rothberg's "implicated subject"; the shame of having witnessed but survived violence results in "desubjectification" (Agamben 1999, 105–6). In shame, passivity and sensibility coexist; it derives from being aware of and indeed moved by one's own passivity (109–11).

In sum, martyrdom's centrality to memory activism around the arson attack derives from the spatially charged way it was experienced as a media event rather than just from its ready assimilability into Alevi martyrology. This experience has turned certain activists identifying personally with the martyrs into "implicated subjects" in Rothberg's terms—into individuals left in much more ambiguous territory than that permitted by the guilt-innocence binary. What might "implication" as such mean for in-person encounters with sites linked to the arson attack and spoken of through the concepts of martyrdom, witnessing, and shame?

In-Person Spatial Testimony in 2010s Sivas

As discussed earlier, I began the fieldwork behind this book just days after the Madımak Hotel's transformation into Science and Culture Center, which introduced a Memory Corner with a list of thirty-seven names, including those of the two members of the crowd that surrounded the hotel during the arson attack. This all-encompassing name list was symptomatic of how the arson attack was historicized in the early 2010s. Examples in this respect included a ruling-party member's statement in Parliament that "the majority of those taken to court" for the arson attack "are as innocent as those set ablaze."[4] They also included one of Turkey's most popular political TV shows, which equated as "two witnesses" both a survivor and a former suspect whose acquittal many of those upholding the victims' legacy have continued to contest, and another such show in which a commentator opined that "being set ablaze" and "setting ablaze" each deserved recognition as a legitimate form of "victimhood" (Çaylı 2012). The broader historical narrative promoted here is that the arson attack was but one episode in a string of conspiracies whose known perpetrators were in effect naive pawns used by clandestine political-criminal networks seeking, as also implied in the Memory Corner, to damage Turkey's national unity (Kenanoğlu 2013). The late 2000s and early 2010s were, therefore, a context in which state-endorsed historical revisionism abused the concept of witness and, even more controversially, the notion of victim, obfuscating subject-positional differences involved in violent histories.

The theme of martyrdom had long enabled those communities upholding the thirty-three festival guests' legacy to underscore the very subject-positional differences in question. Faced with attempts to obfuscate these differences, the theme began to mark ever more visibly the anniversary commemorations held in Sivas. To recall, this annual event, which since the mid-2000s has seen increasingly larger crowds flock to the city from across Turkey and beyond, drew thousands in the early 2010s. The route along which the event proceeded—stretching from Sivas's "Alevi neighborhood" of Alibaba down to the site of the arson attack, where flowers were laid—retraced the trajectory that law enforcement had denied Alibaba's residents in the lead-up to the blaze. The procession was invariably led by "martyrs' families" (relatives of the thirty-three victims [figure 26]) alongside a bus equipped with powerful amplifiers loudly broadcasting songs and anthems associated with the "martyrs" (the historical ones long venerated in Alevism as well as those killed in Sivas). A speaker on the bus

---

4. For the transcript of the session in which these remarks were uttered, see "130'uncu Birleşim" [130th Session], *Türkiye Büyük Millet Meclisi Tutanak Dergisi*, July 2, 2012, http://www.tbmm.gov.tr/tutanak/donem24/yil2/ham/b13001h.htm.

periodically interrupted the music to make brief remarks, many of which concerned the Memory Corner: "Today we march against those who listed murderers alongside our martyrs!" The speaker also cued the crowd on what slogans to shout, most of which featured the arson attack as directly linked to numerous other historical atrocities that are now the subject of Alevi martyrology.

The martyrdom theme was highlighted in 2011 by a group of around thirty young marchers dressed in uniform-like attire comprising red vests and balaclavas, who held up cardboard cutouts of *zülfikar* (figure 27), an icon known as "the sword of Ali," the inaugural Alevi martyr. The same year, commemoration participants coming from Istanbul had prepared a sign that read "Museum of Shame" (see figures 26 and 28). Their plan was to temporarily hang it atop the entrance of the site of the blaze to materialize their disapproval of the outcome of its recent transformation and especially the commemorative name list. The police turned out to have gathered intelligence about this intervention and used it—alongside the

26. "Martyrs' families" leading the commemorative procession in central Sivas as they carry the "Madımak Museum of Shame" signboard produced by memory activists, 2011.

27. Young memory activists holding up placards (in the shape of "the sword of Ali") bearing victims' names, 2011.

28. Activists passing the "Madımak Museum of Shame" signboard from hand to hand to get it past the barricade, 2011.

Science and Culture Center's being "public space" as discussed in chapter 3—as the pretext to barricade the building's forecourt. Only the martyrs' families were allowed past the barricade for the flower-laying ceremony. When the "Museum of Shame" sign was passed forward from hand to hand to ultimately verge on going past the barricade (figure 28), the police teargassed the crowd. The ensuing melee prompted leading Alevi figures to emphasize in their closing speeches that what had just taken place was "a continuation of previous massacres and the centuries-long tyranny of hegemonic powers that slew our martyrs in the past." Pir Sultan Abdal, the sixteenth-century minstrel after whom the 1993 festival targeted by the arsonists was named, featured prominently in these speeches as one such martyr. One activist in her twenties drew the link between Pir Sultan, the arson-attack victims, and the commemoration participants not just ideologically but also spatially, as she suggested that "he was murdered just around the corner from where they teargassed us today and where our martyrs were slain yesterday," pointing to what is now known in Sivas as Dikilitaş Square.

The materially charged impact these martyrological connections have made on memory activism around the arson attack is evidenced by a set of statues commemorating certain Alevi victims in their ancestral villages in Sivas province's Emlek region. Known to locals as the "Martyrs' Monuments" (figure 29), these statues are modeled on a 1978 monument to Pir Sultan Abdal located in Banaz, renowned as the minstrel's native village in rural Sivas (figure 30). Recall that this is where the Pir Sultan Abdal Festival was held thrice before moving to central Sivas in 1993; the monument honoring the minstrel was built as part of preparations for the festival's inaugural episode (M. Demir 2008). The late 1970s was a period when rural-to-urban migration was completing its first generational cycle in Turkey (Zürcher 2005, 226–72). This wave of migration not only included Alevis as a substantial demographic but also profoundly shaped their identity through an unprecedented encounter with and/or categorization as the socioreligious other (Shankland 2003). Alevis encountered an urban Turkey that had little or no room—social or physical—for their rituals and practices. Such profound encounters led newly urbanized

29. The Martyrs' Monuments in the villages of Saraç (*left*), Beyyurdu (*center*), and Kavak (*right*), 2012.

Alevis to reestablish links with their ancestral villages through initiatives like summer festivals that offered an opportunity to not only reunite with fellow believers but also conduct religious service denied in cities (Langer et al. 2011, 112). In the mid-1990s, these initiatives reemerged in response to troubles urban Alevis faced, which followed from those of the 1970s. The Martyrs' Monuments were among the tangible results of this reemergence.

Part of my fieldwork took place in Banaz and villages across the Emlek region, which I visited together with activists of the generation mentioned above. I observed that the similarities between the Martyrs' Monuments and the Pir Sultan Abdal monument in Banaz were not merely formal. They also included the various meanings the monuments were ascribed by villagers. Some of these meanings derived from collective labor and knowledge in the village that had enabled the monuments' construction in conditions of climatic and economic hardship and that the villagers considered reminiscent of the martyrs' perseverance in the face of persecution. Other meanings concerned surrounding landscapes. Many villagers in Banaz spoke of the Pir Sultan monument as spatially referencing

30. The Pir Sultan Abdal monument built in 1978 in the village of Banaz, 2012.

31. One of the streams in rural Sivas that have acquired colloquial names due to their genocide-related associations, 2012.

landforms nearby that they considered witnesses to crucial events in the minstrel's life or in Alevi cosmology. Such was the way in which the villagers across the Emlek region made sense of the location of each Martyrs' Monument.

Some of these conversations around the monuments and the landscapes nearby transitioned into histories other than those of Alevism. An activist in his fifties hailing from the Emlek region referred to a tributary bordering one village as *sevkiyat* (deportation) brook and to another one nearby variably as *kanlı* (bloody) or *karanlı* (corrupted from *karanlık*; dark) brook (figure 31). *Sevkiyat* brook, he explained, is where the region's Armenians had been gathered in 1915 and "deported" eastward by orders of the then Ottoman government. Around this time, *kanlı* brook witnessed the massacre of Armenians from another part of the region; the stream ran bloodred for months. Having to elaborate on these vernacular names prompted the activist to comment on his ancestors' role in them: "My grandpa was tasked with taking them farther east; that's all he did—he didn't kill anyone." "The killers always came from Sunni villages," said another male activist of the same generation who accompanied us. Still another admitted, "Alevis did what they could—many Armenians sought refuge in our villages—but, had we been able to do more back then, what we subsequently experienced might also have been different." Such conversations would then return to the Sivas arson attack, implying its being among the subsequent experiences that could have had a different course had 1915 unfolded differently.[5]

Further instances when sites associated with the Sivas victims prompted segues from the arson attack to various other not necessarily Alevism-related violent episodes like the Armenian genocide took place during the 2012 commemoration in Sivas. Consider the following conversation I had with an activist of the above-mentioned generation on the way to the commemoration. As we chatted about the city's historically significant buildings, he lamented that, while there had been many in the past, now there were few. "Of course, one can always blame insatiable contractors," explained the activist, "but, if you ask me, the real damage was done a long time ago, in 1915, when the Armenians perished; the artisans and master masons were all Armenians, and in their wake, no one was left to build anything of quality." I asked him where his knowledge of and interest in the topic came from. The activist responded by referring to his ancestral village in the southern region of Sivas province and the stories he had heard from its elders. "Thousands of Armenians used to live in the region; they were exiled, massacred in 1915," he explained, referring to the Armenian genocide: "Our elders say Alevis were not involved; all killers were Sunnis. Some even protected the Armenians by hiding them. Be that as it may, could more have been done to prevent what happened? After all, this was not just a catastrophe experienced by a particular people, but a curse upon an entire geography. Imagine, if central Sivas's population were a third Armenian, as it had been before 1915, could a massacre like Madımak take place?" The activist then went on to relay further village-borne stories relating to the Armenian genocide. "The region around our village is famous for its fruit trees—especially apricots—but it is said that, after 1915, even they became useless," he recalled. "Of course. Who would eat the fruits of a geography awash with blood even if the trees yielded them?" the activist concluded.

These remarks continued to reverberate the day after, when the commemoration in Sivas saw police barricades move farther up, by about half

---

5. The conversations mentioned here took place on June 30, 2012.

a kilometer, from where they had been the year before. An hour-long sit-in ensued, throughout which tension levels gradually rose, at times bordering on physical confrontation between the police and the activists (figure 32). I noticed the senior activist shuttle jumpily between the barricades and the crowd performing the sit-in a few dozen meters in front. Ultimately, the police conceded and moved the barricades back to where they had been in 2011. The procession resumed. On the way back, the activist recounted his experience during the sit-in:

> This is so unfair, I thought to myself. Had there been barricades in 1993 right here in these streets, the massacre would have been prevented; yet there were none. With such thoughts going through my mind, I was about to snap and lunge at the police. Then suddenly a kid appeared from between buildings lining the street and walked toward me. He said, "Uncle, calm down. My family has a wonderful apricot grove. It's very calming; let me take you there." I remember strolling with him for a while. Then someone else called out to me; I looked their way. When I turned back, the kid was gone.

It was not possible or even analytically relevant to ascertain whether the activist's experience was a daydream or an actual encounter. What did render it empirically significant, however, was the conversation he and I had had on the way to the commemoration, in which apricot trees had prompted him to reflect on the magnitude of the Armenian genocide's social and spatial impact. Now, in the activist's experience during the impasse in front of the barricades, the same feature of the landscape resurfaced as indexing a space in which to find wisdom vis-à-vis violent histories' likelihood to recur precisely where they have previously occurred.

The activist's remarks therefore recall my observations across the Emlek region and do so for at least two reasons. First, whether in the case of the site of the arson attack and the barricades mounted to render it inaccessible or in the case of the Martyrs' Monuments and the landscapes nearby, the extent to which sites associated with the arson attack serve to remember the thirty-three victims concerns much more than just their formal features. Rather, it derives from the social processes characterizing the construction and/or use of these environments—put differently,

32. Activists' sit-in against the police's placement of barricades farther along the procession route, 2012.

from the extent to which these processes are seen to resemble or contra-dict the values known to have marked the events surrounding the victims' martyrdom. Second, both cases demonstrate that, once these sites are ren-dered a medium that helps evince such cross-historical resemblances and contradictions, the histories across which they operate become capable of engulfing numerous others than just the arson attack and/or events sig-nificant to Alevi cosmology and/or martyrology—other histories such as the Armenian genocide.

7

Testifying to Diyarbakır Prison, Architecturally

"Is it a coincidence that they recently got Kurdish kids to paint pictures on the prison's walls?" asked a senior member of the '78ers Association, rhetorically, as we talked about their campaign to transform the Diyarbakır Prison into a memorial museum. The "kids" in question were the students from the local Dicle University who, as discussed in chapter 4, had responded favorably to the prison administration's request in 2007 to decorate two of the penitentiary's outer walls with duplicates of well-known paintings and education-themed quotations (figure 33). "Is it a coincidence, too, that they got them to do this for free?" continued the senior activist. The questions were rhetorical because the activist was convinced that the project carried echoes of political inmates' experiences in the prison throughout the early 1980s:

> They [the prison administration] forced us to paint all the prison's aisles, from beginning to end, all the way down to the very interiors of our wards, using our money. All our windows were painted in Turkish flags. Our aisles were all filled with slogans like "How happy is the one who says, 'I am Turk'" or "A Turk is worth the world," and with the national anthem, the student oath, and pictures of Kenan Evren [the junta leader]. We were forced not only to paint these but also to pay for the materials.[1]

1. The student oath mentioned here was obligatory for elementary school pupils in the Republic of Turkey and the Turkish Republic of Northern Cyprus (recognized by no other state besides Turkey) until 2013. Pupils were obliged to recite this oath every

33. Works of famous modernist painters reproduced on outer walls of the Diyarbakır Prison compound, 2011.

Might the senior activist's emphasis on coincidence, through which he drew a parallel between his plight in the 1980s prison and the late 2000s project to beautify its outer walls, be considered seriously for what it entails regarding the spatial politics of witnessing state-endorsed violence and commemoration?

The question recalls anthropologist Rosalind Morris's work on histories of state-endorsed violence in Southeast Asia that, she observes, have engendered a particular sort of ghostliness. This ghostliness is partly "a function of technology, of the technologization of life and death, movement and war," as it is "densest in the places where the *accidents* of modernity are likely to occur: highways, railways, and industrialized spaces where heavy machinery is located" (2008, 230; emphasis added). Against the grain of much of the scholarship on remembering and forgetting

morning before class until it was abolished as a result of the government's Democratic Openings and informal peace talks with the PKK. This excerpt is from my interview with the activist on July 9, 2012, in Diyarbakır.

state-endorsed violence, Morris does not attribute this ghostliness to a lack of closure. For her, it is not simply a case where the dead who have been deprived of proper burial now return to haunt the living but rather one where the very distinction between the dead and the living becomes difficult to delineate (231). It is this difficulty that Morris's concept of accidentality seeks to grasp. Accidentality, for her, refers both to accidents in the literal sense—as in apartheid's legacy cropping up through crashes involving speeding cars on South Africa's highways—and, more broadly, to "event[s]" the "anticipation" of which "cannot mitigate" their "occurrence" and that are "the result of a failure internal to technology" (2010, 589). When histories of state-endorsed violence crop up through what Morris calls "accidents of modernity," causality becomes disturbed in a way that not only throws linear temporality into disarray but also differs fundamentally from a cyclical return to an unresolved past. Accidentality as such, she argues, undermines the very sequentiality between the past, present, and future; it hinders violence's localization in the past alone. Accidental encounters in this respect therefore gesture toward the "possibility of a political or ethical opening to the future . . . whose form is not determined a priori" (2008, 236). Appraising this possibility, concludes Morris, requires a shift of methodological focus away from irretrievably lost opportunities often conceptualized as wounds and closer to "poorly anticipated" but always necessarily historically situated encounters that are the stuff of accidents (237).

While Morris's conceptual focus is on the accidental rather than the coincidental per se, I find her insights directly pertinent to coincidences of the sort invoked by the senior activist. The pertinence has not only to do with the etymological link between the Turkish-language words *kaza* and *kazara* that correspond, respectively to the English-language ones of "accident" and "coincidentally" and that feature in conversations of the sort quoted above as memory activists seek meaning in what purport to be unplanned-for and/or unanticipated encounters with histories of state-endorsed violence.[2] More pertinent to my focus on materiality and space

2. In addition to the quotes from my ethnography, a former political inmate's memoir (Bozyel 2014) offers further instances of how these concepts have figured in attempts

is Morris's observation that the specific contexts in which accidents as such occur have much to do with modernity, its technologies, and the sites shaped by the latter. I propose to extend this observation back toward the histories of violence that crop up through accidents as such or to attend to the role technology has played in both the violent episodes being accidentally encountered and the encounters themselves. Doing so requires that technology be understood not necessarily through its most conspicuous manifestations like factories or railways, but rather as an assemblage of artifacts and environments employed in inflicting violence in the modern mode. As ethnic homogenization is a prime example of such violence, penitentiaries like Diyarbakır Prison and mechanisms of torture employed there in the 1980s are foremost among such assemblages.

Take the senior activist's recollection of how the coup-era prison administration forced him and his fellow political inmates to paint the walls of cells and hallways. As indicated by him and by other survivors of Diyarbakır Prison in numerous accounts that proliferated in the early 2010s, these instances of forced painting amounted to a prominent technology of torture in the penitentiary and did so in at least two ways (Güney 2012, 65–67; Aydınkaya 2011, 120; M. Ayata 2011, 363–66; Miroğlu 2009, 117–22). First, the content of the murals comprised nationalist and racist tropes. In addition to the slogans and symbols referenced by the activist quoted above, these tropes included depictions of historical rulers (for example, the republic's founder, Mustafa Kemal Atatürk; various Ottoman sultans; and Seljuk and Hunnic emperors) and events (including the conquest of Constantinople [1453], the siege of Vienna [1683], and the battle of Gallipoli [1915–16]), which state-endorsed nationalisms in Turkey have variously employed to forge a Turkic historiography (Güney 2012, 65–67). The prison's use of such tropes therefore dovetailed with the junta's broader strategy of Turkification (Zeydanlıoğlu 2009). The torturous effect at work here was compounded owing to the fact that the murals enveloped the prisoners' field of vision in much of their daily life and were

---

to find meaning in the unplanned-for or unanticipated encounters of the sort described here.

used by the prison administration to quiz the inmates on aspects of Turkish official historiography, leading to physical torture if officers found the answers unsatisfactory (Miroğlu 2009, 127–28). Second, the prisoners were exploited for resources in terms of both labor and material costs. Therefore, when the senior activist finds the late 2000s painting of the prison's outer walls reminiscent of what they went through in the 1980s, the reminiscence is technologically informed in the sense I have outlined above. This is evident not only in the spatial overlap but also the avowedly preventive-cum-educational function ascribed to the murals—the prison administrator that led the late 2000s art project explained that their objective was to "make people think before committing a crime" and "prevent them from committing a crime."[3] Technology's significance to the parallels the senior activist draws between the late 2000s and early 1980s is also evident in his emphasis that, in both cases, Kurdish resources and labor were used without compensation or remuneration.

What might these poorly anticipated but technologically informed encounters with histories of state-endorsed violence mean for testimony's relationship to subjectivity and space's role in it? Addressing this question requires revisiting the case of four Diyarbakır Prison inmates who self-immolated on May 18, 1982, in protest against torture, and who have since then been remembered as martyrs by members of the pro-Kurdish political movement (Bargu 2014, 173). Forced to paint the aisles and cells in nationalist and racist slogans and symbols, they gradually and surreptitiously stockpiled enough of the highly combustible painting materials to use for self-immolation (Özcan 2011; Aydınkaya 2011, 120). The violent technology of forced painting has since become the stuff of witnessing and bearing witness to state-endorsed violence in 1980s Diyarbakır Prison. This is evident in the particular way the nationalist and racist murals have come to feature in discussions around precisely how to carry out the prison's transformation into a memorial museum, if and when this proves

3. See "Diyarbakır Cezaevi'nin Çehresi Değişiyor" [The Face of Diyarbakır Prison Is Changing], *Haberler.com*, Nov. 21, 2007, http://www.haberler.com/diyarbakir-cezaevi -nin-cehresi-degisiyor-haberi.

34. Nationalist and racist murals from coup-era Diyarbakır Prison, re-created for the film *July 14* (2017). Courtesy of the director Haşim Aydemir.

possible. The murals have long been painted over but remain among the most vividly memorable instruments of the torture that unfolded there (figure 34). Activists have been virtually unanimous in proposing that the murals be restored to their original state. But some have called for their restoration to be guided by principles beyond visual faithfulness to the original. As the senior activist quoted at the beginning of this chapter told me: "We want this original version back so that when our kids see it, they will know very well what we witnessed. But we do not want anyone else to do this. We will do it ourselves; we have the skills to restore it to the way it used to be, because we were its makers." His emphasis on the process rather than just the product of restoration is significant. It indicates that the political potential of the built environment's role in testifying to violence does not only concern physical or visual restoration. What is also at stake in this role is restoration of the agency that violence seeks to take away from its victims or survivors and of subjectivity, which hinges on this agency.

Prioritizing the question of agency means not to dismiss the significance of that which is physical or visual but rather to do full justice to the role of aesthetics in the political potential of spatial testimony. Specifically, it means to avoid reducing this role to a straightforward binarism between representation, symbolism, and imagination, on the one hand, and realism, documentarism, and evidence, on the other. Diyarbakır Prison survivor Mesut Baştürk's science-fiction novel based on his experience in the penitentiary under the junta indicates just why such binarism is best avoided. The novel's protagonist is an actor who stars in a popular political drama, which Baştürk bases on a nationalistic TV series that actually existed and enjoyed its highest ratings in the mid-2000s. The author begins the novel by sending his protagonist back in time, as this is what the script of the drama's forthcoming episode requires. Set in Constantinople in 1453, this episode is supposed to see the actor conquer the city from the Byzantines—the topic of one of the most vividly remembered murals from 1980s Diyarbakır Prison. The actor boards a time machine but *accidentally* ends up in the coup-era prison instead of mid-fifteenth-century Constantinople (Baştürk 2007, 13–15). Following this science-fictional introduction, Baştürk continues his narrative in the manner of a memoir. He has his protagonist undergo the same torture that he and his fellow inmates survived inside the coup-era prison and offers a detailed account of it.

In his novel, Baştürk addresses the question of aesthetics in ways more direct than his stylistic interweaving of fiction and documentary. Toward the end of the book, a conversation between the protagonist and one of his cell mates sees the actor entertain the idea of making a film about the prison once he returns to the 2000s. The protagonist laments the fact that the Kurds have yet to make such a film despite the rich "material" offered by Diyarbakır Prison, contrasting it with the case of the Holocaust and its being the subject of a wide range of dramas (148). This direct reference to the role of interweaving of the imaginary and the documentary in confronting political violence suggests that the author's aesthetic decisions are more than just stylistic garb. Nor are they limited to an urge to comment exclusively and convergently on 1980s Diyarbakır Prison. Baştürk has used the novel to keep the prison alive as an issue through which to engage with the imperative of confronting state-endorsed violence as an infinitely open-ended and self-reflexive task. A case in point is what the author made of his being one of the first witnesses invited in early 2016 to testify before a parliamentary commission set up to investigate 1980s human rights violations at the prison. Baştürk suggested that the committee may have prioritized his testimony because he had written his recollections of torture as a science-fiction novel rather than a conventional memoir offering a documentarian, if personalized, account of the past (Akgün 2016). The author therefore self-reflexively brought into question the political stakes involved in fictionalizing state-endorsed violence, such as its rendering violent histories safer—that is, more bearable and less visceral—to engage with. In so doing, Baştürk underscored how the committee effectively trivialized the trauma associated with the prison by purporting to come to terms with it as a long-past case of violence that was now merely material for good fiction—when in fact the 2010s continued to witness the sort of problems for which the 1980s were infamous.[4]

In this short chapter, I have aimed to further explore the spatiality of spatial testimony and its role in confronting histories of state-endorsed violence as per the critical-analytical objective of part 3. The former inmates of Diyarbakır Prison whose thoughts and work I have discussed in this chapter reiterate what the previous one showed regarding the

4. The complicated relationship between documentarian and imaginational modes of narrating one's subjection to violence is known to have confronted the author Mesut Baştürk immediately after his release from Diyarbakır Prison. In 1987 the renowned author Aziz Nesin, who would later survive the Sivas arson attack explored elsewhere in this book, visited Diyarbakır to find out about torture inside the prison from its victims and survivors. Baştürk and a former cell mate met with Nesin at his hotel and gave him lengthy accounts of the torture they had survived. Observing Nesin's daydreamy silence, they asked if something was wrong. Nesin replied, "Guys, I always thought my imagination is wild but now realize that Kurds' is much wilder than mine" (Karabağlı 2016). Indeed, some of the political inmates of 1980s Diyarbakır Prison also found unbelievable the violent treatment they received inside the penitentiary as they were going through it (Düzel 2003). These experiences suggest that Baştürk's aesthetic decision to merge science fiction and documentarism is not merely a creative preference but rather informed historically in both biographical and social ways.

importance of attending to agency and the right to historicization as a necessary complement to a focus on epistemics. Put differently, in this chapter I have reiterated that what is at stake in spatial testimony is not only the question of producing knowledge on what occurred in the past but also which producers and modes of production emerge out of this process as more authoritative, powerful, and legitimate than others. I have moreover drawn attention to the interplay between technologies of both violence and testimony and their role in victims' and survivors' endeavors to claim the agency to historicize. That these technologies are both devoid of an innate or autonomous politicality *and* carry the potential to be instantaneously politicized if and when placed in the appropriate spatial context renders them conduits of poorly anticipated encounters with histories of violence. The poorly anticipated nature of these encounters becomes manifest not only in the way they occur but also in the effects they yield. So poorly anticipated are the effects that they include exposing victims and survivors as well as perpetrators and the latter's successors to reflection and introspection—recall novelist and survivor Baştürk's grappling repeatedly with the question of fictionalizing an issue so grave as 1980s Diyarbakır Prison. But spatial testimony's potential to help untangle the continuities between violence and commemoration is only ever enhanced as a result of this risk.

Conclusion

My aims in part 3 have been twofold. First, I have aimed to analyze memory activism around the Sivas arson attack and the Diyarbakır Prison in terms of the ways in which activists have mobilized spatial testimony and especially those mobilizations that have become manifest in their remembrance of victims as "martyrs" and their campaigns for museums of "shame." My second aim has been to contribute to the growing literature on the politics of spatiality's role in testifying to state-endorsed violence.

Chapter 6 showed that, in the case of Sivas, the spatial import of the notions of "witness," "martyrdom," and "shame" in question has been informed by televisual mediation, which amplified the presence of assailants outside the hotel and erased that of counterassailants nearby in the "Alevi neighborhood" of Alibaba. But awareness of this amplification and erasure required further spatially charged knowledge—knowledge about the hotel's central location in Sivas and its being within walking distance of Alibaba, about the role of violent histories in making Alibaba the neighborhood that it is today, and about how its residents were treated in the lead-up to the arson attack. Certain televisual witnesses who possessed this sort of knowledge were left oscillating between the two subject-positional extremes of guilt and innocence. It was especially knowledge of how Alibaba's residents were treated in the hours leading to the arson attack that heightened these viewers' sense of enforced passivity—the "shame" through which they witnessed the victims' martyrdom. Those activists campaigning for Diyarbakır Prison's transformation into a memorial museum have also often drawn upon the concept of "shame."[5] There is cause to suggest that this has also been informed by a specific and spatially charged experience, including the forced painting of walls in nationalist and racist tropes discussed in chapter 7. In memoirs, survivors have recounted being forced to chant the slogans of the sort painted on these walls and feeling "shame" as they were walked back to their cells and encountered fellow inmates' glares from behind the bars along the aisles (Güney 2012, 52–53). Survivors have also recounted the self-immolation of the four martyrs as a response to the shame resulting from subjection to the form of torture that forced painting was—a response that former inmates have considered effective as it led the prison administration to take back the paint, thinner, and varnish and halt the torturous practice (Miroğlu 2009, 121–22).

The experience of shame invoked so emphatically by each of these campaigns for a "museum of shame" is therefore not only the stuff of a subject position grounded in a purportedly universally relatable provictim stance that a discrete physical or visually mediated encounter with sites of violence can alone secure. It also has to do with a self-reflexive subjectivity informed by a geographically and socially specific body of spatial knowledge deriving from multiple encounters with these sites. Indeed, working from this specificity might benefit the very universality activist campaigns seek to engage. It might help tap into an array of histories much wider and more universally relatable than can be afforded either by an unambiguous notion of guilt for which one must repent or by the concept of a victim whose agency is solely premised on suffering. In the case of the activists featured in chapter 6, these histories pertained not only to the Sivas arson attack but also to the Armenian genocide and indeed entangled the one in the other. In the case of the torture survivors featured in chapter 7, histories of this sort included nationalist ones employed in torturing political convicts inside the junta-run Diyarbakır prison as well as the specific history of the torture itself.

---

5. See "Diyarbakır Cezaevi Utanç Müzesi Olacak" [Diyarbakır Prison Will Become a Museum of Shame], *CNN Türk*, Sept. 12, 2012, http://www.cnnturk.com/2012/turkiye /09/12/diyarbakir.cezaevi.utanc.muzesi.olacak/676520.0/index.html.

Following from this analysis, I propose to reconsider a tendency characterizing the spatial turn in scholarly explorations of testimony and its cognates. The tendency is to limit testimony's function to the production of knowledge about violent events whose eventhood is considered discrete and spatiotemporally predetermined. My introduction to part 3 ended with a question regarding its potentials and limitations in accounting for the dehistoricization that violence inflicts on victims, survivors, and their sociopolitical heirs. The question meant to acknowledge testimony as a practice that is oriented toward ethics as well as epistemics—as an attempt to reclaim the very agency undermined through violence and its dehistoricizing impact. The empirical analysis I have offered in part 3 has shown this question to be about much more than simply the various registers employed in historicizing a violent event, including the documentarian urge to preserve the site of violence "as is," the memorialization of victims as "martyrs," the performative attempt to resuscitate through commemoration the very spatial knowledge obscured by violence and its televisual mediation, and daydreamy encounters with alterity triggered by limits imposed on such commemorative attempts. Nor is the question explorable only as one of representing the suffering that is assumed to define the identities of victims, survivors, and their familial and sociopolitical heirs. The extent to which spatial testimony challenges violence's dehistoricizing impact also involves asking precisely what sorts of historical moments constitute the violence being commemorated, where and when its eventhood begins and ends, and how the answer to each of these perennial questions affects the extent to which previous answers have challenged or confirmed power relations structured by violent histories. Simply put, it requires asking if and to what extent spatial testimony grants victims, survivors, and their familial and sociopolitical heirs the right to historicization.

It might be worth concluding by way of a return to the dyadic conceptualization of testimony developed by Marc Nichanian and introduced at the beginning of part 3: "testimony as document" versus "testimony as monument." It is worthwhile to recall this conceptualization here for the two insights it offers. Consider, first, Nichanian's criticism of "the era of the witness" for its subjection of testimony to the logic of verifiability. This criticism indicates that the stakes involved in overcoming the era's limitations cannot be reduced—as some of its critics have done—to a clear-cut opposition between the privileging of the human witness as ethically biased and of object witnesses as epistemically oriented. The second insight concerns Nichanian's effort to render troubling histories not only a perpetual preoccupation but also a socially all-encompassing one. This effort helps nuance a prominent strand of critical scholarship that has problematized mainstream approaches to troubling histories for tending toward closure. Examples of this critical scholarship include the burgeoning literature on "confronting the past" in Turkey (Bakıner 2013; Kaya 2015) as well as James E. Young's renowned conceptualization of what a contrarian or "counter" approach to spatial commemoration might entail (Young 2016). The nuance Nichanian helps offer to this scholarship is that the question of avoiding closure does not just concern content; it is not a task met by continually increasing the number and subject-positional diversity of the testimonies fed into projects of confronting the past. Rather, it is a structural question or one that concerns the terms on which the past is confronted. Insofar as this book's focus on materiality, spatiality, and visuality is concerned, these terms are of an *aesthetic* register. Since structuring the terms of a project necessarily requires much greater authority than is required for participating in it, closure is a question that ought to be approached with a keen awareness of power relations—especially the ones shaped by the very violence that is the subject of testimony—and how they might be permeating the aesthetics of commemoration.

Yet part 3 has not only confirmed these two insights but also indicated potential ways of furthering their critical purchase. In complicating the opposition between the ethical mode and the epistemic one, the physical environments discussed above also complicate the regimentation of testimony into categories based exclusively on one or the other of these modes (for example, "testimony as document" versus "testimony as monument"). These environments enable a testimony that both communicates specific subject positions engendered by violence and fosters a sense of subjectivity much more open-ended and evolvable than subject positionality. The environments that manifest this dual testimony are at once realistic and emblematic: they are considered material evidence of violence as well as conduits for an engagement with troubled histories that turns on perspective and imagery rather than epistemic verifiability. In chapter 6, the intertwinement of the ethical and the epistemic or the imaginative and the verifiable derived from the mediated way the arson attack was witnessed by millions. This experience not only led televisual witnesses to identify with the "martyrs" but also implicated them in what unfolded before their eyes, leaving them with a role unassimilable under the relatively less ambiguous categories of victim, perpetrator, and bystander. In chapter 7, the intertwinement of the ethical and the epistemic or the imaginative and the verifiable has involved the technologically informed ghostliness that haunts such mundane acts as painting walls. This intertwinement has thrust witnesses into an open-ended and self-reflexive quest that constitutes the agency to historicize and the sense of subjectivity it underpins. As a result, the range of what is witnessable through each site of state-endorsed violence has expanded from histories that are the subject of campaigns for memorial museums to ones that are both more distant and more recent. Part 3 has shown the Armenian genocide to be among the more distant histories but has only hinted at what the more recent ones might involve. The book's coda will detail the latter.

Coda

Throughout the first half of the 2010s, Turkey's global image remained associated with peace and democracy—an association that the political and media establishment's approach to confronting the past had, since the late 2000s, sought to substantiate. But toward the middle of the decade, this image began to deteriorate rapidly. In late 2015, war flared up between the army and Kurdish insurgents. In mid-2016, a faction in the military attempted a failed coup. By the end of that year, the country's global image had deteriorated so profoundly that mainstream commentators declared "the fall of Turkey" (Brown 2016). In this coda, which stands in lieu of a conventional conclusion, I discuss some of the developments that underpinned this deterioration and how they relate to the topic and arguments of this book. I begin by reflecting on an episode from late 2012. The episode brought my fieldwork in central Sivas to an abrupt end and exposed me directly—in a much more personal way than researchers generally experience—to the tensions between democracy and injustice, peace and violence, and did so several years before commentators declared Turkey's fall. The significance of this episode, however, is not limited to its exposing me directly to the tensions I had observed in the field. The episode is also significant because of the questions it raised regarding the dynamics between the two main figures of anthropological fieldwork: fieldworker and interlocutor.

Before I unpack this twofold significance, allow me to reiterate the main arguments of this book. In the early 2010s, Turkey's sites of state-endorsed violence became the foremost arena where competing approaches to confronting the past became materially, spatially, and visually manifest. The political and media establishment's approach was one of indexing the entire nation as victims, whereas memory activists (including survivors and victims' families) sought to underscore the specific identity of the victims whose legacy they upheld. When the establishment's approach became manifest at sites of violence, the manifestation was such that it not only denied memory activists the recognition they sought but also portrayed them as the actual victimizers (part 1). Activists responded by continuing to foreground the specificity of victimhood and did so by appropriating the very sociospatial mechanisms the authorities employed to deny them their demands even as they constantly repudiated the idealization of each such mechanism (part 2), two examples being public space and the memorial museum. Throughout this process, the sociopolitical function of victimhood became less associated with demands for recognition and more with claims to agency. The agency in question involved, particularly, the ability and freedom to make connections across various episodes of violence and, in so doing, build alliances across diverse sociopolitical constituencies, including those episodes that might implicate one's own kin in violent histories (part 3).

In 2014 a leading activist—the chairperson of an association of survivors of the 1980 coup—offered a most succinct expression of this increasing emphasis on agency during his opening address at the annual "September 12 Museum of Shame" exhibition that the association organized. Criticizing both right-leaning figures' attempts to generalize and depoliticize victimhood and left-wing activists' risk of reducing themselves to objectified victims, the chairperson declared, "We are interlocutors (*muhatap*), not victims (*mağdur*)."[1] I consider the chairperson's reference to being "interlocutors" noteworthy not only because it indexes

---

1. For further details of the chairperson's opening address, see "Utanç Müzesi'nde Abdi İpekçi ve Ahmet Kaya'nın da Eşyaları Sergilenecek" [Museum of Shame Will Also Exhibit Abdi İpekçi and Ahmet Kaya's Belongings], *T24*, Sept. 4, 2014, http://t24.com.tr/haber/aile-bakanligi-seda-sayani-rtuke-sikayet-etti,269759. For further details of the debate that Turkey's veteran leftists have had over being victims versus being interlocutors, see Pekdemir 2016.

the agency of a stakeholder over the passivity of a demandant. I find the reference noteworthy also because it mobilizes a term that is central to anthropological fieldwork (the methodological mainstay of this book) and that indexes individuals inhabiting the field. Therefore, as I reflect below on the events that brought my fieldwork at a site of violence to an abrupt end, I ask how scholarship on political violence that draws on fieldwork might approach victimhood's association with agency (evident in both the chairperson's "interlocutor" reference and the argumentative arc of this book) as more than just empirical data and as a call for methodological reconsideration.

In late August 2012, I returned to Sivas hoping to conduct daily observations inside the Science and Culture Center inaugurated the year before. I wanted to observe, more closely than before, how visitors responded to the building's new program and how staff members negotiated these responses. My daily presence in this socially and physically intimate, historically troubling, and politically contested space was impossible without formal approval. I thus contacted the governorship, as a deputy governor had overseen the building's recent transformation and was now responsible for its day-to-day management. When I went to see the deputy governor, it seemed useful that I had already spoken to him several times over the past year, had visited the building, and had interviewed its staff. It also seemed useful that my name and birthplace did not mark me as a member of one of Turkey's historically marginalized communities—he asked me more than once what my last name is and where I am from. After a twenty-minute conversation, the deputy governor approved my request and phoned the Science and Culture Center staff to inform them. Mirroring the lack of written documentation on the building's recent transformation, he delivered his approval only orally. During our meeting, I had repeatedly offered to apply in writing, but once I secured approval I ceased to insist. I thus began conducting my daily observations inside the Science and Culture Center. I did not know, however, that they would end abruptly with my expulsion from the building and detention on the street by the police and with the authorities' confiscating my notes and threatening to prosecute me.

35. The part of the Science and Culture Center known as the Children's Library.

What seems to have triggered the escalation that brought my field-work to an abrupt end is my bearing witness to exchanges between visitors and employees of the Science and Culture Center. Many of these exchanges involved visitors' responses to noncommemorative parts of the building. Some responded to these parts as if they carried commemorative significance. A case in point was the Children's Library located in the first floor (figure 35). Parents with young children, who constituted a significant demographic among the building's visitors, were particularly drawn to this library. Its colorful interiors received favorable commentary from both parents and kids. But the arson attack continued to haunt this library despite its lack of direct references to the event. Two parents in their midthirties examined the faith section of the Children's Library and asked why there were no books here on Alevism. Other parts of the building whose noncommemorative function failed to prevent commemorative interpretations included the air well and the staircase (figure 36). These are spaces indelibly associated with victims' and survivors' attempts to find refuge from harm. The staircase, as documented in some of the most

36. The Science and Culture Center's only publicly viewable
and accessible staircase.

widely circulated photographs of the arson attack, sheltered victims as
they were held captive by the assailants outside (figure 37). This fact has
led numerous cultural works on the arson attack to architecturally center
around staircases.[2] The air well has figured prominently in survivors' tes-

2. This is the case in the two best-known plays on the atrocity, *Simurg* and *Sivas '93*,
both of which were conceived to mark the fifteenth anniversary of the atrocity and toured

37. Eventual victims and survivors sheltering in Madımak Hotel's staircases minutes before the blaze. Courtesy of late photographer Battal Pehlivan's brother İsmail Pehlivan.

timonies as the only route available to them as they strove to flee the blaze; indeed, it enabled forty-two to escape death (Yıldırım 1993).[3]

During my daily observations, I encountered many visitors who asked to see the original staircase where some of the eventual survivors and victims had sought shelter. Some raised the question almost immediately upon entering the building, implying that the staircase's commemorative significance is higher than the Memory Corner's despite the latter's prescribed function. Others compelled the employees to explain why the staircase is not there anymore. Employees, in turn, tended to confine their responses to brief technical explanations: after all, the entire building had been refurbished as per the government's orders, and the staircase was no exception. But, on what would turn out to be my last day in the building, one employee felt obliged to engage with these inquiries more directly. This interaction occurred when a man and two women in their

---

extensively across Turkey and Europe. *Simurg*'s protagonist is a survivor who lost his brother in the arson attack. The most crucial moments of the play unfold when the protagonist visits the Madımak Hotel more than a decade after the arson attack and walks up and down its staircase, experiencing episodes of hallucination and fluctuating between the past and the present. *Sivas '93* is conceived minimally as regards stage and costume design. All actors are dressed in plain black, and the play includes no other element of stage design except a couple of flights of stairs around which action revolves. Another case in point is the 2012 documentary *Menekşe'den Önce* (literally, Before Menekşe, referring to one of the youngest Sivas victims). It presents interviews with survivors, many of which are conducted in staircases. A memorial proposed in 2010 for the native village of the youngest Sivas victim, Murat Gündüz, also centered on the staircase as an architectural element. During my conversation with them on September 6, 2011, the memorial's designers told me of their motivation to "relate the experience of visitors to that of the victims and survivors." For a textual example of the staircase's commemorative significance, see Tüleylioğlu 2012.

3. During my fieldwork inside the building, I noticed that the staff ate their lunch in the Fairy Tale room, which looks to the air well, but also drew the curtains that are otherwise open. I inquired into this later with a staff member, who replied, "When you are eating, you surely do not want to see such a place that gives you shivers. . . . I also always feel extremely uncomfortable whenever I have to climb to the upper floors." Such remarks demonstrate that parts of the building unimbued with any commemorative function have nevertheless continued to trigger imagery relating to the arson attack.

early fifties walked together into the building. One of the women directly approached a staff member and said they wished to see the place where Arif Sağ (a famous Alevi musician who survived the arson) escaped. The employee responded favorably and told them to follow him. He took the visitors up the stairs to the part of the building now called the Fairy Tale room, serving primary school students. The employee pointed to the air well adjacent to the room. He informed them that tens of people ran away through this air well to the neighboring BBP headquarters. This triggered a discussion between the employee and the three visitors about the arson attack and who was really behind it. The employee embarked on a personal interpretation of the arson attack as a conspiracy that targeted the whole nation. He went on to ask if the visitors would wish to also see the notorious staircase. The visitors followed him to the staircase. Here, they asked what had happened to the original staircase and why the space now looked the way it did—for instance, why the Olympic rings had been put there. He replied that such design decisions were made by the government so as to be equidistant to all segments of society. Unconvinced, the visitors brought up the recent lapsing (owing to the statute of limitations) of one of the court cases on the arson attack, highlighting the paradox between it and the social equidistance spoken of by the employee. The debate heated up as the visitors descended the stairs. They left the building complaining indignantly.

Immediately after this exchange, the Science and Culture Center's director walked up angrily to the employee, next to whom I happened to be standing. Having apparently overheard his conversation with the three visitors, the director began a rebuke. He told the employee to avoid telling people what happened where: After all, how could architectural features from 1993 remain intact when the building's refurbishment was so thorough? If anyone asks about the stairs, the director said, the employee must tell them that he does not know anything, that this is a Science and Culture Center, and that kids are being educated here—otherwise, there would be no way out of it. He especially emphasized that the employee must refrain from entertaining such questions as who escaped, where and how they escaped, who got chased, who chased them, and who lost their lives where. The director seemed to address these remarks to employees in general, particularly to the employee involved in the exchange that triggered his commentary. But, throughout most of his rebuke, he looked at me. I expressed my discomfort and asked, "Sir, may I ask why you're looking at me? I don't tell anyone anything, anyway." He replied that he of course was not addressing me but rather speaking in general terms so that the staff understood and were made aware of sensitive issues. This concluded the exchange, and we all went our separate ways. A few minutes later (about an hour before the institution's closing time), however, the tension evolved to engulf me in a much more direct way.

> I'm sitting at a desk in the Children's Library jotting down some notes. I notice the director approach me from the back. He addresses me as his "friend," says he wants to see what I have been doing and writing, and grabs my notebook. After a quick glance at it, he begins to scold angrily: What sorts of things am I writing? Am I going to get him into trouble! I should follow him upstairs, he instructs, and says he wants to inspect what I have been doing and writing. He runs up the stairs to his office. Appalled and helpless, I follow.
>
> What follows is an hour-long diatribe in which the director goes through almost every single one of my notes, questioning my identity, my research, and even the building itself. What I am doing has nothing to do with scientific research, he says. He was told that I was interested in architecture, but now that he has seen my notes he is convinced that this is not the case. For all he knows, I am not actually interested in architecture but in messing around.
>
> I respond that "the notes are all very much about architecture, since they concern the ways in which visitors experience the building." But I fail to appease the director. Do you know what, he says, this building itself has nothing to do with architecture! What is there for me to study here that concerns architecture, anyway? This is kamusal [public] space, he stresses. According to him, the people who come here are illiterate, ignorant peasants. What would they know or care about architecture? This is kamusal space, and I therefore cannot conduct this kind of research here.
>
> Reaching the peak of his diatribe, the director threatens to confiscate my notebook and report me to the deputy governor and the police. I am shocked. "How come, sir? You cannot confiscate a personal item," I reply as he reaches for his phone. I follow by calling my roommate, the only

person I know in Sivas. The director asks if I, too, am making calls. Go ahead, he says, call whomever you want—who would I be calling anyway that could be of help? I explain that I am calling my roommate who is a native of Sivas and an academic himself. Seeing that I know a local seems to give the director second thoughts about confiscating my notebook. He suddenly decides to tear out and confiscate the pages that he thinks include my notes from the past ten days and returns the rest of the notebook to me. The director then shows me the door, saying that, if necessary, he will report me to the authorities.

I go down the stairs to pack up and leave the building. I say good-bye to every single member of staff, including the two policemen. I tell everyone that the director has obviously misunderstood my research. I express regret that things turned out this way but also hope that I might return soon to continue the conversation. I give my email address and mobile number to one of the two employees with whom I had the most detailed conversations, telling him to keep in touch. I go out to a nearby café to wind down and inform my roommate of my whereabouts so that he can join me.

When he arrives, I recount to him in detail what I just experienced. He says that we should go to the police to report the incident, as the confiscation of my notes is entirely illegal. We could go to the precinct in Alibaba, he suggests. He has heard they are trustworthy there, explains my roommate, invoking Alibaba's well-known reputation as Sivas's "Alevi neighborhood." I, on the other hand, have in mind the recently increasing number of academics jailed upon indictments that lack factual basis (Ziflioğlu 2012a). Recent changes in the law mean that they could spend months in prison awaiting trial while the police looked for evidence to substantiate their indictment (Jones 2012; Eissenstat 2012). I therefore fear upsetting the authorities further and tell my roommate that, before all else, I would like to catch my breath and reflect on what happened. He says that he could at least go to the Science and Culture Center to talk to the director himself and leaves. He returns after about a quarter of an hour, saying that the director presented to him the same arguments he had to me: that my research was neither scientific nor about architecture and that the building's being public space was a hindrance to the sort of observations I wished to conduct there. My roommate is convinced that there is no chance of having a reasonable conversation with the director.

According to him, we should discuss the matter with the deputy governor and see what he thinks.

Just as we are discussing how to best pursue the matter, I receive a call on my mobile from the employee to whom I had given my phone number before leaving the building. He suggests that the director now regrets what he has done and wants to return my notes. The director told him to kindly ask that I come back to the building to get my notes back, says the employee. I thank him and hang up. Seeing how distressed I am, my roommate suggests that I stay and rest and that he pay a quick visit to the building, collect my notes, and rejoin me at the café. I agree.

But a few minutes after leaving, he calls to say that there is an air of turmoil at the Science and Culture Center: perhaps they have realized how unlawfully they acted and are afraid that I will press charges. At any rate, they now want me to go over there in person because they would like to apologize, says my roommate. Accepting the invitation, I walk the couple of minutes from the café to the building. As I approach my roommate waiting for me at the entrance, I notice the two policemen watching the building start walking toward us. They surround us as if preparing for an arrest, but then only ask for our identity cards. "Why? What have we done?" we ask. One of the policemen says all they want to do is run a regular check—it should take no longer than a minute. We hand them our identity cards.

The so-called regular check turns out to take about forty-five times the duration suggested by the police. First, one of the policemen goes into the patrol car, looking extremely alarmed. He speaks on his radio, mobile phone, and car phone, using all possible means of communication available. The other officer stays with us, as if to keep us from escaping. He puts on his sunglasses and stands in a serious posture with his arms crossed, as if to distinguish himself from the person I had come to know over the past several days. The atmosphere is one of extreme panic. A team of undercover policemen arrives at the scene as reinforcement.

As we wait outside the building for the police to complete their checks, a lawyer friend of my roommate runs into us. We recap the events for him. Witnessing the dubious procedure the police are following, he stays with us to see how the "regular check" is going to proceed. He speaks with the policemen to understand exactly what sort of information they are after. After three-quarters of an hour, the police finally say they are done and return our papers. They tell us we are free to go, providing no further information whatsoever on the sort of checks they ran. The story about the director being remorseful and wishing to return my notes turns out to have been a trap.

That evening, my roommate and I reflect on the experience. He acknowledges his naïveté in initially suggesting that we report the confiscation of my notes to the police. I tell him that, regardless of whether I ultimately decide to file an official complaint, I first wish to raise the matter with the deputy governor who had authorized my work inside the Science and Culture Center. The next morning, we go to the deputy governor's office to request a meeting with him. His secretary tells us that he is away attending meetings across town but should be back in about two hours. We decide to kill time at the courtyard of Buruciye Madrassa, the centuries-old complex that also happens to be where the first instances of physical aggression unfolded on the day of the arson attack.

As we are sitting in the café now situated in the building's courtyard, the deputy governor coincidentally turns up with his entourage. Surprised, I walk up to him: "Sir, I happen to be waiting to meet with you." Before I can speak any further, the deputy governor interrupts and rehearses the arguments that the director had presented to me the day before. He then suggests that I return to London, have the embassy look through my documents and stamp them, and then mail them here for the governorship's review. I remind him that "when I initially asked if more papers or official letters than the ones I had brought were required, you yourself approved my research confirming that no further documents were necessary." That was then; this is now, he replies.

Before we go our separate ways, there is one final issue that my roommate and I raise: the director's unlawful confiscation of my notes. Just as we begin to utter the word notes, *the deputy governor interrupts us. Pointing to his chest pocket, he says he has my notes and will keep them as evidence. If I continue to insist on raising the issue, he will not hesitate to report me to the local prosecutor. Faced with this outright threat, I decide to book a flight and leave Sivas at the earliest possible opportunity.*

That night, I share my version of the events with my roommate's coffee-shop circle and, later, with friends and family. The coffee-shop circle, some members of which are supporters of the Turkish-Islamist party BBP, treats my becoming persona non grata less as a personal matter than as an event with social and historical significance or one that has directly to do with the arson attack. For an elementary school teacher in his early thirties who is also a member of the BBP's youth organization, my expulsion epitomizes the authorities' unwillingness to "investigate Madımak properly." The man even offers to mobilize his organization to publicize my predicament: Would you want me to inform the guys and organize a demonstration? Let us march to Madımak and chant, "The AKP do not want to find out what really happened here!"

The next morning, I meet with an Alevi journalist in her midforties who was the first activist I had met in the field. She happens to be sitting with a member of Parliament for Sivas from the main opposition party, Cumhuriyet Halk Partisi (CHP; Republican People's Party) who is the province's only opposition MP. Having listened to my story, the journalist remarks that I must have now found out about how it feels to be traumatized even at the sight of Madımak. Both she and the MP then reiterate the point many have made throughout my fieldwork regarding the authorities' unwillingness to allow anything on the arson attack to be researched. Finally, they propose to publicize the episode by organizing a press conference with me, the journalist, the MP, and representatives of the local Alevi association involved in the campaign around the arson attack.

The first significance of my expulsion is empirical. Although the entire episode may seem no more than a crash course on the harsh realities of fieldwork—expulsions from the field being not uncommon, especially for anthropologists (Owens 2003)—in my case, it serves not simply as an example of denial of access to empirical material but rather as such material itself.[4] This is evident not only in the authorities' argument as to why they wanted me out—the building's being "public space"—which reiterates the role that conventional imaginaries of spatial publicness play in extending violent histories into the future (part 2). It is also evident in the reaction the expulsion elicited from the BBP youth organization member. His reaction reiterated that the authorities' nationalization of victimhood, grounded in understandings of Turkey's histories of state-endorsed violence as conspiracies plotted by outsiders against insiders, has not simply

---

4. For a detailed and critical discussion of denial of access, and how it might serve as empirical material for research that focuses on spatial and visual politics, see Çaylı 2020.

appeased but, in fact, perpetuated conspiracy theoretical historicization (part 1). In sum, this final episode of fieldwork exposed me to some of what I had observed over the past two years regarding how, in depoliticizing victimhood, conspiracy theoretical historicizations of state-endorsed violence have produced further forms of victimization (some perceived and fueled by the same conspiracy theoretical historicizations in question; others embodied and deriving from direct experience of assaults, injustice, and marginalization inflicted spatially and visually).

How I myself followed up on my expulsion is another aspect that renders the episode significant, and it is this significance that I would like to consider a call for methodological reconsideration. I hesitated to follow through with the Alevi memory activist's invitation to publicize my predicament for fear of working up my expulsion into a claim to victimhood. I hesitated, in other words, to add to the already long list of such claims, which had been in circulation and mutual competition throughout the late 2000s and early 2010s, albeit with varying degrees of grounding in embodied experience—a context already dominated by those claims based more on perception than on embodiment. After much thought, I followed up by writing and submitting an official letter to the governorship nine months after the event, in which I recapped the entire episode and demanded that my access to the building be reinstated (appendix 1). I did so against the advice of many family members and friends, who suggested that getting back in touch with the authorities would be in vain and might trigger even further predicament. The reply I received six months later ended with a rejection but also elaborated on the Science and Culture Center project and its main commemorative element, thus serving as the first publicly accessible and official record of the authorities' rationale behind the building's transformation. "A Memory Corner has been constituted inside the building," read the reply, "in memory of the saddening events that took place at this site and that the entire country would rather not remember" (appendix 2), recording in writing the authorities' identification of those communities bent on remembering as the nation's other.

This written correspondence between me and the authorities, I suggest, evidences my adoption of the memory activists' insistence on rational-critical methods, which they combined with those approaches involving direct action and performance such as protests and commemorations. In speaking of rational-critical methods here, I have in mind, for instance, the activists' insistent demands for state-sponsored memorial museums to be built at sites of violence, despite their awareness of the political limitations of remembrance through such official institutions—something they continually demonstrated through direct collective action. A similar point could be made about the activists' attitude toward existing models of public space: making the most of them as sociospatial infrastructures while also problematizing their idealization. Another case in point is the lawsuits activists filed against the Memory Corner's all-encompassing name list (alongside staging protests against it) and doing so despite being repeatedly let down by the law since the arson attack. That I adopted this insistence on rational-critical methods helped rectify, if partially, my previous reliance on performances—rather than written expressions—of rapport and consent when requesting permission to conduct research inside the Science and Culture Center.

My adoption of some of the rational-critical methods I had learned from memory activists is cause for rethinking the agency of interlocutors in anthropological fieldwork, particularly in the case of research on violence and its commemoration where questions around victimhood and its commonplace associations with passivity and objectification become salient (Stølen 2007; Fassin and Rechtman 2009; Jensen and Ronsbo 2014). Since the cultural turn of the 1970s, a growing number of anthropologists have preferred to refer to the individuals among whom fieldwork is conducted not as "informants" but rather as "interlocutors" (Van Maanen 1988). Not unlike the activist cited at the beginning of this coda, they consider the latter term to better reflect these individuals' agency—in the particular case of this anthropological debate: *epistemic* agency (Ingold 2014, 392). More recently, the same concern for acknowledging agency has led other anthropologists to prefer the term *collaborator* over the first two, as they have sought to position interlocutors on a par with fieldworkers as active agents (Gay y Blasco and Wardle 2019, 168–91). Hierarchizing such terms is undoubtedly not without contention, primarily because it risks a false equivalence between what ought to be differentially obligated types of epistemic agency, researchers' primary obligation being toward critical analysis of and through the field, whereas interlocutors' is directly toward the field itself (Bourdieu 2003).

The aftermath of my expulsion confirms the differences between these primary obligations while also calling for further consideration of the dynamics between them. It indicates that, just as scholarship would ideally be expected to furnish those inhabiting the field with novel perspectives on it and thus help them better address their obligations to it, so might interlocutors' methods and experience guide researchers in addressing their critical-analytical obligations. To return this point to victimhood is not only to reiterate what much of contemporary scholarship on suffering has already emphasized regarding the importance for scholars to learn from victims without suppressing the latter's empirical experience with a focus on rationality and critical detachment (Enns 2012, 184; Govier 2015, 82; Tietjens Meyers 2016, 195). It also means to nuance these emphases by indicating that criticality and rationality are not so much a scholarly preserve as they are always also at work in how interlocutors grapple with and respond to experience that scholars deem empirically significant. Hence scholars' imperative to learn from interlocutors' rational-critical expertise as well as their empirical experience. Indeed, understood as such, this expertise might prove particularly useful in situations where the empirical experience of scholars is found to approximate the experience of interlocutors.[5]

The "Fall" of Turkey?

As indicated at the beginning of this coda, the abrupt end to my fieldwork in Sivas was followed by a period in which the political and media establishment's interest in "confronting the past" gradually waned. In its

---

5. With respect to anthropologically informed cultural geography, the point I am making here resonates with Watson and Till's call to use anthropological fieldwork in ways that "legitimate expert knowledges beyond the limits of academic institutions and settings" (2010, 130). As such, it also calls into question Duncan and Duncan's argument that the critical potential of anthropological fieldwork hinges on replacing "the idea of the researcher as an expert decoder" with a sort of "expertise" that is oriented toward "reception and audience" and that attends to the visceral rather than the rational (2010, 231).

stead, mainstream politics and media increasingly became conducive to violence's acceleration in a physical and readily observable register. The unjustifiable use of tear gas and blockading of peaceful protest narrated in chapters 3 and 4 became a countrywide practice around the time of the Gezi Park protests (Çaylı 2016b). In 2015, pro-Kurdish peace activists were targeted by suicide bombers on two occasions, one of which was the deadliest attack on civilians in Turkey's history. War in Turkey's Kurdistan flared up in August 2015, as PKK-affiliated groups dug ditches and mounted barricades in city centers and the central government conducted raids accompanied by successive localized round-the-clock curfews, resulting in thousands losing their homes (Çaylı 2016a). A petition signed by academics (including myself), which called on the authorities to end these curfews and raids, was met with a witch hunt by the government and its supporters, causing those signatories based in Turkey to lose their jobs and passports (Sertdemir Özdemir, Mutluer, and Özyürek 2019). In July 2016, an attempted coup unleashed its own episode of violence, whose direct and indirect effects on how the country is run continue to this day. These effects include a system of executive presidency inaugurated in 2017, which has given the administration the power to clamp down on any dissident voice it considers a threat (Sertdemir Özdemir and Özyürek 2019).

Both the Gezi Park protests and the 2016 coup attempt have rapidly become the subject of a body of scholarship in their own right, not least among spatially and visually focused scholars of memory (Whitehead and Bozoğlu 2016; Houston 2018; Evered 2019; Apaydın 2019; Carney 2019; Hammond 2019, 2020). This scholarship is incisive in its understanding of the publics of commemoration and protest and nuanced in its political contextualization and analysis of the events. Specifically, it nuances the platitude that Turkey has slid toward authoritarianism by unpacking the limitations as well as achievements that mark the authorities' response to both Gezi protests and the coup attempt and by giving voice to marginalized groups and to how they have contended with these responses. However, this scholarship has unlocked only partially the critical and analytical promises of its incisive and nuanced approach owing to a methodological decision characterizing it. This decision is to spotlight Gezi and the coup each as something of a milestone for commemoration and protest in 2010s Turkey—indeed, an emergent tendency in this scholarship is to think of one of these events through the other (Houston 2018; Carney 2019; Hammond 2019). Thus omitted from the analysis of memory and violence are the discourses and practices of "confronting the past" that are discussed in this book and that not only indelibly marked the prelude to the mid-2010s but also continued to reverberate in the latter part of the decade. This omission has risked reproducing a methodological slippage that *Victims of Commemoration* has sought to problematize. Namely, the slippage involves the associating of activism exclusively with that which is unscripted and spontaneous (for example, Gezi) and abandoning to the realm of institutional or government-led politics that which is rational-critical and that which requires long-term or large-scale mobilization, organization, and planning. The improvisations characterizing government-endorsed commemorative practice versus the levelheaded and persistent campaigning of the activists discussed in this book have decisively thrown this sort of an association and abandonment into disarray.[6]

It is therefore worth adding to the urgent conversation emerging from the burgeoning literature on memory and violence in 2010s Turkey by revisiting how the sites and practices discussed in *Victims of Commemoration* have fared in the late 2010s. Throughout these years, the activist campaigns to turn Diyarbakır Prison into a museum and the site of the Sivas arson attack into a "museum of shame" proper have continued unabated. The Diyarbakır Prison has, moreover, continued to serve as a medium of the state's carrot-and-stick attitude toward pro-Kurdish demands. In 2013, the '78ers Foundation presented a petition with one hundred thousand signatures to Parliament, which reiterated the demand for Diyarbakır Prison's

6. It is possible to raise a similar point about Christopher Houston's (2020) otherwise excellent and newly published ethnography on the spatial underpinnings and consequences of late 1970s and early 1980s violence in Istanbul and how they have shaped the city and its left-leaning activist politics to this day. In prioritizing the agency of individuals and their personal recollections in its exploration of activist politics, the ethnography tends to sideline the sociopolitical legacy of movements deriving from the large-scale and long-term mobilization, organization, and planning they undertake.

transformation into a memorial museum.[7] Two years later, the Kurdish-run metropolitan municipality set up a "coordination center" in central Diyarbakır to research and document human rights violations inside the prison during the 1980s and to push for its transformation into a memorial museum.[8] That same year, the prime minister paid a visit to Diyarbakır on the campaign trail ahead of the June 7 general election and said, "We are transforming the jailhouse that carries extremely painful memories into a museum" (S. Kaplan 2015). It soon turned out, however, that the "jailhouse" he was talking about was not the notorious Diyarbakır Prison but another penitentiary, smaller and older than the latter and located within the city's historic citadel that had opened as a history and archaeology museum just days before the 2015 general election (S. Kaplan, Ayaydın, and Dağ 2015). In late 2015 and early 2016, when war flared up across Turkey's Kurdistan and the government replaced democratically elected pro-Kurdish mayors with unelected and centrally appointed "caretakers," the building hosting the "Diyarbakır Prison coordination center" that had been recently established by the metropolitan municipality was handed over to the association of army veterans and deceased soldiers' relatives (Karakaş 2016; Oruç 2018).

Amid the war, the parliamentary commission investigating torture in coup-era Diyarbakır Prison began holding its first official meetings with survivors. Mesut Baştürk, whose science-fiction novel based on his memories of 1980s Diyarbakır Prison was discussed in chapter 7, was among the people invited. He lamented that, contrary to the commission's name bearing the word *confrontation*, there is no one to be confronted, as those individuals responsible for the torture have not been summoned. Baştürk also compared 2016 to the early 1980s: "Our cells and hallways were decorated in Turkish flags and slogans like, 'How happy is the one

7. See "Turn Diyarbakır Prison into Museum: Petition," *Hürriyet Daily News*, Apr. 19, 2013, http://www.hurriyetdailynews.com/turn-diyarbakir-prison-into-museum-petition--45189.

8. For more on this coordination center, see "Diyarbakır Cezaevinin Müzeye Dönüş-mesi İçin Adımlar Atılıyor" [Steps Taken toward Transforming Diyarbakır Prison into a Museum], *Evrensel*, May 15, 2015, http://www.evrensel.net/haber/112843/diyarbakir-cezaevinin-muzeye-donusmesi-icin-adimlar-atiliyor.

who says I'm a Turk.' And now the special forces of the gendarmerie and the police [deployed in the mid-2010s urban war] paint similar slogans on walls in streets. It is as if I am reliving the period. Had there been a confrontation with what occurred then, this would not have taken place" (Akgün 2016). In 2017 the "Museum of Shame" put together annually by former political convicts was held for the sixth time in Ankara. One difference from previous years was that the personal belongings and photographs of the peace activists killed in the suicide bomb attacks of 2015 were added to the exhibits. A representative of the Revolutionary '78ers Federation, the organizers of the exhibition, admitted that "we do not want new items to be added to the Museum of Shame; we wish that, when a kid goes out to the street, no mother languishes, wondering, 'Is [my] kid going to come back?'"[9]

The wake of the failed coup in 2016 has seen calls for the restoration of capital punishment, whose abolition was represented by Ulucanlar Prison Museum's central exhibit, the caged-up gallows. Leading figures from the alliance of right-wing political parties, which has not only kept President Erdoğan in power but also imbued him with executive powers since the failed coup, have threatened to reimpose the death penalty. The threats soon engulfed Ulucanlar, too, when a progovernment TV channel ran a segment on the museum. Speaking in front of the gallows, the reporter reminded viewers that "Ulucanlar has been transformed from a prison into a museum" and "capital punishment was altogether abolished in 2004." "But," he suggested, "today the Turkish public wants and awaits the execution of certain individuals." Regarding precisely whom "the public wants hanged right here on this gallows," the reporter named not only the PKK's jailed leader Abdullah Öcalan and the exiled cleric Fethullah Gülen who allegedly plotted the failed coup of 2016—both portrayed as archvillains by mainstream politicians and media—but also the leader of the main opposition party CHP and "every single citizen who betrays this

9. See "12 Eylül Utanç Müzesi'ne Yeni Eşyalar Gelmesin!" [Don't Let New Objects Arrive at September 12 Museum of Shame], *T24*, Sept. 10, 2017, https://t24.com.tr/haber/12-eylul-utanc-muzesine-yeni-esyalar-gelmesin,437198.

land." "Yet," he lamented, "in 2004, capital punishment was unfortunately abolished in Turkey."[10]

In using this coda to draw an arc from the final episode of my fieldwork to more recent developments in Turkey, my intention has been neither to suggest my expulsion as a foreshadowing of what mainstream scholarly accounts have considered Turkey's fall from grace nor to cast myself as an early victim of the country's supposed slide from peaceful democracy to violent authoritarianism (Sarfati 2017). There never was any socially all-encompassing grace to fall from in the first place, nor were the relations between peace and violence or democracy and authoritarianism so sweepingly antithetical, as has been suggested in recent mainstream analyses of Turkey's contemporary politics. Recall the Alevi journalist who saw in my predicament a "trauma" she had experienced all along, although it may have come as a shock to others. My intention in drawing this arc, however, is not just to reiterate this point about sociopolitical privilege and disadvantage. It is to clarify why commemoration is so central to the aspiration, if only ever asymptotic, of eradicating such privilege and disadvantage. If spaces of commemoration do not just represent violence but are also structured by it—if violence *at once* structures the spatial methods used in commemoration *and* hides under their guise—it is from a problematization of this methodological nexus and structurality that any aspiration toward the ever-emergent nonviolent and just community must also begin.

10. For more on this segment and the responses it triggered, see "Akit sunucusu: 'Kamuoyu Kılıçdaroğlu'nun idamını istiyor'; CHP: 'Hesabını yargıda vereceksiniz'" [Akit Reporter: The Public Wants Kılıçdaroğlu's Execution; CHP: You Will Pay for This in Court], *Euronews*, Mar. 19, 2019, http://tr.euronews.com/2019/03/19/akit-sunucusu-kamuoyu-kilicdaroglu-nun-idamini-istiyor-chp-hesabiniyargida-vereceksiniz.

Appendixes

References

Index

Appendix A

The author's letter to Sivas governorship, seeking permission to continue research inside the Science and Culture Center (English translation, followed by Turkish)

Republic of Turkey, Governorship of Sivas

To Mr. Ömer Kalaylı, Deputy Governor in charge
of the Provincial Directorate of National Education

Date: 1 November 2013

Dear Mr. Ömer Kalaylı,

Since March 2011, I have been pursuing my doctoral education at University College London, which is located in London, the capital of the United Kingdom. As part of my doctoral work, I have conducted research in 2011 and 2012 at the Sivas Special Provincial Administration Science and Culture Center, of which your deputy governorship is in charge. During that research, I met with your predecessor Mr. Veysel Çiftçi on numerous occasions and, with his approval and permission, had the opportunity to visit the Science and Culture Center several times.

However, in the most recent research trip I made, which took place in September 2012, Mr. Çiftçi requested that I produce official documents approved by the Education Counsellor of the Turkish Embassy in London, explaining my research and confirming my student status at UCL. He stated that, unless I present these documents to your deputy governorship, I would be unable to continue my research.

Please find attached proof of my student status and a detailed explanation of my research written by my thesis supervisor, both of which have been validated by the Education Counsellor of the Turkish Embassy in London. Also attached is a copy of my identity card, attesting to my citizenship of the Republic of Turkey. Under these circumstances, I wish to be able to continue my research at the Science and Culture Center (in September 2014, instead of the date of September 2013 stated in my supervisor's letter—the postponement being the result of the unexpectedly lengthy process of validating documents). I remain with thanks and kindly request that you address the matter.

Regards,
Eray Çaylı
Return address

TÜRKİYE CUMHURİYETİ SİVAS VALİLİĞİ

İl Milli Eğitim Müdürlüğü'nden sorumlu Vali Yardımcısı Sn. Ömer
Kalaylı'nın dikkatine

Tarih: 1 Kasım 2013

Sayın Ömer Kalaylı,

İngiltere'nin başkenti Londra'daki "University College London"
adlı üniversitede Mart 2011'de başladığım doktora eğitimimi halen
sürdürmekteyim. Doktoram kapsamında, 2011 ve 2012 yılları yaz
aylarında, vali yardımcılığınıza bağlı Sivas İl Özel İdaresi
Bilim ve Kültür Merkezi ile ilgili araştırmalar yapmış, bu
araştırmalarım sırasında selefiniz Sn. Veysel Çiftçi ile birçok
kez görüşmüş ve kendisinin izni ve onayıyla Bilim ve Kültür
Merkezi'ni de birçok kez ziyaret etme imkanı bulmuştum.

Ancak bu ziyaretlerin 2012 Eylül ayına denk gelen sonuncusunda,
Sn. Çiftçi, benden, doktoramı sürdürdüğüm şehir olan Londra'daki
Türkiye Cumhuriyeti Büyükelçiliği'ne bağlı Eğitim Müşavirliği'nce
tasdiklenmiş, araştırmamı açıklayan ve okuduğum okulda kaydım
olduğunu teyit eden belgeleri talep etmiştir ve şayet bu
belgeleri makamınıza sunmazsam araştırmama devam edemeyeceğimi
belirtmiştir.

Ekte, öğrenci belgemin ve doktora tez danışmanım tarafından
kaleme alınan araştırmam hakkındaki daha detaylı bir dilekçenin,
T.C. Londra Büyükelçiliği Eğitim Müşavirliği'nce onaylanmış
nüshalarını, tarafınıza gönderiyorum. Ayrıca şahsıma ait nüfus
kağıdının çift taraflı bir kopyasını da ekte bulabilirsiniz. Bu
koşullar altında, (belgelerin düzenlenmesi ve tasdiği beklenenden
çok daha uzun sürdüğünden, bahsi geçen 2013 yılı yerine) 2014
Eylül ayında araştırmamı yapabilmeyi umuyorum. Teşekkür eder ve
gereğinin yapılmasını arz ederim.

Saygılarımla,
Eray Çaylı

Adres: ███████████████████████████████

38. The author's letter to Sivas governorship, seeking permission to continue
research inside the Science and Culture Center (Turkish).

Appendix B

The Sivas authorities' response to the author's letter (English translation, followed by Turkish)

Republic of Turkey
SIVAS SPECIAL PROVINCIAL ADMINISTRATION
Directorate of Human Resources and Education
Number: 50951556-000-3158   26/02/2014

Subject: Eray Çaylı

Dear: Eray ÇAYLI
      Concerning: Your letter dated 01.11.2013
      In the above-mentioned letter you state that you are currently pursu-
ing your doctoral education at University College London (UCL), and ask
for permission to carry out the research duty, which you have been given
by your school, at the Sivas Special Provincial Administration Science and
Culture Center in the month of September 2014.
      The building in question has been transformed into a science and
culture center, which predominantly serves primary and secondary school
pupils, and includes a children's library and devices for science-technology
experiments.
      Moreover, a memory corner has been constituted inside the building,
in memory of the saddening events that took place at this site and that the
entire country would rather not remember.
      For these reasons, the building has been found unsuitable for the
research you are planning to carry out, given its current state and the way in
which it is being used, and thus your proposal has been found inadmissible.

Kindly submitted for your information.

> It is confirmed that this letter has been e-signed as
> part the Law No. 5070   Alpaslan CEYHAN
> Assistant to the General Secretary
> 27/02/2014
> Name-Surname: Bekir GEMİCİ
> Title: Chief
> Signature: _____

*This document has been e-signed. In order to see the original visit https://
www.e-icisleri.gov.tr/EvrakDogrulama and enter the code (b9VaHi-P8UssK
7iF1Tb-Aaq64B-gmLL30SL)

Akdeğirmen Mah. M. Akif Ersoy Cad. 580480 For detailed information contact E. ÇEVİKDOĞAN
Telephone: (346)2230116 Fax: (346)2247980
e-mail: Electronic Web: www.icisleri.gov.tr

T.C.
SİVAS İL ÖZEL İDARESİ
İnsan Kaynakları ve Eğitim Müdürlüğü

Sayı   : 50951556-000-3158
Konu : Eray ÇAYLI   26/02/2014

Sayın:Eray ÇAYLI

İlgi : 01.11.2013 tarihli dilekçeniz.

İlgi tarihli dilekçenizde Londra Üniversitesi Koleji (UCL)'de doktora eğitimini sürdürmekte olduğunuz ve okulunuzca verilen araştırma görevini 2014 Eylül ayında İl Özel İdaresine bağlı Bilim ve Kültür Merkezinde yapmak üzere izin talep etmektesiniz;

Söz konusu bina ağırlıklı olarak ilk ve ortaöğretim öğrencilerine hizmet veren, içerisinde çocuk kütüphanesi ve fen-teknoloji deney aletlerinin bulunduğu bilim kültür merkezine dönüştürülmüştür.

Ayrıca; bina içerisinde geçmişte bu alanda meydana gelen ve tüm ülkenin hatırlamak istemediği üzücü olaylar anısına bir de anı köşesi oluşturulmuştur.

Bu nedenlerle; binanın mevcut durumu ve kullanım şekli itibariyle yapmayı planladığınız araştırma için uygun olmadığı kanaatine varıldığından talebiniz uygun görülmemiştir.

Bilgilerinizi rica ederim.

Bu evrakın 5070 Sayılı Kanun
gereğince E-İMZA ile imzalandığı
tasdik olunur.
23.03.2014

Adı-Soyadı : Bekir GEMİCİ
Ünvanı   : ŞEF

Alpaslan CEYHAN
Genel Sek. Yard.

*Bu belge elektronik imzalıdır. İmzalı suretinin aslını görmek için https://www.e-icisleri.gov.tr/EvrakDogrulama adresine girerek (b9VaHi-P8UssK-7iF1Tb-Aaq64B-gmLL30SL) kodunu yazınız.

Akdeğirmen Mah. M. Akif Ersoy Cad. 58040   Ayrıntılı bilgi için irtibat: İ.ÇEVİKDOĞAN
Telefon: (346)223 01 16 Faks: (346)224 79 80
e-posta: Elektronik Ağ: www.icisleri.gov.tr

39. The Sivas authorities' response to the author's letter (Turkish).

References

Films

Başaran, Tunç, director. 1989. *Don't Let Them Shoot the Kite.* 100 minutes.
Bezar, Miraz, director. 2009. *Min Dît* [I Have Seen]. 102 minutes.
Güney, Yılmaz, director. 1983. *Duvar* [The Wall]. 117 minutes.
Özbakır, Aynur, director. 2010. *İki Temmuz (July the Second).* 48 minutes.
Özçelik, Murat, director. 2010. *Ölücanlar* [Dead Souls]. 91 minutes.
Yalçın, Soner, director. 2013. *Menekşe'den Önce* [Before Menekşe]. 70 minutes.

Fiction Writing

Baştürk, Mesut. 2007. *Esat, Polat ve Azat* [Esat, Polat and Azat]. Istanbul: Tevn.
Güney, Yılmaz. 2019 [1977]. *Soba, Pencere Camı ve İki Ekmek İstiyoruz* [We Want a Stove, a Windowpane and Two Loaves of Bread]. Istanbul: İthaki.
Rushdie, Salman. 1988. *Satanic Verses.* London: Viking.

TV Series

Giritlioğlu, Tomris, producer. 2009–10. *Bu Kalp Seni Unutur Mu?* [Would This Heart Forget You?]. 17 episodes.

Theater

Doğan, Serdar, writer and director. 2008. *Simurg.*
Erkal, Genco, writer and director. 2008. *Sivas '93.*
Zenderlioğlu, Berfin, and Mirza Metin, writer and director. 2011. *Disko 5 No'lu* [Disco No. 5].

Other Sources

Açıkgöz, Namık. 2004. "Bir Kelimenin Anlam Zıtlaşması Macerası" [The Adventure of a Word's Contested Semantics]. *Radikal,* July 18, 2004. http://www.radikal.com.tr/radikal2/bir-kelimenin-anlam-zitlasmasi-macerasi-871619/.

Agamben, Giorgio. 1998. *Homo Sacer: Sovereign Power and Bare Life.* Stanford, CA: Stanford Univ. Press.

———. 1999. *Remnants of Auschwitz: The Witness and the Archive.* Translated by Daniel Heller-Roazen. New York: Zone Books.

Aguilera, Carolina 2014. "Memories and Silences of a Segregated City: Monuments and Political Violence in Santiago, Chile, 1970–1991." *Memory Studies* 8 (1): 102–14.

Ahıska, Meltem, and Biray Kolluoğlu Kırlı. 2006. "Editors' Introduction." *New Perspectives on Turkey* 34: 5–8.

Akbulut, A. Kürşad. 2006. "13 Yıl Sonra 2 Temmuz" [July 2 after 13 Years]. *Anadolu*, July 4, 2006, 1.

Akgün, Reyhan. 2016. "Mağdurlar: Diyarbakır Cezaevi ile Yüzleşilmeli" [Victims: Diyarbakır Prison Must Be Confronted]. *Bas News*, Mar. 5, 2016. http://www.basnews.com/index.php/tr/news/kurdistan/262452.

Akgün Yüksekli, Berrin, and Aysu Akalın. 2011. "Space as a Projection of Spatial Practices: An Urban Park in Western Anatolia in the Early-Republican Period." *Middle Eastern Studies* 47 (4): 641–54.

Aksoy, Ozan. 2014. "The Music and Multiple Identities of Kurdish Alevis from Turkey in Germany." *CUNY Academic Works*, Feb. 1, 2014. http://academicworks.cuny.edu/gc_etds/5.

Alan, Serkan. 2019. "Sırrı Süreyya Önder'in İsmi 'Ulucanlar Müzesi'nden Kaldırıldı!" [Sırrı Süreyya Önder's Name Removed from "Ulucanlar Museum"!]. *Gazete Duvar*, May 17, 2019. http://www.gazeteduvar.com.tr/gundem/2019/05/17/sirri-sureyya-onderin-ismi-ulucanlar-muzesinden-kaldirildi/.

Alkan, Nezahat. 2007. "Ulucanlar Cezaevi'nin Kültür Merkezi Yapılması İçin Proje Yarışması: Jüride Eski Tüfekler Var" [Competition of Projects to Turn Ulucanlar Museum into a Culture Center: Veterans in Jury]. *Birgün*, Mar. 13, 2007. http://v3.arkitera.com/h15086-ulucanlar-cezaevinin-kultur-merkezi-yapilmasi-icin-proje-yarismasi-juride-eski-tufekler-var.html.

Alpar, Zeynep. 2011. "Hüseyin'in Hikâyesi" [Hüseyin's Story]. *Radikal İki*, Feb. 6, 2011. http://www.radikal.com.tr/radikal2/huseyinin-hikyesi-1039214.

Altan, Sanem. 2009. "Diyarbakır'da işkenceye tanıklık eden imam ve askerler konuşsun" [The Imams and the Soldiers Who Witnessed Torture in Diyarbakır Must Speak Out]. *Vatan*, Aug. 30, 2009. https://www.gazetevatan.com/gundem/diyarbakir-da-iskenceye-taniklik-eden-imam-ve-askerler-konussun-256585.

Altındağ Belediyesi. 2010. *Ulucanlar Cezaevi Müze ve Kültür Sanat Merkezi: Ulucanlar Prison Museum, Culture and Art Center*. Ankara: Altındağ Belediyesi.

Anderson, Patrick. 2004. "To Lie Down to Death for Days." *Cultural Studies* 18 (6): 816–46.

Apaydın, Veysel. 2019. "Heritage, Memory and Social Justice: Reclaiming Space and Identity." In *Critical Perspectives on Cultural Memory and Heritage: Construction, Transformation and Destruction*, edited by Veysel Apaydın, 84–97. London: UCL Press.

Appadurai, Arjun. 1990. "Disjuncture and Difference in the Global Cultural Economy." *Theory Culture Society* 7 (2–3): 295–310.

Arendt, Hannah. 1970. *On Violence*. New York: Harcourt, Brace.

Arınç, Bülent. 2011. "Mandate for a New Turkey." *Guardian*, June 13, 2011. http://www.theguardian.com/commentisfree/2011/jun/13/mandate-for-a-new-turkey.

Arsu, Şebnem. 2011. "Turkey Disqualifies 12 Pro-Kurdish Politicians from Parliamentary Election." *New York Times*, Apr. 18, 2011. http://www.nytimes.com/2011/04/19/world/europe/19turkey.html.

Asimovic Akyol, Riada. 2016. "Turkish Women in Police Force Allowed to Wear Headscarves." *Al-Monitor*, Sept. 2, 2016. http://www.al-monitor.com/pulse/originals/2016/09/turkey-headscarf-ban-women-police-officers.html.

Assmann, Aleida, and Sebastian Conrad, eds. 2010. *Memory in a Global Age: Discourses, Practices and Trajectories*. Basingstoke: Palgrave Macmillan.

Aşut, Attila. 1994. *Sivas Kitabı: Bir Topluöldürümün Öyküsü* [The Sivas Book: A Mass Murder Story]. Ankara: Edebiyatçılar Derneği.

Ayata, Bilgin, and Serra Hakyemez. 2013. "The AKP's Engagement with Turkey's Past Crimes: An Analysis of PM Erdoğan's 'Dersim Apology.'" *Dialectical Anthropology* 37 (1): 131–43.

Ayata, Muzaffer. 2011. *Diyarbakır Zindanları* [Diyarbakır Dungeons]. Vol. 1. Istanbul: Aram.

Aydın, Suavi, and Jelle Verheij. 2012. "Confusion in the Cauldron: Some Notes on Ethno-religious Groups, Local Powers and the Ottoman State in Diyarbekir Province, 1800–1870." In *Social Relations in Ottoman Diyarbekir, 1870–1915*, edited by Joost Jongerden and Jelle Verheij, 15–54. Leiden: Brill.

Aydınkaya, Fırat. 2011. *Ölüm Koridoru: Diyarbakır Cezaevi'nden Notlar—Hamit Kankılıç ile söyleşi* [Death Hall: Notes from Diyarbakır Prison—Interview with Hamit Kankılıç]. Istanbul: Avesta.

Aytekin, Eraydın, Halife Yalçınkaya, Hilal Özdemir, Gökhan Ceylan, Hakan Kaleli, and Bülent Tatlı. 2010. "Devlet İlk Kez Madımak'ta" [State at Madımak for the First Time]. *Posta*, July 2, 2010. http://www.posta.com.tr/devlet -ilk-kez-madimakta-haberi-35394.

Baer, Marc David. 2013. "An Enemy Old and New: The Dönme, Anti-Semitism, and Conspiracy Theories in the Ottoman Empire and Turkish Republic." *Jewish Quarterly Review* 103 (4): 523–55.

Bakıner, Onur. 2013. "Is Turkey Coming to Terms with Its Past? Politics of Memory and Majoritarian Conservatism." *Nationalities Papers* 41 (5): 691–708.

Bargu, Banu. 2014. *Starve and Immolate: The Politics of Human Weapons*. New York: Columbia Univ. Press.

Barry, Andrew. 2013. *Material Politics: Disputes along the Pipeline*. Oxford: Wiley-Blackwell.

Başkaya, Devran. 2006. "Sivas Davası Yeniden Açılsın!" [The Sivas Case Must Be Reopened]. *Alevilerin Sesi* 96: 6.

Bastian, Misty L. 2003. "'Diabolic Realities': Narratives of Conspiracy, Transparency, and 'Ritual Murder' in the Nigerian Popular Print and Electronic Media." In *Transparency and Conspiracy: Ethnographies of Suspicion in the New World Order*, edited by Harry G. West and Todd Sanders, 65–91. Durham, NC: Duke Univ. Press.

Batuman, Bülent. 2015. "'Everywhere Is Taksim': The Politics of Public Space from Nation-Building to Neoliberal Islamism and Beyond." *Journal of Urban History* 41 (5): 881–907.

Baykan, Ayşegül, and Tali Hatuka. 2010. "Politics and Culture in the Making of Public Space: Taksim Square, 1 May 1977, Istanbul." *Planning Perspectives* 25 (1): 49–68.

Beeley, Brian. 1970. "The Turkish Village Coffeehouse as a Social Institution." *Geographical Review* 60 (4): 475–93.

Benli, Mesut Hasan. 2016. "Danıştay'dan Madımak kararı" [Madımak Verdict from the Council of State]. *Hürriyet*, Oct. 18, 2016. http://www.hurriyet.com .tr/gundem/danistaydan-madimak-karari-yanan-ile-yakanayni-yerde-olmaz -40252462.

Bevan, Robert. 2006. *The Destruction of Memory: Architecture at War*. London: Reaktion.

Biner, Zerrin Özlem. 2011. "Multiple Imaginations of the State: Understanding a Mobile Conflict About Justice and Accountability from the Perspective of Assyrian-Syriac Communities." *Citizenship Studies* 15: 3–4.

———. 2020. *States of Dispossession: Violence and Precarious Coexistence in Southeast Turkey.* Philadelphia: Univ. of Pennsylvania Press.

Boano, Camillo. 2011. "'Violent Spaces': Production and Reproduction of Security and Vulnerabilities." *Journal of Architecture* 16 (1): 37–55.

Bond, Lucy, and Jessica Rapson, eds. 2014. *The Transcultural Turn: Interrogating Memory between and beyond Borders.* Berlin: De Gruyter.

Bourdieu, Pierre. 2003. "Participant Objectivation." *Journal of the Royal Anthropological Institute* 9 (2): 281–94.

Boynueğri, Gamze. 2017. "Ülkücüler'in Koğuşu Açılıyor" [The Nationalists' Ward Opens]. *Ülkücü Medya*, Aug. 9, 2017. http://www.ulkucumedya.com /ulkuculerin-kogusu-aciliyor-96883h.htm/.

Bozarslan, Felat, Bayram Bulut, and Serdar Sunar. 2012. "Diyarbakır'da Olaylar Çıktı" [Incidents Erupt in Diyarbakır]. *Hürriyet*, July 15, 2012. http://www .hurriyet.com.tr/gundem/diyarbakirda-olaylar-cikti-20984523.

Bozarslan, Felat, and Serdar Sunar. 2012. "Demirtaş'tan Erdoğan'a Ağır Benzetme" [Damning Comparison from Demirtaş to Erdoğan]. *Milliyet*, July 19, 2012. http:// www.milliyet.com.tr/siyaset/demirtastan-erdogana-agir-benzetme-1569237.

Bozdoğan, Sibel. 2001. *Modernism and Nation Building: Turkish Architecture in the Early Republic.* Seattle: Univ. of Washington Press.

Bozgeyik, Burhan. 1993. "Adına 4 Gün Şenlik Yapılan Pir Sultan Kimdir?" [Who Is Pir Sultan, in Whose Name a Four-Day Festival Is Being Held?]. *Hakikat*, July 2, 1993, 2.

Bozyel, Bayram. 2014. *Diyarbakır 5 No.lu* [Diyarbakır No. 5]. Istanbul: İletişim.

Brown, Eric. 2016. "The Fall of Turkey." *American Interest*, Dec. 7, 2016. http:// www.the-american-interest.com/2016/12/07/the-fall-of-turkey/.

Butler, Judith. 2004. *Precarious Life: The Politics of Mourning and Violence.* London: Verso.

Butz, David. 2010. "Autoethnography as Sensibility." In *The Sage Handbook of Qualitative Geography*, edited by Dydia DeLyser, Steve Herbert, Stuart Aitken, Mike Crang, and Linda McDowell, 138–55. London: Sage.

Çakır, Bawer. 2009. "Diyarbakır Zindanı Müze Olsun, İşkenceciler Yargılansın" [Let Diyarbakır Prison Become a Museum, Let the Torturers Be Brought to Court]. *Bianet*, Aug. 24, 2009. https://m.bianet.org/biamag/siyaset/116628 -diyarbakir-zindani-muze-olsun-iskenceciler-yargilansin.

Çamuroğlu, Reha. 1998. "Alevi Revivalism in Turkey." In *Alevi Identity: Cultural, Religious and Social Perspectives*, edited by Tord Olsson, Elisabeth Özdalga and Catharina Randvere, 79–84. Istanbul: Swedish Research Institute.

Carney, Josh. 2019. "Projecting 'New Turkey' Deflecting the Coup: Squares, Screens, and Publics at Turkey's 'Democracy Watches.'" *Media, Culture and Society* 41 (1): 138–48.

Carrier, Peter. 2005. *Holocaust Monuments and National Memory: Cultures in France and Germany since 1989.* Oxford: Berghahn.

Çaylı, Eray. 2012. "Tanıklığı Sorgulamak" [Interrogating Witnessing]. *Agos Kitap/Kirk*, Apr. 13, 2012. http://www.metiskitap.com/catalog/text/85628.

———. 2016a. "Bear Witness: Embedded Coverage of Turkey's Urban Warfare and the Demarcation of Sovereignty against a Dynamic Exterior." *Theory & Event* 19 (1). http://muse.jhu.edu/article/610225.

———. 2016b. "Inheriting Dispossession, Mobilizing Vulnerability: Heritage amid Protest in Contemporary Turkey." *International Journal of Islamic Architecture* 5 (2): 359–78.

———. 2020. "Introduction: Field as Archive / Archive as Field." *International Journal of Islamic Architecture* 9 (2): 251–61.

Cemal, Hasan. 2003. *Kürtler* [Kurds]. Istanbul: Doğan.

Cengizkan, Ali. 2004. *Ankara'nın İlk Planı, 1924–25 Lörcher Planı* [Ankara's First Plan, the 1924–25 Lörcher Plan]. Ankara: Arkadaş.

Cesari, Chiara de, and Ann Rigney, eds. 2014. *Transnational Memory: Circulation, Articulation, Scales.* Berlin: De Gruyter.

Chakrabarty, Dipesh. 1998. "Minority Histories, Subaltern Pasts." *Economic and Political Weekly* 33 (9): 373–79.

———. 2000. *Provincializing Europe: Postcolonial Thought and Historical Difference.* Princeton, NJ: Princeton Univ. Press.

Chalfont, Lord, Jacques Soustelle, Norman Podhoretz, Gerhard Lowenthal, George Will, and Michael Elkins. 1980. "Political Violence and the Role of the Media: Some Perspectives." *Political Communication* 1 (1): 79–99.

Çınar, Alev. 2005. *Modernity, Islam and Secularism in Turkey: Bodies, Places and Time.* Minneapolis: Univ. of Minnesota Press.

Colomina, Beatriz. 1993. "War on Architecture: E.1027." *Assemblage* 20:28.

Comaroff, Jean, and John Comaroff. 2003. "Transparent Fictions; or, The Conspiracies of a Liberal Imagination: An Afterword." In *Transparency and Conspiracy: Ethnographies of Suspicion in the New World Order*, edited by Harry G. West and Todd Sanders, 287–99. Durham, NC: Duke Univ. Press.

Coşkun, Zeki. 1995. *Aleviler, Sünniler ve . . . Öteki Sivas* [Alevis, Sunnis and . . . the Other Sivas]. Ankara: İletişim.

Cuff, Dana, Anastasia Loukaitou-Sideris, Todd Presner, Maite Zubiaurre, and Jonathan Jae-an Crisman. 2020. *Urban Humanities: New Practices for Reimagining the City.* Cambridge, MA: MIT Press.

Dalkılıç, Neslihan, and Fatma Meral Halifeoğlu. 2011. "Erken Cumhuriyet Döneminde Diyarbakır'da Kamu Binaları: 1923-1950 Dönemi" [Public Buildings in Early Republican Era Diyarbakır: 1923-1950]. *Mimarlık* 358: 74–84.

Das, Veena. 2007. *Life and Words: Violence and the Descent into the Ordinary.* Los Angeles: Univ. of California Press.

Dean, Jodi. 2000. "Theorizing Conspiracy Theory." *Theory and Event* 4 (3). http://muse.jhu.edu/article/32599.

de Certeau, Michel. 1984. *The Practice of Everyday Life.* Berkeley: Univ. of California Press.

Delaney, Carol. 1991. *The Seed and the Soil: Gender and Cosmology in Turkish Village Society.* Los Angeles: Univ. of California Press.

Deliktaş, Aydın. 2000. "2 Temmuz Sendrumu [sic] ve Olağanüstü Günler" [July 2 Syndrome and Extraordinary Days]. *Hakikat*, July 4, 2000.

Demir, Kurthan. 2015. "Sivas Katliamı Kurbanları Kadıköy'de Anıldı" [Commemoration of Sivas Massacre Victims in Kadıköy]. *Habertürk*, June 28, 2015. http://www.haberturk.com/gundem/haber/1096417-sivas-katliami-kurbanlari-kadikoyde-anildi.

Demir, Murtaza. 2008. "Pir Sultan Abdal Anıtı Nasıl Dikildi?" [How Was the Pir Sultan Abdal Monument Erected?]. *Banaz Köyü*, Mar. 18, 2008. http://www.banazkoyu.com/index.php?option=com_content&task=view&id=83&Itemid=60.

De Tapia, Stéphane. 2011. "Turkish Extreme Right-Wing Movements: Between Turkism, Islamism, Eurasism, and Pan-Turkism." In *The Extreme Right in Europe: Current Trends and Perspectives*, edited by Uwe Backes and Patrick Moreau, 297–320. Göttingen: Vandenhoeck and Ruprecht.

Deutsche, Rosalyn. 1996. *Evictions: Art and Spatial Politics.* Cambridge, MA: MIT Press.

Dikeç, Mustafa. 2017. *Urban Rage: The Revolt of the Excluded.* New Haven, CT: Yale Univ. Press.

Doğan, Soner. 2007. *Sivas: 2 Temmuz 1993* [Sivas: 2 July 1993]. Istanbul: Ekim.

Douglass, Ana, and Thomas A. Vogler. 2003. "Introduction." In *Witness and Memory: The Discourse of Trauma*, edited by Ana Douglass and Thomas A. Vogler, 1–53. New York: Routledge.

Dressler, Markus. 2013. *Writing Religion: The Making of Turkish Alevi Islam*. New York: Oxford Univ. Press.

Duncan, Nancy, and James Duncan. 2010. "Doing Landscape Interpretation." In *The SAGE Handbook of Qualitative Geography*, edited by Dydia DeLyser, Steve Herbert, Stuart Aitken, Mike Crang, and Linda McDowell, 225–47. London: Sage.

Düzel, Neşe. 2003. "Üç Yılını 'Cehennem'de Geçirdi" [He Spent Three Years in "Hell"]. *Radikal*, June 23, 2003. http://www.radikal.com.tr/turkiye/uc-yilini-cehennemde-gecirdi-673856/.

Eissenstat, Howard. 2012. "In Turkey: The Ivory Tower Besieged." *Amnesty USA*, Nov. 14, 2012. http://blog.amnestyusa.org/europe/in-turkey-the-ivory-tower-beseiged.

Ekinci, Oktay. 1993. "Katliamın Tanığı Olduğu Gibi Korunsun." *Cumhuriyet*, July 10, 1993.

Ellis, John. 2000. *Seeing Things: Television in the Age of Uncertainty*. London: I. B. Tauris.

Elver, Hilal. 2012. *The Headscarf Controversy: Secularism and Freedom of Religion*. New York: Oxford Univ. Press.

Enns, Diane. 2012. *The Violence of Victimhood*. University Park: Pennsylvania State Univ. Press.

Eral, Sadık. 1995. *Çaldıran'dan Çorum'a Anadolu'da Alevi Katliamları* [Alevi Massacres in Anatolia from Çaldıran to Çorum]. Istanbul: Yalçın.

Ergun, Ayça, and Aykan Erdemir. 2010. "Negotiating Insider and Outsider Identities in the Field: 'Insider' in a Foreign Land; 'Outsider' in One's Own Land." *Field Methods* 22 (1): 16–38.

Erll, Astrid. 2011. "Travelling Memory." *Parallax* 17 (4): 4–18.

Ertür, Başak. 2016. "The Conspiracy Archive: Turkey's Deep State on Trial." In *Law, Violence, Memory: Uncovering the Counter-Archive*, edited by Stewart Motha and Honni van Rijswijk, 177–94. Abingdon: Routledge.

Eskin, İsmail, and Gülsen Aslan. 2010. "Diyarbakır'a Mazlum ve Kemal Anıtı" [Mazlum and Kemal Monument in Diyarbakır]. *Evrensel*, Sept. 12, 2010.

Evered, Kyle T. 2019. "Erasing the Place of Dissent: Inscriptions and Eliminations of Gezi Park Graffiti." *Area* 51 (1): 155–65.

Ewalt, Joshua P. 2011. "Mapping Injustice: The World Is Witness, Place-Framing, and the Politics of Viewing on Google Earth." *Communication, Culture & Critique* 4: 333–54.

Farmer, Paul. 2004. "An Anthropology of Structural Violence." *Current Anthropology* 45 (3).

Fassin, Didier. 2008. "The Humanitarian Politics of Testimony: Subjectification through Trauma in the Israeli-Palestinian Conflict." *Cultural Anthropology* 23 (3): 531–58.

Fassin, Didier, and Richard Rechtman. 2009. *The Empire of Trauma: An Inquiry into the Condition of Victimhood.* Princeton, NJ: Princeton Univ. Press.

Feldman, Allen. 1991. *Formations of Violence: The Narrative of the Body and Political Terror in Northern Ireland.* Chicago: Univ. of Chicago Press.

———. 2015. *Archives of the Insensible: Of War, Photopolitics, and Dead Memory.* Chicago: Univ. of Chicago Press.

Felman, Shoshana. 1991. "In an Era of Testimony: Claude Lanzmann's Shoah." *Yale French Studies* 79:39–81.

Foote, Kenneth E. 2003. *Shadowed Ground: America's Landscapes of Violence and Tragedy.* Austin: Univ. of Texas Press.

Fortun, Kim, and Michael Fortun. 1999. "Due Diligence and the Pursuit of Transparency: The Securities and Exchange Commission, 1996." In *Paranoia within Reason: A Casebook on Conspiracy as Explanation*, edited by George E. Marcus, 157–92. Chicago: Univ. of Chicago Press.

Fenster, Mark. 2008. *Conspiracy Theories: Secrecy and Power in American Culture.* Minneapolis: Univ. of Minnesota Press.

Fraser, Nancy. 1990. "Rethinking the Public Sphere: A Contribution to the Critique of Actually Existing Democracy." *Social Text* 25–26: 56–80.

Galtung, Johan. 1969. "Violence, Peace, and Peace Research." *Journal of Peace Research* 6 (3): 167–91.

Gay y Blasco, Paloma, and Huon Wardle. 2019. *How to Read Ethnography.* London: Routledge.

Givoni, Michal. 2011. "Witnessing/Testimony." *Mafte'akh* 2e: 147–70.

Göçek, Fatma Müge. 2011. *The Transformation of Turkey: Redefining State and Society from the Ottoman Empire to the Modern Era.* London: I. B. Tauris.

Göçek, Fatma Müge, and Murat Özyüksel. 2012. "The Ottoman Empire's Negotiation of Western Liberal Imperialism." In *Liberal Imperialism in Europe*, edited by Matthew P. Fitzpatrick, 193–217. Basingstoke: Palgrave Macmillan.

Göle, Nilüfer. 1994. "Towards an Autonomization of Politics and Civil Society in Turkey." In *Politics in the Third Turkish Republic*, edited by Metin Heper and Ahmet Evin, 213–22. Boulder, CO: Westview Press.

Govier, Trudy. 2015. *Victims and Victimhood*. Ontario: Broadview Press.

Guida, Michelangelo. 2008. "The Sèvres Syndrome and 'Komplo' Theories in the Islamist and Secular Press." *Turkish Studies* 9 (1): 37–52.

Günbulut, Şükrü. 1994. "Madımak Yangınında Vurgulamak İstediklerim" [What I Wish to Emphasize Regarding the Madımak Fire]. In *Sıvas Kitabı: Bir Topluöldürümün Öyküsü*, edited by Attila Aşut, 205–11. Ankara: Edebiyatçılar Derneği.

Gündoğdu, İnan. 2011. "Gerçeğin Sineması" [Cinema of Truth]. *Radikal İki*, Apr. 10, 2011. http://www.radikal.com.tr/radikal2/gercegin-sinemasi-1045826.

Güney, Süleyman. 2012. *Diyarbakır'da Neler Oldu? Kemal Yamak, Kenan Evren ve Ben* [What Happened in Diyarbakır? Kemal Yamak, Kenan Evren and I]. Istanbul: Pêrî.

Gürpınar, Doğan. 2013. "Historical Revisionism vs. Conspiracy Theories: Transformations of Turkish Historical Scholarship and Conspiracy Theories as a Constitutive Element in Transforming Turkish Nationalism." *Journal of Balkan and Near Eastern Studies* 15 (4): 412–33.

Habermas, Jürgen. 1991. *The Structural Transformation of the Public Sphere: An Inquiry into a Category of Bourgeois Society*. Cambridge, MA: MIT Press.

Hakyemez, Serra. 2017. "Margins of the Archive: Torture, Heroism, and the Ordinary in Prison No. 5, Turkey." *Anthropological Quarterly* 90 (1): 107–38.

Hammond, Timur. 2019. "The Politics of Perspective: Subjects, Exhibits, and Spectacle in Taksim Square, Istanbul." *Urban Geography* 40 (7): 1039–54.

———. 2020. "Making Memorial Publics: Media, Monuments, and the Politics of Commemoration Following Turkey's July 2016 Coup Attempt." *Geographical Review* 110 (4): 536–55.

Hamsici, Mahmut. 2017. "2010 Referandumu: 'Evet,' 'Hayır' ve 'Boykot' Cepheleri Ne Demişti?" [The 2010 Referendum: What Had "Yes," "No" and "Boycott" Camps Said?]. *BBC News Türkçe*, Apr. 5, 2017. http://www.bbc.com/turkce/haberler-turkiye-39462061.

Harvey, Penny, and Hannah Knox. 2015. *Roads: An Anthropology of Infrastructure and Expertise*. Ithaca, NY: Cornell Univ. Press.

Hauser, Mark W., Whitney Battle-Baptiste, Koji Lau-Ozawa, Barbara L. Voss, Reinhard Bernbeck, Susan Pollock, Randall H. McGuire, Uzma Z. Rizvi, Christopher Hernandez, and Sonya Atalay. 2018. "Vital Topics Forum: Archaeology as Bearing Witness." *American Anthropologist* 120 (3): 535–48.

Herscher, Andrew. 2008. "Warchitectural Theory." *Journal of Architectural Education* 62 (1): 35–43.

———. 2010. *Violence Taking Place: The Architecture of the Kosovo Conflict.* Stanford, CA: Stanford Univ. Press.

———. 2011. "From Target to Witness: Architecture, Satellite Surveillance, Human Rights." In *Architecture and Violence: Reception and Reproduction,* edited by Bechir Kenzari, 127–48. Barcelona: Actar.

———. 2014a. "In Ruins: Architecture, Memory, Countermemory." *Journal of the Society of Architectural Historians* 73 (4): 464–69.

———. 2014b. "Surveillant Witnessing: Satellite Imagery and the Visual Politics of Human Rights." *Public Culture* 26 (3): 469–500.

Hess, Reinhard. 2007. "Alevi Martyr Figures." *Turcica* 39: 253–90.

Hightower, Ben, and Scott East. 2018. "Protest in Progress/Progress in Protest." *M/C Journal: A Journal of Media and Culture* 21 (3). http://journal.media-culture.org.au/index.php/mcjournal/article/view/1454.

Hirsch, Eric, and Charles Stewart. 2005. "Introduction: Ethnographies of Historicity." *History and Anthropology* 16 (3): 261–74.

Holm, Nicholas. 2009. "Conspiracy Theorizing Surveillance: Considering Modalities of Paranoia and Conspiracy in Surveillance Studies." *Surveillance & Society* 7 (1): 36–48.

Houston, Christopher. 2018. "Plotters and Martyrs: The Justice and Development Party's (AKP) Constituting of Political Actors in the 15 July Coup Event." *Politics, Religion & Ideology* 19 (4): 531–45.

———. 2020. *Istanbul, City of the Fearless: Urban Activism, Coup d'État, and Memory in Turkey.* Berkeley: Univ. of California Press.

Hunt, Jamer. 1999. "Paranoid, Critical, Methodical: Dalí, Koolhaas, and . . ." In *Paranoia within Reason: A Casebook on Conspiracy as Explanation,* edited by George E. Marcus, 21–38. Chicago: Univ. of Chicago Press.

Huyssen, Andreas. 1995. *Twilight Memories: Marking Time in a Culture of Amnesia.* London: Routledge.

Iğsız, Aslı. 2008. "Documenting the Past and Publicizing Personal Stories: Sensescapes and the 1923 Greco-Turkish Population Exchange in Contemporary Turkey." *Journal of Modern Greek Studies* 26 (2): 451–87.

İnan, Mert. 2012. "Dağkapı adı değişsin Şeyh Said Meydanı olsun" [The Name Dağkapı Should Be Changed as Şeyh Said Square]. *Vatan*, Mar. 14, 2012. https://www.gazetevatan.com/gundem/dagkapi-adi-degissin-seyh-said-meydani-olsun-436850.

Ingold, Tim. 2014. "That's Enough about Ethnography!" *HAU: Journal of Ethnographic Theory* 4 (1): 383–95.

Iveson, Kurt. 2007. *Publics and the City*. Oxford: Blackwell.

Jameson, Fredric. 1988. "Cognitive Mapping." In *Marxism and the Interpretation of Culture*, edited by Cary Nelson and Lawrence Grossberg, 347–58. Urbana: Univ. of Illinois Press.

Jensen, Steffen, and Henrik Ronsbo. 2014. *Histories of Victimhood*. Philadelphia: Univ. of Pennsylvania Press.

Jones, Dorian. 2012. "Turkish Pre-trial Detention a Form of Punishment?" *Deutsche Welle*, Feb. 23, 2012. http://www.dw.de/turkish-pre-trial-detention -a-form-of-punishment/a-15760002.

Jongerden, Joost. 2003. "Violation of Human Rights and the Alevis in Turkey." In *Turkey's Alevi Enigma: A Comprehensive Overview*, edited by Paul. J. White and Joost Jongerden, 71–93. Leiden: Brill.

Kaçmaz, Metin. 2009. "16 Yıldır Kapanmayan Yara" [16-Year-Long Festering Wound]. *Alevilerin Sesi* 129: 9.

Kaiser, Susana. 2002. "Escraches: Demonstrations, Communication and Political Memory in Post-dictatorial Argentina." *Media, Culture & Society* 24 (4): 499–516.

Kaplan, İsmail. 2008. "Neden Para İle Madımak Müzesi Olmaz?" [Why Will Money Not Make Madımak a Museum?]. *Alevilerin Sesi* 119: 52.

Kaplan, Sema. 2015. "Diyarbakır Cezaevi Müzeye Dönüşüyor" [Diyarbakır Prison Is Becoming a Museum]. *Hürriyet*, Jan. 26, 2015. http://www.hurriyet.com .tr/diyarbakir-cezaevi-muzeye-donusuyor-37046026.

Kaplan, Sema, Özgür Ayaydın, and Maşallah Dağ. 2015. "Diyarbakır'da 'İçkale Müze Kompleksi' Açıldı" ["Citadel Museum Complex" Opens in Diyarba-kır]. *Anadolu Ajansı*, May 25, 2015. http://www.aa.com.tr/tr/kultur-sanat /diyarbakirda-ickale-muze-kompleksi-acildi/43644.

Karabağlı, Hülya. 2016. "Aziz Nesin, Diyarbakır Cezaevi'nde Olanlara İnanmayıp 'Kürtlerin Hayal Dünyası Benimkinden Geniş' Dedi!" [Aziz Nesin Did Not Believe in What Had Taken Place at Diyarbakır Prison and Said "Kurds" Imagination Is Wilder than Mine!]. *T24*, May 10, 2016. http://t24.com.tr /haber/aziz-nesin-diyarbakir-cezaevinde-olanlara-inanmayip-kurtlerin -hayal-dunyasi-benimkinden-genis-dedi,339707.

Karaca, Banu. 2011. "Images Delegitimized and Discouraged: Explicitly Political Art and the Arbitrariness of the Unspeakable." *New Perspectives on Turkey* 45: 155–83.

Karaca, Ekin. 2012. "İnsan Olan Diyarbakır'da Yaşananlara Tepki Gösterir" [If One Is Human One Must React to What Took Place in Diyarbakır]. *Bianet*,

July 17, 2012. http://www.bianet.org/bianet/insan-haklari/139763-insan-olan
-diyarbakir-da-yasananlara-tepki-gosterir.

Karakaş, Burcu. 2016. "Hani Diyarbakır Cezaevi müze olacaktı?" [Was Diyarbakır Prison Not Supposed to Become a Museum?]. *P24*, Dec. 19, 2016. http://
platform24.org/yazarlar/1922/hani-diyarbakir-cezaevi-muze-olacakti.

Karaköse, Nayat. 2007. "12 Eylül Karanlığı Yırtılsın" [Let the Darkness of September 12 Rip]. *Bianet*, Sep. 10, 2007. https://bianet.org/kadin/siyaset/101677
-12-eylul-karanligi-yirtilsin.

Kaya, Duygu Gül. 2015. "Coming to Terms with the Past: Rewriting History
through a Therapeutic Public Discourse in Turkey." *International Journal of
Middle East Studies* 47: 681–700.

Keenan, Thomas. 2004. "Mobilizing Shame." *South Atlantic Quarterly* 103 (2):
435–49.

Kenanoğlu, Ali. 2013. "'Yak Ulan Yak' Diyen Mağdurlar" [The Victims Who Said
"Burn, Man, Burn!"]. *Evrensel*, Nov. 1, 2013. http://www.evrensel.net/yazi
/69694/yak-ulan-yak-diyen-magdurlar.

Kennedy, Rosanne, and Maria Nugent. 2016. "Scales of Memory: Reflections on
an Emerging Concept." *Australian Humanities Review* 59: 61–76.

Kenzari, Bechir. 2011a. "Introduction." In *Architecture and Violence: Reception
and Reproduction*, edited by Bechir Kenzari, 12–18. Barcelona: Actar.

———. 2011b. "Construction Rites, Mimetic Rivalry, Violence." *Architecture
and Violence: Reception and Reproduction*, edited by Bechir Kenzari, 149–74.
Barcelona: Actar.

Kezer, Zeynep. 2012. "Of Forgotten People and Forgotten Places: Nation-Building
and the Dismantling of Ankara's Non-Muslim Landscapes." In *On Location:
Heritage Cities and Sites*, edited by D. Fairchild Ruggles, 169–91. New York:
Springer.

Kirişçi, Kemal. 1999. "Turkey and the Mediterranean." In *The Foreign Policies of
the EU's Mediterranean States and Applicant Countries in the 1990s*, edited
by Stelios Stavridis, Theodore Couloumbis, Thanos Veremis, and Neville
Waites, 250–94. London: Palgrave Macmillan.

Kırlı, Cengiz. 2004. "Coffeehouses: Public Opinion in the Nineteenth-Century
Ottoman Empire." In *Public Islam and the Common Good*, edited by Dale E.
Eickelman and Armando Salvatore, 75–97. Leiden: Brill.

Koerbin, Paul. 2011. "Pir Sultan Abdal: Encounters with Persona in Alevi Lyric
Song." *Oral Tradition* 26 (1): 191–220.

Konuralp, Okan. 2012. "Diyanet 1000 'mele'yi atadı" [Diyanet Has Assigned 1000 'Mele's to Duty]. *Hürriyet,* June 22, 2012. https://www.hurriyet.com.tr /gundem/diyanet-1000-mele-yi-atadi-20816924.

Korkmaz, Atilla, and Hüseyin Kaçar. 2009. "Diyarbakır Cezaevi işkencenin üssüydü" [Diyarbakır Prison Was the Epicenter of Torture]. *Sabah,* Aug. 22, 2009. https://www.sabah.com.tr/gundem/2009/08/22/diyarbakir_cezaevi_iskencenin _ussuydu.

Kusow, Abdi M. 2003. "Beyond Indigenous Authenticity: Reflections on the Insider/Outsider Debate in Immigration Research." *Symbolic Interaction* 26 (4): 591–99.

Langer, Robert, Thomas Quartier, Udo Simon, Jan Snoek, and Gerard Wiegers. 2011. "Ritual as a Source of Conflict." In *Ritual, Media, and Conflict,* edited by Ronald L. Grimes, Ute Husken, Udo Simon, and Eric Venbrux, 93–132. New York: Oxford Univ. Press.

Lennartz, Karl. 2001–2. "The Story of the Rings." *Journal of Olympic History* 10: 29–61.

Levy, Daniel, and Natan Sznaider. 2006. *The Holocaust and Memory in the Global Age.* Philadelphia: Temple Univ. Press.

Linenthal, Edward T. 2001. *Preserving Memory: The Struggle to Create America's Holocaust Museum.* New York: Columbia Univ. Press.

Low, Setha. 2017. *Spatializing Culture: The Ethnography of Space and Place.* London: Routledge.

Loyd, Jenna M. 2012. "Geographies of Peace and Antiviolence." *Geography Compass* 6 (8): 477–89.

Maessen, Enno. 2014. "Reassessing Turkish National Memory: An Analysis of the Representation of Turkish National Memory by the AKP." *Middle Eastern Studies* 50 (2): 309–24.

Marchand, Laure, and Guillaume Perrier. 2015. *Turkey and the Armenian Ghost: On the Trail of the Genocide.* Montreal and Kingston: McGill-Queen Univ. Press.

Marcus, George E., ed. 1999. *Paranoia within Reason: A Casebook on Conspiracy as Explanation.* Chicago: Univ. of Chicago Press.

Marcus, George E., and Michael G. Powell. 2003. "From Conspiracy Theories in the Incipient New World Order of the 1990s to Regimes of Transparency Now." *Anthropological Quarterly* 76 (2): 323–34.

Mélikoff, Irène M. 2004. "Hasluck's Study of the Bektashis and Its Contemporary Significance." In *Archaeology, Anthropology, and Heritage in the Balkans and Anatolia: The Life and Times of F. W. Hasluck, 1878–1920.* Vol. 1, edited by David Shankland, 297–308. Istanbul: Isis Press.

Mills, Amy. 2010. *Streets of Memory: Landscape, Tolerance, and National Identity in Istanbul.* Athens: Univ. of Georgia Press.

Miroğlu, Orhan. 2009. *Dijwar: Faili Meçhul Cinayetler ve Diyarbakır Cezaevi'ne Dair Her Şey* [Dijwar: Unsolved Murders and Everything about Diyarbakır Prison]. Istanbul: Everest.

Mitchell, Don. 2003. *The Right to the City: Social Justice and the Fight for Public Space.* New York: Guilford.

Morris, Rosalind C. 2008. "Giving Up Ghosts: Notes on Trauma and the Possibility of the Political from Southeast Asia." *Positions* 16 (1): 229–58.

———. 2010. "Accidental Histories, Post-historical Practice? Re-reading Body of Power, Spirit of Resistance in the Actuarial Age." *Anthropological Quarterly* 83 (3): 581–624.

Muradoğlu, Abdullah. 2009. "Diyarbakır Hapishanesi" [Diyarbakır Prison]. *Yeni Şafak*, Aug. 25, 2009. https://www.yenisafak.com/yazarlar/abdullah-muradoglu/diyarbakir-hapishanesi-18269.

Mustafa, Daanish, Katherine E. Brown, and Matthew Tillotson. 2013. "Antipode to Terror: Spaces of Performative Politics." *Antipode* 45 (5): 1110–27.

Myers, Greg. 2006. "'Where Are You From?': Identifying Place." *Journal of Sociolinguistics* 10 (3): 316–39.

Navaro-Yashin, Yael. 2002. *Faces of the State: Secularism and Public Life in Turkey.* Princeton, NJ: Princeton Univ. Press.

———. 2003. "'Life Is Dead Here': Sensing the Political in 'No Man's Land.'" *Anthropological Theory* 3 (3): 107–25.

Nefes, Türkay Salim. 2013. "Political Parties' Perceptions and Uses of Anti-Semitic Conspiracy Theories in Turkey." *Sociological Review* 61 (2): 247–64.

———. 2015. "Understanding Anti-Semitic Rhetoric in Turkey through the Sèvres Syndrome." *Turkish Studies* 16 (4): 1–16.

Negt, Oskar, and Alexander Kluge. 2002. *Public Sphere and Experience: Toward an Analysis of the Bourgeois and Proletarian Public Sphere.* Cambridge, MA: Harvard Univ. Press.

Neyzi, Leyla. 2002. "Remembering to Forget: Sabbateanism, National Identity, and Subjectivity in Turkey." *Comparative Studies in Society and History* 44 (1): 137–58.

Neyzi, Leyla, and Haydar Darıcı. 2015. "Generation in Debt: Family, Politics, and Youth Subjectivities in Diyarbakır." *New Perspectives on Turkey* 52: 55–75.

Nichanian, Marc. 2009. *The Historiographic Perversion*. Translated by Gil Ani-
djar. New York: Columbia Univ. Press.

Ögelman, Nedim, Jeannette Money, and Philip Martin. 2002. "Immigrant Cohe-
sion and Political Access in Influencing Foreign Policy." *SAIS Review* 22 (2):
145–65.

Olick, Jeffrey K. 2008. "From Collective Memory to the Sociology of Mnemonic
Practices and Products." In *Cultural Memory Studies: An International and
Interdisciplinary Handbook*, edited by Astrid Erll, Ansgar Nünning, and
Sara B. Young, 151–61. Berlin: De Gruyter.

Oliver, Kelly. 2000. "Beyond Recognition: Witnessing Ethics." *Philosophy Today*
44 (1): 31–43.

———. 2001. *Witnessing: Beyond Recognition*. Minneapolis: Univ. of Minnesota
Press.

———. 2003. "Subjectivity and Subject Position: The Double Meaning of Witnessing." *Studies in Practical Philosophy* 3 (2): 132–43.

Oral, Mahmut. 2012. "Diyarbakır Savaş Alanı" [Diyarbakır Was a Warzone].
Cumhuriyet, July 15, 2012.

Oruç, Mehmet Şah. 2018. "78'liler Derneği Başkanı Alkan: 12 Eylül'ün Zihniyeti
Bugün Hala Sürüyor" [President of 78'ers Association: The Mind-Set of September 12 Has Continued to This Day]. *Yeni Yaşam*, Sept. 10, 2018. http://
yeniyasamgazetesi.com/78liler-dernegi-baskani-alkan-12-eylulun-zihniyeti
-bugun-hala-suruyor.

Owens, Geoffrey Ross. 2003. "What! Me a Spy? Intrigue and Reflexivity in Zan-
zibar." *Ethnography* 4 (1): 122–44.

Öz, Işıl. 2012. "Tüleylioğlu: Madımak 'Yak Ula Yak' Diye Ateşe Verildi" [Tü-
leylioğlu: Madımak Was Set Ablaze with Chants of "Burn, Man, Burn"].
T24, Mar. 3, 2012. http://t24.com.tr/haber/tuleylioglu-madimak-yak-ula-yak
-cigliklariyla-atese-verildi,198445.

Özbayar, Gürem F., and Zeynep Kutlu. 2010. "Ulucanlar Cezaevi Dönüşüm
Süreci" [The Transformation Process of Ulucanlar Prison]. *TMMOB Mimarlar Odası Ankara Şubesi Bülten* 77: 31–39.

Özbayar, Gürem F., Zeynep Kutlu, and Figen Kıvılcım. 2008. "Ankara Ulucanlar
Merkez Kapalı Cezaevi: Bir Düşün Gerçeğe Dönüşümü" [Ankara Ulucan-
lar Central Prison: A Dream Come True]. *TMMOB Mimarlar Odası Ankara
Şubesi Bülten* 61: 36–40.

Özbek, Meral. 2005. "Giriş: Kamusal Alanın Sınırları" [Introduction: The Boundaries
of Public Space]. In *Kamusal Alan*, edited by Meral Özbek, 19–91. Istanbul: Hil.

Özcan, Nazan. 2011. "Duvarların Dili Çözüldü" [The Walls Have Begun to Talk]. *Radikal İki*, Jan. 16, 2011. http://www.radikal.com.tr/radikal2/duvarlarin-dili -cozuldu-1036882.

Özer, Eray. 2015. "13'ümde Alevi Olduğumu Öğrendim" [I Learnt I'm Alevi at 13]. *Cumhuriyet*, Mar. 22, 2015. http://www.cumhuriyet.com.tr/haber/yasam /233608/13_umde_Alevi_oldugumu_ogrendim.html.

Özkoçak, Selma, 2007. "Coffee Houses: Rethinking the Public and Private in Early Modern Istanbul." *Journal of Urban History* 33: 965–86.

Öztürk, Muhsin. 2011. "Sivas'ta O Gün" [That Day in Sivas]. *Aksiyon*, July 4, 2011. https://birdeburadandinleyin.blogspot.com/2013/01/sivasta-o-gun-muhsin -ozturk-ibrahim.html.

Özyürek, Esra. 2006. *Nostalgia for the Modern: State Secularism and Everyday Politics in Turkey*. Durham, NC: Duke Univ. Press.

———. 2007. *The Politics of Public Memory in Turkey*. Syracuse, NY: Syracuse Univ. Press.

———. 2009. "The Light of the Alevi Fire Was Lit in Germany and Then Spread to Turkey: A Transnational Debate on the Boundaries of Islam." *Turkish Studies* 10 (2): 233–53.

Pekdemir, Melih. 2016. "Hiç Heveslenme! Mağdur Olmayız, Muhatabız" [Worry Not! We Will Not Be Victims, We Are Interlocutors]. *Birgün*, June 20, 2016. http:// www.birgun.net/haber/hic-heveslenme-magdur-olmayiz-muhatabiz-116810.

Pelkmans, Mathijs, and Rhys Machold. 2011. "Conspiracy Theories and Their Truth Trajectories." *Focaal* 59: 66–80.

Perrier, Guillaume. 2011. "Turkish Authorities Launch Raids to Censor Book before Publication." *Guardian*, Apr. 5, 2011. http://www.guardian.co.uk/world /2011/apr/05/turkey-censorship-ahmet-sik-perrier.

Raj, Dhooleka S. 2003. *Where Are You From? Middle-Class Migrants in the Modern World*. Berkeley: Univ. of California Press.

Rancière, Jacques. 2004. *The Politics of Aesthetics: The Distribution of the Sensible*. Translated by Gabriel Rockhill. London: Continuum.

Razon, Na'amah, and Karen Ross. 2012. "Negotiating Fluid Identities: Alliance-Building in Qualitative Interviews." *Qualitative Inquiry* 18 (6): 494–503.

Rigney, Ann. 2012. *The Afterlives of Walter Scott: Memory on the Move*. New York: Oxford Univ. Press.

———. 2015. "Cultural Memory Studies: Mediation, Narrative, and the Aesthetic." In *Routledge International Handbook of Memory Studies*, edited by Anna Lisa Tota and Trever Hagen, 65–76. London: Routledge.

Robinson, Firdevs, and Burak Baktir. 2000. "28 Die in Turkish Battle for Jails." *Guardian*, Dec. 24, 2000. http://www.theguardian.com/world/2000/dec/24 /theobserver.

Rothberg, Michael. 2009. *Multidirectional Memory: Remembering the Holocaust in the Age of Decolonization*. Stanford, CA: Stanford Univ. Press.

———. 2013. "Multidirectional Memory and the Implicated Subject: On Sebald and Kentridge." In *Performing Memory in Art and Popular Culture*, edited by Liedeke Plate and Anneke Smelik, 39–58. Abingdon: Routledge.

———. 2019. *The Implicated Subject: Beyond Victims and Perpetrators*. Stanford, CA: Stanford Univ. Press.

Ryang, Sonia. 1997. "Native Anthropology and Other Problems." *Dialectical Anthropology* 22 (1): 23–49.

Saldanha, Arun. 2012. "Aestheticism and Post-humanism." *Dialogues in Human Geography* 2 (3): 276–79.

Sancar, Mithat. 2007. *Geçmişle Hesaplaşma* [Reckoning with the Past]. Istanbul: İletişim.

Sarfati, Yusuf. 2017. "How Turkey's Slide to Authoritarianism Defies Modernization Theory." *Turkish Studies* 18 (3): 395–415.

Sargın, Güven Arif. 2004. "Displaced Memories; or, The Architecture of Forgetting and Remembrance." *Environment and Planning D: Society and Space* 22 (5): 659–80.

Sarlo, Beatriz. 2005. *Cultura de memoria y Giro subjetivo: Una discusión* [Culture of Memory and the Subjective Turn: A Discussion]. Buenos Aires: Siglo Veintiuno.

Schäfers, Marlene. 2018. "'It Used to Be Forbidden': Kurdish Women and the Limits of Gaining Voice." *Journal of Middle East Women's Studies* 14 (1): 3–24.

———. 2019. "Archived Voices, Acoustic Traces, and the Reverberations of Kurdish History in Modern Turkey." *Comparative Studies in Society and History* 61 (2): 447–73.

Schuppli, Susan. 2013. "Dusting for Fingerprints and Tracking Digital Footprints." *Photographies* 6 (1): 159–67.

———. 2014. "Entering Evidence: Cross-Examining the Court Records of the ICTY." In *Forensis*, edited by Forensic Architecture, 279–314. Berlin: Sternberg Press.

Sertdemir Özdemir, Seçkin, Nil Mutluer, and Esra Özyürek. 2019. "Exile and Plurality in Neoliberal Times: Turkey's Academics for Peace." *Public Culture* 31 (2): 235–59.

Sertdemir Özdemir, Seçkin, and Esra Özyürek. 2019. "Civil and Civic Death in the New Authoritarianisms: Punishment of Dissidents through Juridical Destruction, Ethical Ruin, and Necropolitics in Turkey." *British Journal of Middle Eastern Studies* 46 (5): 699–713.

Sfeir, Antoine. 2007. *The Columbia World Dictionary of Islamism.* Translated by John King. New York: Columbia Univ. Press.

Shankland, David. 2003. *The Alevis in Turkey: The Emergence of a Secular Islamic Tradition.* London: Routledge.

Şimşek, Hülya, ed. 2000. *Yalanları Parçalayan Ulucanlar Katliamı: Adalet, İnsan Hakları, Demokratikleşme* [The Ulucanlar Massacre That Tore Lies Apart: Justice, Human Rights, Democratization]. Istanbul: Tutuklu Aileleri Bülteni.

Sökefeld, Martin. 2002. "Alevi *Dedes* in the German Diaspora: The Transformation of a Religious Institution." *Zeitschrift für Ethnologie* 127 (2): 163–86.

Spector, Tom. 2014. "Publicness as an Architectural Value." *Journal of Architecture and Urbanism* 38 (3): 180–86.

Spence, Louise, and Aslı Kotaman Avcı. 2013. "The Talking Witness Documentary: Remembrance and the Politics of Truth." *Rethinking History* 17 (3): 295–311.

Springer, Simon. 2011. "Public Space as Emancipation: Meditations on Anarchism, Radical Democracy, Neoliberalism and Violence." *Antipode* 43 (2): 525–62.

Staeheli, Lynn A. 2010. "Political Geography: Democracy and the Disorderly Public." *Progress in Human Geography* 34 (1): 67–78.

Stevens, Quentin, and Karen A. Franck. 2016. *Memorials as Spaces of Engagement: Design, Use and Meaning.* London: Routledge.

Stewart, Charles. 2012. *Dreaming and Historical Consciousness in Island Greece.* Cambridge, MA: Harvard Univ. Press.

Stewart, Kathleen. 1999. "Conspiracy Theory's Worlds." In *Paranoia within Reason: A Casebook on Conspiracy as Explanation,* edited by George E. Marcus, 13–19. Chicago: Univ. of Chicago Press.

Stølen, Kristi Anne. 2007. *Guatemalans in the Aftermath of Violence: The Refugees' Return.* Philadelphia: Univ. of Pennsylvania Press.

Stoneall, Linda. 1983. "Where Are You From? A Case of Rural Residential Identification." *Qualitative Sociology* 6 (1): 51–65.

Şulul, Ömer. 2012. "Şanlıurfa'da BDP'nin Yasaklı Diyarbakır Mitingi İçin Denetim" [Measures in Şanlıurfa Due to BDP's Banned Diyarbakır Demonstration]. *Hürriyet,* July 14, 2012. http://www.hurriyet.com.tr/gundem/sanliurfada -bdpnin-yasakli-diyarbakir-mitingi-icin-denetim-20984927.

Suner, Asuman. 2009. "Silenced Memories: Notes on Remembering in New Turkish Cinema." *New Cinemas: Journal of Contemporary Film* 7 (1): 71–81.

———. 2011. "A Lonely and Beautiful Country: Reflecting upon the State of Oblivion in Turkey through Nuri Bilge Ceylan's *Three Monkeys.*" *Inter-Asia Cultural Studies* 12 (1): 13–27.

T.C. Devlet Bakanlığı. 2010. *Madımak Değerlendirme Toplantısı* [Madımak Assessment Meeting]. Ankara: Başak.

Tahincioğlu, Gökçer. 2010. "'Üç Fidan'ın Darağacı Sergilenecek" [The Three Saplings' Gallows Will Be Exhibited]. *Milliyet*, Aug. 31, 2010. http://www.milliyet.com.tr/gundem/uc-fidan-in-daragaci-sergilenecek-1283072.

Takeyuki, Tsuda. 2015. "Is Native Anthropology Really Possible?" *Anthropology Today* 31 (3): 14–17.

Tambar, Kabir. 2014. *The Reckoning of Pluralism: Political Belonging and the Demands of History in Turkey*. Stanford, CA: Stanford Univ. Press.

———. 2017. "The Uncanny Medium Semiotic Opacity in the Wake of Genocide." *Current Anthropology* 58 (6): 762–84.

Tanboğa, Mehmet, and Fevzi Yetkin. 2011. *Dörtlerin Gecesi* [The Night of the Four]. Istanbul: Aram.

Tanyeri-Erdemir, Tuğba. 2012. "Sivas: A Tale of Painful Indifference." *Hürriyet Daily News*, Mar. 16, 2012. http://www.hurriyetdailynews.com/sivas-a-tale-of-painful-indifference--16122.

Taşpınar, Ömer. 2005. *Kurdish Nationalism and Political Islam in Turkey: Kemalist Identity in Transition*. London: Routledge.

Taştekin, Fehim. 2014. "What Does Erdogan Mean by 'Alevis without Ali'?" *Al-Monitor*, June 2, 2014. http://www.al-monitor.com/pulse/originals/2014/06/turkey-erdogan-alevi-sunni-sectarian-cemevi-sabahat-akkiraz.html.

Taussig, Michael. 1997. *The Magic of the State*. New York: Routledge.

Tietjens Meyers, Diana. 2016. *Victims' Stories and the Advancement of Human Rights*. New York: Oxford Univ. Press.

Törne, Annika. 2015. "'On the Grounds Where They Will Walk in a Hundred Years' Time': Struggling with the Heritage of Violent Past in Post-genocidal Tunceli." *European Journal of Turkish Studies* 20. http://journals.openedition.org/ejts/5099.

Tosun, Funda. 2012. "Sivil Şehitlik Tartışılıyor" [Civilian Martyrdom Debated]. *Agos*, Mar. 31, 2012. http://www.agos.com.tr/tr/yazi/1047/sivil-sehitlik-tartisiliyor.

Tschumi, Bernard. 1996. *Architecture and Disjunction*. Cambridge, MA: MIT Press.

Tüleylioğlu, Orhan. 2010. *Yüreklerimiz Hâlâ Yangın Yeri: Sivas, 2 Temmuz 1993* [Our Hearts Are Still Ablaze: Sivas, July 2, 1993]. Ankara: Umag.

————. 2012. *Merdivende Üç Şair* [Three Poets on Stairs]. Istanbul: Kırmızı Kedi.

Türkiye İnsan Hakları Vakfı. 2004. *2003 Türkiye İnsan Hakları Raporu* [2003 Turkey Human Rights Report]. Ankara: Buluş.

Tyner, James A., Joshua F. J. Inwood, and Derek H. Alderman. 2014. "Theorizing Violence and the Dialectics of Landscape Memorialization: A Case Study of Greensboro, North Carolina." *Environment and Planning D: Society and Space* 32 (5): 902–14.

Ünalın, Çetin, ed. 2010. *Tanıkların Ulucanlar'ı: Sözlü Tarih* [The Witnesses' Ulucanlar: Oral History]. Ankara: TMMOB Mimarlar Odası Ankara Şubesi.

Üngör, Uğur Ümit. 2011. *The Making of Modern Turkey: Nation and State in Eastern Anatolia, 1913–1950.* New York: Oxford Univ. Press.

Ünsal, Fikret. 1995. *Figüran Aziz* [Aziz the Walk-on]. Sivas: Anadolu.

————. 2003. "Asala'nın Oyununa Gelmeyin" [Don't Be Fooled by Asala]. *Anadolu*, July 30, 2003.

Van Bruinessen, Martin. 1996. "Kurds, Turks and the Alevi Revival in Turkey." *Middle East Report* 200: 7–10.

Van der Linden, Harry. 2012. "On the Violence of Systemic Violence: A Critique of Slavoj Žižek." *Radical Philosophy Review* 15 (1): 33–51.

Van Maanen, John. 1988. *Tales of the Field: On Writing Ethnography.* Chicago: Univ. of Chicago Press.

Verstraete, Pieter. 2013. *IPC-Mercator Policy Brief: The Standing Man Effect.* Istanbul: Istanbul Policy Center.

Wagner-Pacifici, Robin. 2010. "Theorizing the Restlessness of Events." *American Journal of Sociology* 115 (5): 1351–86.

————. 2015. "Reconceptualizing Memory as Event: From 'Difficult Pasts' to 'Restless Events.'" In *Routledge International Handbook of Memory Studies,* edited by Anna Lisa Tota and Trever Hagen, 22–27. London: Routledge.

Wagner-Pacifici, Robin, and Barry Schwartz. 1991. "The Vietnam Veterans Memorial: Commemorating a Difficult Past." *American Journal of Sociology* 97 (2): 376–420.

Warner, Michael. 2005. *Publics and Counterpublics.* New York: Zone Books.

Watson, Annette, and Karen E. Till. 2010. "Ethnography and Participant Observation." In *The SAGE Handbook of Qualitative Geography,* edited by Dydia DeLyser, Steve Herbert, Stuart Aitken, Mike Crang, and Linda McDowell, 121–37. London: Sage.

Weheliye, Alexander G. 2014. *Habeas Viscus: Racializing Assemblages, Biopolitics, and Black Feminist Theories of the Human.* Durham, NC: Duke Univ. Press.

Weizman, Eyal. 2010. "Forensic Architecture: Only the Criminal Can Solve the Crime." *Radical Philosophy* 164: 9–24.

———. 2014. "Introduction: Forensis." In *Forensis*, edited by Forensic Architecture, 9–34. Berlin: Sternberg Press.

Welat, İrfan. 2010. *Auschwitz'den Diyarbakır'a 5 Nolu Cezaevi* [Prison No. 5 from Auschwitz to Diyarbakır]. Istanbul: Aram.

Wells, Karen. 2007. "The Material and Visual Cultures of Cities." *Space and Culture* 10 (2): 136–44.

West, Harry G., and Todd Sanders. 2003. "Power Revealed and Concealed in the New World Order." In *Transparency and Conspiracy: Ethnographies of Suspicion in the New World Order*, edited by Harry G. West and Todd Sanders, 1–37. Durham, NC: Duke Univ. Press.

Whitehead, Christopher, and Gönül Bozoğlu. 2016. "Protest, Bodies, and the Grounds of Memory: Taksim Square as 'Heritage Site' and the 2013 Gezi Protests." *Heritage & Society* 9 (2): 111–36.

Wieviorka, Annette. 2006. *The Era of the Witness.* Ithaca, NY: Cornell Univ. Press.

Wilpert, Czarina. 1990. "Religion and Ethnicity: Orientations, Perceptions and Strategies among Turkish Alevi and Sunni Migrants in Berlin." In *The New Islamic Presence in Western Europe*, edited by Tomas Gerholm and Yngve Georg Lithman, 88–106. New York: Mansell.

Wolf, Diane L. 1996. *Feminist Dilemma in Fieldwork.* Oxford: Westview Press.

Yalçınkaya, Halife, and Gökhan Ceylan. 2011. "İşte Yeni Madımak!" [Here Is the New Madımak!]. *Radikal*, June 30, 2011. http://www.radikal.com.tr/turkiye/iste_yeni_madimak-1054628.

Yavuz, Deniz, ed. 2010. *Tevkifhaneden Müzeye Ulucanlar* [Ulucanlar from Prison to Museum]. Ankara: Özel.

Yavuz, M. Hakan. 2009. *Secularism and Muslim Democracy in Turkey.* Cambridge: Cambridge Univ. Press.

Yıldırım, Ali. 1993. *Ateşte Semaha Durmak* [Whirling in the Face of Fire]. Ankara: Yurt.

Yildiz, Ali Aslan, and Maykel Verkuyten. 2011. "Inclusive Victimhood: Social Identity and the Politicization of Collective Trauma among Turkey's Alevis in Western Europe." *Peace and Conflict: Journal of Peace Psychology* 17: 243–69.

Yıldız, Mehmet. 2011. "Olaylı Anma" [Eventful Commemoration]. *Takvim*, July 3, 2011. http://www.takvim.com.tr/Siyaset/2011/07/03/olayli-anma.

Yılmaz, Ali Abbas, and Yılmaz Yiğitler. 2019. "Rant Uğruna Kentsel Kırım" [Profit-led Urbicide]. *Tigris Haber*, May 13, 2019. http://www.tigrishaber.com /video-rant-ugruna-kentsel-kirim-56140h.htm.

Young, James E. 2016. *The Stages of Memory: Reflections on Memorial Art, Loss, and the Spaces Between*. Amherst: Univ. of Massachusetts Press.

Zerubavel, Eviatar. 2003. *Time Maps: Collective Memory and the Social Shape of the Past*. Chicago: Univ. of Chicago Press.

Zeydanlıoğlu, Welat. 2009. "Torture and Turkification in the Diyarbakır Military Prison." In *Rights, Citizenship and Torture: Perspectives on Evil, Law and the State*, edited by John T. Parry and Welat Zeydanlioglu, 73–92. Oxford: Inter-Disciplinary Press.

Ziflioğlu, Vercihan. 2012a. "PEN Turkey Gives Prize to Scribes Behind Bars." *Hürriyet Daily News*, Mar. 8, 2012. http://www.hurriyetdailynews.com/pen -turkey-gives-prize-to-scribes-behind-bars-15504.

———. 2012b. "Trial on Sivas Massacre Dropped Despite Protests." *Hürriyet Daily News*, Mar. 14, 2012. http://www.hurriyetdailynews.com/trial-on-sivas -massacre-dropped-despite-protests-15939.

Zırh, Besim Can. 2016. "Alevilikte Şehadet: Kerbela'dan Gezi'ye Hüseyin'in Tarih Dışına Taşan Nefesi." In *"Öl Dediler Öldüm": Türkiye'de Şehitlik Mitleri*, edited by Serdar M. Değirmencioğlu, 89–110. Istanbul: İletişim.

Žižek, Slavoj. 2008. *Violence: Six Sideways Reflections*. London: Picador.

Zürcher, Erik Jan. 2005. *Turkey: A Modern History*. London: I. B. Tauris.

Index

Page numbers in italics signify photos or other illustrations.

221

Eray Çaylı, PhD (University College London, 2015), studies the spatial and visual politics of violence in Turkey and beyond. Çaylı is Leverhulme Early Career Fellow (2018–22) at London School of Economics and Political Science where he also teaches his own graduate-level courses on violence, visuality, racism, and racialization. His most recent publications include special issues that he has guest-edited for the *International Journal of Islamic Architecture* and for the *Journal of Visual Culture* as well as the volume *Architectures of Emergency in Turkey: Heritage, Displacement and Catastrophe* (2021) that he coedited with Pınar Aykaç and Sevcan Ercan. *Victims of Commemoration* is his first monograph. For more, please see http://www.eraycayli.com.